'EAT THE HEART OF THE INFIDEL'

‘Eat the Heart of the Infidel’

The Harrowing of Nigeria and the Rise of Boko Haram

ANDREW WALKER

HURST & COMPANY, LONDON

First published in the United Kingdom in 2016 by
C. Hurst & Co. (Publishers) Ltd.,
41 Great Russell Street, London, WC1B 3PL

Printed in the United States of America

Distributed in the United States, Canada and Latin America by
Oxford University Press, 198 Madison Avenue, New York, NY 10016,
United States of America.

A Cataloguing-in-Publication data record for this book
is available from the British Library.

ISBN: 9781849045582

This book is printed using paper from registered sustainable
and managed sources.

www.hurstpublishers.com

CONTENTS

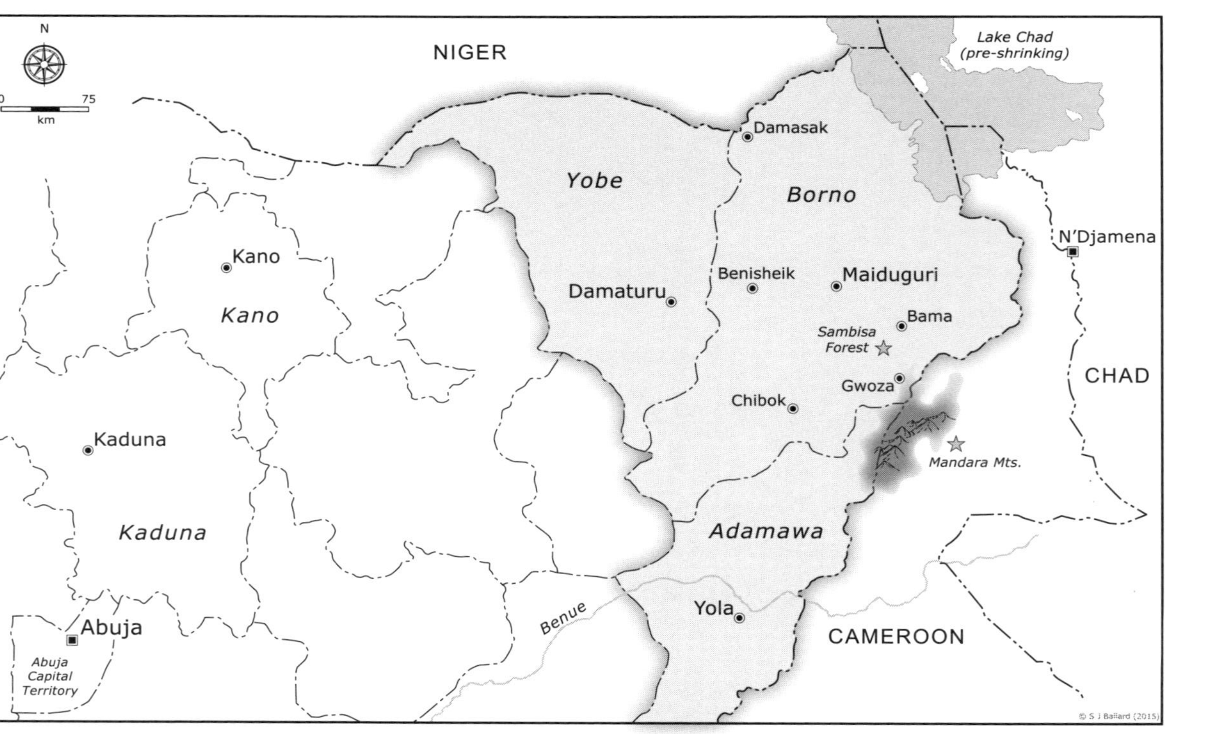

Modern Nigeria

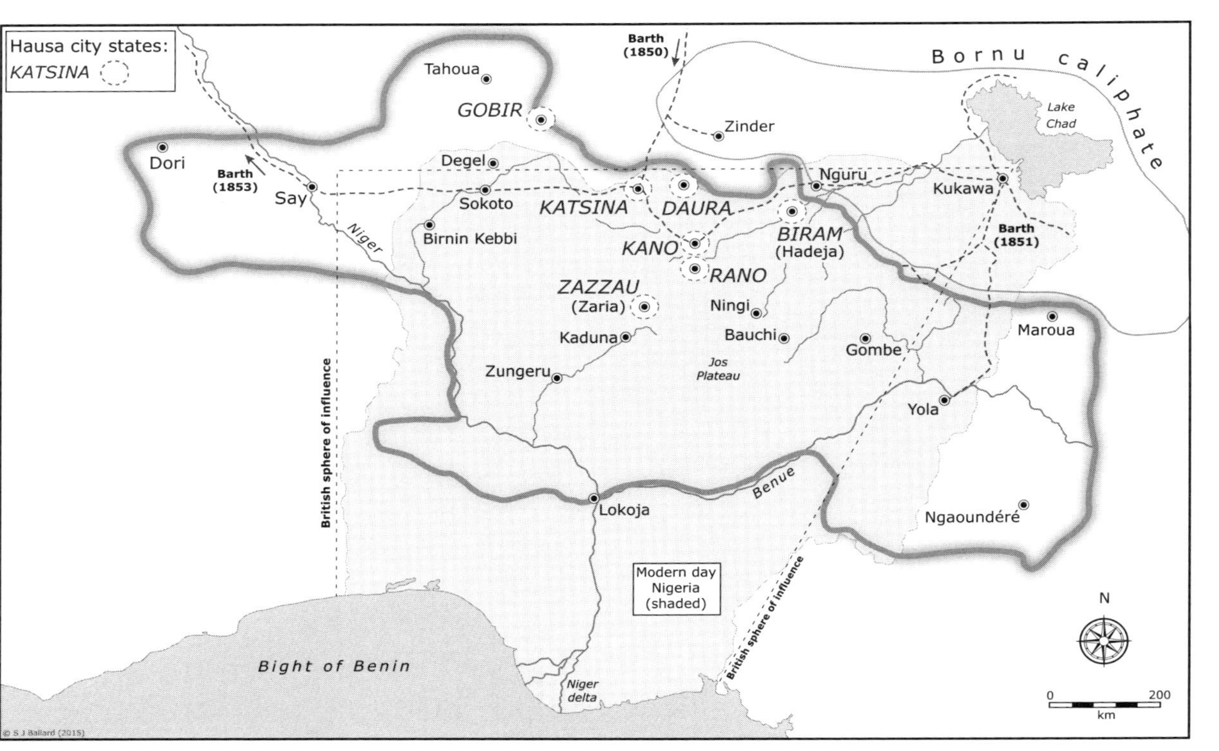

Sokoto Caliphate (in the 1850s)

PREFACE

THE STRANGE TALE OF JOHN HENRY DOROGU

A story, a story; let it go, let it come.
(This is how the storytellers begin their tales in northern Nigeria.)

In a village in north eastern Nigeria, a child stands frozen in fear.

The men had been welcomed as guests. They had seemed harmless. He had even given them water. But the strangers had deceived them. When everyone's guard was down, in a flash they showed their true faces and now the boy is very scared. Too scared to run.

Although he is young, maybe only eight years old, he knows their reputation. He knows now these are the men who destroyed the other villages, who brought suffering to the people of the other villages. The boy knows what it means that these men have come to his village, and now they are in his home.

> At that moment guns were fired, all the strangers started to capture their 'hosts'. My father had told me to go with him to a certain gate but my head was all mixed up. I didn't know what to do, with the result that the Bornu man who had been in my father's house finally caught me. The Hausa man captured my father and someone else captured my father's wife, although who it was I do not know. All the children in town were crying. Mothers were separated from their children and husbands from their wives. And thus we were led away.
>
> As we were leaving the town he [my captor] dragged me through some thorns. Both he and I were in the briers [...] The briars pricked my feet so they were all bloody. He mounted his horse and then lifted me up and put me on the back. I really couldn't pay any attention to whether the thorns had pricked my feet or not since

> I was absorbed in worrying about what was going to happen to me. I saw a friend of mine riding on the back of his master's horse, and I called to him "do you see? We have become slaves." He replied, "There is nothing we can do except put our trust in God's works."
>
> When we arrived at the war camp, we dismounted. As I was looking around, I saw my father's wife being led to the chief by a man with a knife in his hand. I felt my feet itching and then noticed my feet were all bloody. They brought some nuts for us, but we didn't eat any. We weren't hungry because we were so unhappy. After they carried off everything from our town, they set it on fire. Chicken eggs were exploding like guns, as the fire reached everywhere. The fire continued burning in the town even to the next day.
>
> They took us before their chief in order to show him the slaves they had captured. When he had seen all of us they took us away.
>
> This was the beginning of slavery for me.[1]

In a little over five years Nigeria has been devastated by violence foisted on the people of the north east by a group of fanatical Islamists. They have killed tens of thousands of people, chased over a million and a half of them from their homes, and kidnapped hundreds, possibly thousands, of young Nigerians. Those who escaped the clutches of this group told stories of horror, of rape and of murder.

But the account above did not occur in 2015. This boy who was enslaved was named Dorogu. He was seized from his home in a village near Lake Chad around 1849. What happened to him is one of the most remarkable tales in Nigerian history.

Dorogu was seized along with some two or three hundred others from his village and those surrounding it. He suspects that were betrayed, sold by their own liege lords. On his way to the slave pits of Zinder where he would be sold, he passed through one of his family's villages where he saw his grandmother. "When she saw me her whole body trembled. She asked me 'Where is Adamu?' I said 'I don't know.' Then I simply said 'Goodbye'."[2] It was the last time he would see his family.

That we can read Dorogu's account today is because this small boy was then sold on, eventually, to a man from Bornu who presented him as a servant to a German explorer called Adolf Overweg. Overweg became fond of the young boy, and bought his freedom, along with another servant, an eighteen year-old called Abegga.

But sometime during his journey around Lake Chad, Overweg contracted a fever that sent him into seething convulsions of madness. He jabbered incoherently and no man could hold him down. The disease, which could possibly have been the neurological phase of Trypanosomiasis, otherwise known as Sleeping Sickness, caused him great fits of uncontrollable spasmodic movement. In one of these he ran headlong into a tree and fell into a fire. Soon afterwards he died of the fever.[3]

Before his death Overweg had made his travelling companion, another German named Heinrich Barth, promise that he would not let the boys be taken back into slavery. So they travelled with Barth for the remainder of his journey. Dorogu was a bright and curious boy, and Barth who was otherwise a gruff and dyspeptic Prussian, seems to have enjoyed his company. According to later accounts, Barth, who was a fine linguist, talked with Dorogu for hours about the meanings of Hausa words and sayings while they were in the saddle on the way to Timbuktu and back across the Sahara. At his journey's end Barth brought both boys back with him to England.

They were probably the first Hausa people ever to lay eyes on London.

The two boys were the objects of keen Victorian curiosity: they went on tour, were presented to Queen Victoria, and later to Frederick William IV, the King of Prussia.

In London, Dorogu stayed with another linguist, the Reverend JF Schön, who had been part of a mission to southern Nigeria fifteen years earlier with the freed slave Samuel Ajayi Crowther, the man who would become the first African Archbishop.

Schön later said of Dorogu:

> Never was there an African coming to this country that was of greater use; full of information for his age, probably not more than sixteen or seventeen years old, energetic and lively in his habits, always ready to speak. He began relating stories to me, or rather dictating them, giving me a description of his own life and travels in Africa in his own language, very often dictating to me for hours together and even until late in the night; so that I had soon a Hausa Literature of several hundred pages before me.[4]

This book transcribed by Schön was rediscovered in the 1960s, during a period in which European scholars sought out Hausa biographies in the vernacular. Dorogu's life story became the basis for the 1971 book *West African Travels and Adventures*. In it, Dorogu's voice is preserved. The young man has the flair and verbal skill of a fine story-teller. At one point he challenges Schön playfully, and Schön records it:

> Now I have told you many stories. Do you like them, you lover of the Hausa language? Have you discovered any new words? If you find a new word you jump for joy. As far as I'm concerned, if I got gold I would jump for joy because gold has

> value, but what value have words? I am tired of talking; I am going to sleep. If I talked the whole night, you would keep on writing throughout the night. Sleep well, you lover of the Hausa Language. Tomorrow morning, if I get a lot more money, I will tell you many stories. Sleep well. I cannot add another word now.[5]

He also talks about the curious people who have taken him into their homes, and observes the rituals they have constructed that make up what it means to be "civilised": table manners, how to speak to a lady, how one should comport oneself in a friend's house during a genteel society event.

In the book there is reproduced a rare photograph of the boy. Dorogu, standing, leans on his older friend Abbega, who is seated. In the picture they both wear the fez caps Barth bought them in Tripoli. Abegga looks shy, less confident. The older boy is reticent perhaps, and holds back, shielding himself with a stiff expression slightly turned away from the camera. Dorogu, on the other hand, is in a confident pose, hand planted on his hip. The younger boy looks directly out at the photographer, seemingly in a moment of curious consideration. It is as if his eyes are about to narrow, his lips purse over his slightly buck-teeth as he mulls something over, before aiming a well lofted question at the observer. His look has an enigmatic quality to it, as if the more the camera drew in from him, the more Dorugu himself acquired.

In his years in England the boy had become a Christian, baptised "John Henry Dorogu" and was the subject of much curiosity and public comment. But homesickness had begun to take its toll. Eight years after Barth had brought him over the Sahara, he travelled back to Nigeria by boat to Lagos, and disappeared from history.

At that point there was no British colonial territory of Nigeria, and nor would there be for half a century. In the southern part of the country was a myriad of kingdoms and communities and trading posts in the forests below the confluence of the Niger and Benue rivers. There had been longstanding contact between this part of the world and Europe; indeed before the outlawing of the trade it had been where slaves' transatlantic miseries had begun. The enforcement of abolition, a role the British appointed themselves, drove their colonial progress northward.

Above the confluence of the rivers, in what is now northern Nigeria, at that time there existed two caliphates, Islamic states ruled by theocratic aristocracies and their vassals. The Bornu caliphate, on the western shore of Lake Chad, was the remnant of a very old lineage, whose adoption of Islam was contemporaneous with the Norman conquest of England. The other caliphate, whose centre was hundreds of miles to the west of Bornu, was a younger order; an upstart state which had been thrust into being by an insurgent band of jihadists.

When the British came to northern Nigeria at the turn of the twentieth century, only one of these powers remained. The Bornu Caliphate had crumbled, leaving only the other, based around Sokoto. This was a culture with its own proud and written history, which drew its inspiration and strength from Islam. It has been said that this, the Sokoto Caliphate, was one of the greatest achievements in governance of the pre-colonial period.

The Caliphate's economy was based on slavery, and what's more its ruling echelons disdained the British. They refused to recognise them or come to any sort of deal with the invaders. The people of Sokoto feared that their world was about to be brought crashing down.

They were half right, at least. By 1904 the British had toppled the Sultan of Sokoto. But instead of replacing them with British officers, a bold experiment was set underway; the rulers were replaced with the colonists' own handpicked local potentates. Could the land which the British Government eyed as a bountiful future resource, be managed by local elites in the interest of the Empire, rather than of the Caliphate?

A key part of the experiment was the colony's education policy. If the locals were educated in the correct manner, then perhaps the next generation of local rulers would ensure that the right sort of development happened in West Africa. The Colonial Office appointed an unusual man to head this experiment, a Swiss-born missionary, explorer and anthropologist named Hans Vischer who had a unique approach to colonial administration.

Vischer's idea was that in order to succeed in developing Africa, the children of the elite would need to be educated in a modern syllabus, in a manner that simultaneously preserved what he thought of as being the natural "native" character. This would "enable them to use their own moral and physical forces to their best advantage. Widen their mental horizon without destroying their respect for race and parentage."[6] In his dealings he was a considerate and well-meaning man, he abjured the usual colonial officers' attitude of despising Africans and was known to argue openly with colleagues who he felt had disrespected them.

Nevertheless, Vischer believed that the white man was indispensable if West Africa were fully to abolish the slave trade—which was still prevalent in northern Nigeria up until the 1920s—and if prosperity was to come through free trade.

He felt a balance between modern education and tradition was needed. Maintaining cultural sensitivity, he believed, would aid the African's transition to a modern state. Vischer's goal was to train up an indigenous elite to continue the improving work of modernity, after what he saw as the inevitable end of British colonialism.[7]

Although Vischer was granted great personal respect in Kano, where he was called *dan Hausa*—the son of a Hausa-speaker, testimony to his language skills—the old Sokoto elite were sceptical about the new education. In their circles, this foreign education would be dubbed *boko*, meaning sham, fraudulent, or misleading. They believed it would lead to the righteous being taken away from their true calling, which was Islam. Few among those of the old aristocracy sent their children to the new school that Vischer founded in 1909 in the Nasarawa district of Kano, the ancient commercial capital of northern Nigeria. Eventually, over time, the meaning of the word *boko* would shift and come to be understood as anything to do with "Western" education.[8]

The children who did attend Vischer's school in the years before 1912 would have encountered a teacher, who in a way could have been an example of what Vischer was trying to avoid. He was an old Hausa man, who spoke fluent, even cut-glass English and had the impeccable Victorian manners to accompany it. The old man was popular with the colonial staff, who would visit him on off days in the hope he would recall some tales of his fascinating, eventful life.

And he had plenty to tell, if he were so minded. He had been a curious and inquisitive boy, who at a very young age had been captured into slavery in the most brutal manner. After a time he had been sold into the service of a party of European travellers, who included a very single-minded German explorer. Freed from slavery he had even been taken from his land to live in England for a time, with the grumpy white man.

Like a magical link to the past, the teacher at Kano's elite "boko" school was Dorogu, the freed slave boy who Barth took to London in fulfilment of his promise to a dying friend.

Little is known about Dorogu's adult life between leaving London and his employment in Kano. He had been a factotum in the British colonial administration since its establishment in Lokoja, at the confluence of the Niger and the Benue rivers. When the British moved north to Zungeru (in current day Niger State) to topple the Sultan, Dorogu travelled with them, teaching British officers Hausa and translating for them.

In old age, Dorugu still had a quick wit and gentle manners, according to Vischer's wife Isabelle, who wrote a daily diary. But something seems to have had changed in him; the boy who had travelled half the world, been introduced to European royalty, helped compile the first Hausa-English dictionary, and who was possessed with the talent to tell stories, had grown into a quieter, more reticent man. Visitors to his home, who came to hear him recount his life's tales, were often disappointed; in his old age, unlike his youth, he rarely talked about his experiences and travels.[9]

Although he had returned to his homeland, did he feel somehow removed from it too? He lived his old age in Kano, in the Hausa heartland. But he lived among foreigners, speaking their language and worshipping a Christian God.

In her diary Isabelle Vischer recorded old Dorogu's final days. She notes his thin frame and his paper thin skin. Until the end his speech was "careful and correct, without hint of an accent". His death was "graceful and unlaboured", she said. He died being attended to by his wife, who fed him spoons of pap and dribbled water on his lips. "She looked after him to the end" Isabelle wrote, "showing unlimited selflessness."

But in death, kind, intelligent, correct, quiet, reliable Dorogu offered only enigmas to his adoring, foreign friends and colonial employers.

In another entry to her diary some days later, Isabelle reveals that Dorogu might not have been all that he seemed to the white men he lived so closely with: "I fear that during his lifetime Dorogu succumbed to the sin of avarice!" she wrote a week after his death. Among his possessions were found objects that the faithful translator had filched from his adopted people; a collection of old—unopened—biscuit boxes, small jars of jam from England, a dozen pairs of spectacles lifted from the desks of former commanding officers. He had pinched their clothes too; they were found still bearing the original owner's initials on their name-tags.

These items do not seem to have been taken for any sort of material gain; Dorogu apparently acquired a considerable amount of money and rolls of gold and silver pieces during his lifetime. No one had been aware of his trinket collection, which he never displayed.

Did they hold some sort of symbolic power for him, keepsakes taken from these colonial authority figures? Perhaps they were tokens he needed to maintain a mixed identity? Or were they small acts of resistance or rebellion?

There was a final mystery for Dorogu's foreign employers to mull; his widow. As well as the money, the silver and the gold, Dorogu's widow was also entitled to his pension. Dorogu had remained a Christian all his adult life, but his widow's religion was unknown by his employers. It was explained to her that if she opted to be Christian, like her husband, she could take all of his estate in full. If she declared she was a Muslim, however, she would receive only that portion allotted her by an *Alkali*, an Islamic judge, in line with *sharia* rules on inheritance.

Much to Isabelle Vischer's surprise "not only did she declare she was a Moslem," Vischer wrote, "but she even distributed as alms the little that she did inherit."

"She will continue her humble existence in obscurity..." the diary entry concluded.[10]

In January 2015, a large part of north-eastern Nigeria had been taken over by a fanatical Islamist jihadi insurgency dubbed *Boko Haram*, which means "Western education is forbidden". Their leader Abubakar Shekau, who had become familiar through his grisly videos in which he challenged the Nigerian government in Abuja, accusing them of being infidels and threatening to slit their throats, had declared that a new Islamic state had been formed in the north east, and that the towns they held were now "nothing to do with Nigeria".[11] Daily news stories brought fresh tales of horror from the north east, the group's fighters took more and more territory, more and more people fled for their lives.

Nigeria seemed powerless to stop it. In the midst of all this the country was about to hold an election. As it drew near, the person who manages a Twitter account for the candidate of the All Progressives Congress, Retired General Muhammadu Buhari, sent out a somewhat despairing tweet: "We must ask ourselves these questions—how did we become like this? How did we get to this point? What kind of country have we become?"

Unlikely as it may seem, the issues of the complex identity of an old teacher who died over a hundred years ago, the strange tale of John Henry Dorogu, can help us answer these questions and help us understand the war that is tearing northern Nigeria apart.

* * *

To explain why this is so, I will first have to delve into history, to tell the stories of three different men, and the kinds of world they wanted to build. Each of these individuals believed themselves to have a moral mission on earth. Those missions, their fantasies of how the world should be, have outlived them; influencing our idea of how we see the land we call northern Nigeria, and how Nigerians see themselves.

The first of these three men was born the son of an unremarkable itinerant religious teacher. But he died the spiritual leader of a new empire.

PART 1

1

IF YOU CAN'T BEAT THEM, SHUN THEM

In the hot, dusty, dry season of 1804, Muslims across the Hausa kingdoms of Gobir and Kebbi were hurriedly packing their worldly belongings into woven travelling sacks and preparing to flee their homes. In the pre-dawn darkness, by the flickering light of smoky, groundnut-oil lamps, they gathered their households, their wives, children and property (which would have included slaves) and prepared to travel dangerous trails and pathways. It was approaching the hottest part of the year, when walking in the middle of the day would be arduous. Food was scarce, there would be little for the journey and little prospect of procuring any where they were heading. February heralds the onset of the hungry season, when stores begin to be depleted before the rains return in June, and a new growing season can start. On the way, men on horseback armed with spears would be guarding the roads, on the lookout for the fleeing Muslims on the orders of the *Sarkin* Gobir.[1] The penalty for being discovered would be terrible. Once they left, there would be no way back.

What had necessitated this drastic course of action? In the northeast marches of Gobir a group of Islamic purists, led by an Islamic scholar known by his followers as *Shehu*,[2] had declared war against the tyrannous ruler of Gobir in his walled capital of Alakawa. For the followers of the Shehu, to remain where they were meant facing the coming anger and retribution of the most militarily powerful of the fourteen Hausa city states.

The young, despotic Yunfa, who had not long ago succeeded his uncle as Sarkin Gobir, was already known as a sadistic, angry ruler. The forces of Gobir had sacked one town, slaying Muslim men and carrying away their families and property. In response, the Shehu declared he was going to remove himself and his followers from "among the heathen".[3] They would leave Degel, the small village above the Rima River where he lived, and establish a new world dedicated to Islamic purity.

They feared Yunfa's revenge against the Shehu's community, the Dar-ul Islam, would be bloody; men slain and families enslaved. Although it was permissible for Muslims to take slaves from among the polytheistic pagan unbelievers—who they considered barely human—it was another matter altogether for a Muslim to be so treated. Their property and livestock would be seized, they would be forced to work on other men's fields, or as concubines in their beds, or given as tribute to another Hausa *Sarki*, or transported by caravan across the Sahara desert, from where few returned. The thought was horrifying.

For years, Islamic reformist sentiments, led in the main by Fulanis like the Shehu against the Hausa Sarkis had been rising. The band of reformers under the Shehu had been gaining popularity, even among polytheistic unbelievers, who had been flocking to hear him speak and to convert to Islam.[4] Hausa rulers had been resisting. Resentment had been building on both sides, and now the breaking point had been reached. The Shehu, who was an old man of fifty, gathered his family and meagre belongings (consisting mostly of books) and, with the help of Tuareg allies, escaped the clutches of Gobir's army.[5]

Among the followers of the Shehu who lived in the homesteads and cattle camps of Gobir, as far as the walled city of Kebbi and even in Alakawa, the Sarkin Gobir's own capital,[6] this was not an act of cowardice; the Shehu was not deserting them. His son Mohammed Bello, aided by a band of Tuareg horsemen, rode through the country with a message calling on Islamic clerics, *mallams*, to join the community and bring their followers to their new camp. "Let them come out from among the workers of evil," the letter penned by Bello said, "let them rise up with haste. Little by little, war is going to break out in this place, a dust-raising war."[7] To have a hope of survival, the community had to move beyond Gobir's reach. Although Degel was on the fringes of the land that Yunfa controlled, it was too close. The withdrawal was not simply a tactical manoeuvre however, it was a metaphor.

In Bello's letter, presumably written in concert with the Shehu, he said; "Tell them my desire, I will not accept humiliation, for disgrace is a heavy burden to bear. If I am harassed in a town I will leave that town, I will not sit down in a house that is impure." To the Muslims this was a clear reference to the Hijra, the flight of the Prophet Mohammed, from the corrupted city of Mecca to set up a community in Medina. Later, when he wrote an account of that time, Bello referred to it as his father's "Hijra". The Shehu was not running away, but nor was it simply a tactical retreat; it was an example, a movement of religious dynamism. People followed.

The Sarkin Gobir was so alarmed by the numbers of people leaving his own court that he closed the roads and ordered his provincial vassals to harass Muslims wherever they were to be found.[8] Although the number of people who answered this call and fled Gobir is not known, it must have been considerable. The Shehu headed away from Degel on 21 February 1804. Two months later, in the sweltering heat of April when it can reach 40 degrees Celsius at midday, people were still arriving at the new camp. It was at a place called Gudu, thirty miles from Degel as the crow flies, and a much longer route over the rocky scrub and around the dry riverbeds.

"Some of our folk reached us with families and their property," wrote Bello later, "others with their families and no property. Others again by themselves alone without their families or goods."[9]

There were attempts to negotiate a settlement and thereby avoid war. Sarki Yunfa sent his Wazir to the Shehu, pleading with him that all would be forgiven if the Shehu called off the rebellion and returned to his previous life as a roaming preacher. When the Wazir returned to Alakawa, the walled capital of Gobir, the Shehu sent with him a boy named Wodi, holding a message containing the community's terms. The Shehu would return on two conditions; that Yunfa make efforts to purify the faith and that all that had been seized by Gobir, the relatives and property belonging to the Muslims, must be returned to them, but really there was nothing to negotiate. There was no trust between them and no common ground to look toward.

The Sarkin Yunfa considered himself a Muslim; he prayed and fasted and paid *zakat*, the tithe of charity. He gathered his own court *mallams*, his learned scholars, and asked them what he should do. Wodi told the Shehu's companions "They said to Sarkin Gobir, 'You are in the right, Shehu and his people are in the wrong.'"[10]

When they heard this, the Shehu and his close companions looked about their new encampment, which was by a pool of water, with steep ridges on all sides. It was more suited to resisting attack than Degel was, but the war would come to them soon. They would have to attack before their enemies reached them at Gudu, or risk being overrun. There was much that needed doing, among which was the need to elect a leader of their community. Although he declined at first, out of a sense of modesty, there was only one obvious choice.

One by one, the companions gave the Shehu a salute of homage; a raised fist, thumb uppermost.[11]

The Shehu was known to be an intensely spiritual man, both a scholar and a visionary. He had excelled during his Islamic education, gaining not only many prestigious mentors, but also his own following while he was still being educated.[12] Many believed him to be a man of prophecy, a reformer whose coming was ordained by God.

Today, little is known about his origins other than his father Mohammed was a travelling Fulani preacher with a good reputation as a scholar.[13] The Fulani were—and many still are—nomadic pastoralists, cattle herders moving their beasts from pasture to pasture. But over the generations they had begun to settle, making a name for themselves as *mallamai*, preachers and theologians. Many of the *mallams* of the royal courts were Fulani. But Mohammed's own community were not from high places, the courts of the kings. His base was drawn from among the Fulani herdsmen whose small hamlets and cattle camps he passed through, leading them in prayer and teaching their sons the Qur'an.

He was known by them as "the learned one"—*Fodiye* in Fulfulde, the language of the Fulani. His son was Othman bin Mohammed, known according to the Fulani naming convention as "son of the learned one"—dan Fodiyo.

As a boy, Othman dan Fodiyo was taught by his father to recall the Qur'an from memory.[14] He and his brother Abdullah, and probably their age mates too, would sit on reed mats spread on the ground and listen to their father intone the words in Arabic, and repeat them. At first they would have learned the words without understanding what they meant. As they recited in the entrance room of their father's house, or perhaps in the shade under a neem tree, all around them would have been wooden tablets with the suras inscribed in Arabic. Every day they would have worked from the first sura to the last, and then would have recited them in in reverse order to the second sura.

When the boys were ready, they would have stood in front of an examiner, possibly Mohammed, or another man called a *karamokos* who travelled around the Fulani communities especially for this purpose, and recited the verses in their entirety. Only when that could be done without error did they move on to further studies.[15]

The process of education in Islamic knowledge was at that time rigid, in that it was judged by how well students could adhere to the precepts forged in Medieval Arabia and handed down from scholar to pupil for generations. However it was also individualistic in that anyone who can recite the Qur'an without error may consider himself a teacher.[16] It follows that some teachers would have been better than others. The apt student, one who has in mind becoming a master in his own right, must seek out new mentors in different aspects of Islamic learning to complete his overall education. In West Africa, and particularly in the nomadic Fulani tradition, these masters must have also moved around to demonstrate their prowess and acquire a following.

It was a crowded field. From the booming land-ports of the Sahara, where caravans of salt going south passed trains of slaves going north, to the market villages where farmers brought surplus produce to trade, to the walled cities where the Hausa kings held court under the shade of deep green trees among the ochre mud enclosures, there was seemingly an unquenchable thirst for the words of itinerant wise-men. The arrival of a new and persuasive orator, or the return of an old favourite, would cause consternation in the town as people flocked to see him and possibly share his, or her,[17] secret knowledge.

Take this evocative scene, quoted by Mohammed Bello in his biographical work on the time, *Infaq al Maisri*, "The Wages of the Fortunate":

> [T]here came a certain man one night. In the morning people hastened to him in crowds. I went forth with the people. I heard someone saying, 'He is a saint, one of the saints of God'. Another said he is a reformer of religion. When he came to the town we found the people gathered together. The headman of the town, Muhammadu dan Sherif came too with his followers. As the people thronged and pressed together it was difficult to see the man. Finally he entered a building and put his arm through the window. People came and touched his hand and passed on. Each one that touched his hand said he had found satisfaction of his wants. I touched the man's hand and came away. After a few days I heard news that he had gone to some place and fallen into a well and was killed. It appeared he was a madman, he was enslaved by evil spirits and so perished.[18]

This was written by a scholar Bello names as Hasanalusi, who he says authored fifty works debunking the teachings of false prophets. Although it was a hundred and seventy years before Bello was writing, he evidently recognised this scene all too well.

For most, life was a pretty terrifying prospect. The sheer extent of the occult, the vast panorama of what was unknown, was by itself enough to crush the weak and feeble. Death could strike at any moment, without explanation or warning. Life could be snuffed out in a painful instant, or the end could be drawn out in horrific, weeping, sore-covered suffering. Relationships with those closest to you could not altogether be relied on, malevolent forces could conspire to make enemies out of friends. The powerful could simply take what they wished from the weak, rigid hierarchies prevented any redress. It was not surprising that people flocked to men who professed secret knowledge of how to navigate the unknown and the unknowable.

For the most part, these individuals were little more than travelling hucksters, medicine men who would arrive at the market with a wheelbarrow of acrid herbs and a satchel full of charms for the panoply of ailments that afflicted the people. Even today, these are a familiar sight. At any market in northern Nigeria there will be several people selling miracle cures, magic potions for love, or faultless medicines for men's vigour, standing in the shade of a tree, their wares spread out on a blanket or wrapped in little plastic bags, barking their provenance from a raspy bullhorn. Others were journeymen preachers, who eked a living from their audiences' contributions and patrimony. They could be found running schools for children to memorise the Qur'an and acting as community mediators. Others still were court-dwelling clerics who ministered to the elite in their cloistered precincts, from where the common folk were excluded and access to the rulers was jealously guarded by slaves and eunuchs; for access to the rulers was itself power.

What they preached was Islam, to a degree. It was also mixed with other things; old ways that could not be released, or would not let go.

What people believed in this part of the world before the coming of Islam would have been a cult-like belief, centred around a secretive priesthood who revered animal totems.[19] Before the advent of Islam, it is thought that the leadership was believed to be responsible only to the animal totem of the community.[20] The fate of the priestly monarch was linked intimately to the totem. In times of strife, when the monarch's leadership was challenged, rites and sacrifices were made to the totem of the town, inviting it to a face-off with the community's high-priest. According to the anthropologist Arthur Tremearne, crocodiles were frequent totems of villages and the rites often involved the priest going out to sit among them by the riverside, perhaps overnight. If the man survived the encounter, then all was well. If he died, then one of the challengers would take his place. Depending on the community's culture, these rites could also be on a cyclical basis, with a leader having an alloted period, after which he was ritually murdered in the name of the totem. But this was a practice that, even by the Shehu's time, had mostly died out.[21]

The best accounts of the beliefs of pagan Hausas, known as the *Maguzawa*, were recorded a hundred years after the life of the Shehu. They show the world was a place of competing spirits; of rock, earth and tree, and also of long dead ancestors, each with their own characters and personalities. These spirits, called *boruruka*—*bori* in the singular—could enter inside you at any moment. They were the explanation for every aspect of life, responsible for everything, from disease to bad luck. They made family members disagreeable and argumentative, and had the power to delay the rains or bring them early, devastating rural communities. Life was a fearful and complicated web of taboos and ritual.[22]

Once a *bori* had entered inside a human body, it would compete with spirits already living there for control. This included a struggle with the essential spirit—the equivalent to the soul—which entered the body at birth. Powerful *bori* would simply overpower the spirit and kill the body, much like we understand a disease to do. Such was the similarity between the concepts of the *bori* and disease that Tremearne, in 1915, wrote: "the *bori* is a bacillus".[23] Just as people who work with infectious diseases are afraid of a virus, so the Hausa were afraid of *bori*. Probably more so, because the world was full of these risks. *Bori* could be opportunistic, they lived in malevolent places where people felt ill-at-ease, such as in water, or in strange groves in the bush, where they waited to pounce.

They could also be summoned by the desires and caprice of other people. Envious suitors were constantly on the lookout to rob people of their good fortune, their natural endowments, health or hard-won success. Malevolent people could summon *bori* to do evil deeds to those they didn't like or envied just by giving the *bori* the name of the person they wished to harm.

The body was vulnerable because its defence, the soul, was not permanently attached to it. It lived in the shadow and it could be captured by a wizard, or *maiya*. The wizard only had to utter the right words and step on the shadow and it was his.[24] The essential spirit could also leave the body at its own whim, to seek temporary relief of its human host. If the soul was thirsty in the night, for example, it could transform itself and fly away in search of refreshment.[25] What, otherwise were dreams? How else could the night-time chirruping of birds and flapping of wings, when all other birds had gone to roost,[26] be explained? Wizards could trap these souls as they flitted among the trees. When someone fell ill, among the first things to be done was search the nearby trees for entrapped birds and free them.[27]

Once a wizard had the essential spirit, he would eat it. Without the soul, the host body would be at the mercy of the other spirits inside. If the wizard was not forced to return the soul, the body would sicken and die. Protection of the essential spirit and the body against all kinds of spiritual and temporal attacks was a constant concern.

But wizards were not the only worry. Under the right circumstances, any person could summon a malevolent *bori*. At the heart of pagan Hausa belief, indeed of most beliefs that predate the monotheistic religions of Judaism, Christianity and Islam, is the acceptance of the presence and influence of one's enemies at all times. According to these animist creeds, human feelings of desire—like jealousy, envy and covetousness, are not only experienced in the mind or the soul of the person, they can make things happen in the real world. Although these powerful feelings could be damaging, they were accepted as a normal part of life; they were even anticipated. In *Maguzawa* belief there was no moral reproof for succumbing to what monotheistic religious authorities call sin, there was only the use of ritual to protect oneself from the harmful effects of these forces. If you were properly protected, the evil spirit would go elsewhere—maybe even to return and plague the sender. For someone to refuse to take the correct precautions was madness.

For the *Maguzawa* it was prudent to consult *bori* practitioners and procure charms of protection. These *bori* adepts were known as *bokaye*, and were distinct from wizards in that, where wizards were hidden and secretive beings, *bokaye* were openly members of the community. They tended the *Gidan Tsafi*, the house of spirits, a room dense with the incense of burning lumps of tree sap and smelling thickly of leather. Only the *bokaye* dared enter the *Gidan Tsafi* as it contained the physical manifestations of many of the most powerful *bori* held in tanned leather pouches or bottles. Anyone entering without the necessary fortitude to resist would be overcome immediately.[28]

Charms recorded by Tremearne offered by these adepts, who were as likely to be women as men, went from the benign to the cruel. Four cowrie shells tied in the hair of a child, for instance, were thought to snag spirits inside their jagged, toothy curls and prevent them from entering the body. The influence of the spirits could also be assuaged with parts of animals, like the teeth of a horse or the tusks of a boar, or parts of a crocodile or lion. Once affected by an evil wisher, the roots of trees, pounded into a paste were sought as effective cures. "Another excellent method," Tremearne noted, "is to touch the naked body, especially that of a child, with a red hot iron."[29]

Islam's arrival in the Hausa city-states in the fifteenth century is indicated by the appearance of Muslim names among the genealogies of Hausa kings.[30] But Islam did not completely supplant pagan beliefs, nor did it wipe animism away, rather it fused with it.

Islam came from two directions. It was brought to the Hausa from the east by the conquests of the city states by both the empires of Kanem and Bornu and from the west by Askia, ruler of the Songhai empire. As it came it replaced some things; the old concept of leadership—responsible only to the spirit totem—was replaced with one where subjects were answerable to a new clique of privileged elite civil servants and rulers (these men were perhaps relieved that they would no longer have to offer themselves up to a crocodile as a sacrifice). For some time Islam remained solely the preserve of the Hausa aristocracy, who left the small folk to their old ways.

But for the Muslim who also wished to remain protected against the harsh old spirits, there were Islamically acceptable methods available to them. Verses of the Qur'an were sewn into a leather packet and worn around the body. Arabic script was also stitched into clothing, usually undergarments, or inscribed on jewellery and worn. Another form of protection was given when verses of the Qur'an were written in charcoal on a wooden board, the type used in Qur'anic schools to memorise suras. This board was then washed with water, carrying the charcoal with it into a vessel, from where it was drunk. The drinker was protected by literally ingesting holy words. These Islamicised rites were administered by the kind of journeyman *mallams* who travelled from one mosque to another, dependent on the small contributions given to them by children learning the Qur'an by rote, or a minor trade like rope making.[31]

Endless debate circled these wise men on the quality and provenance of their wisdom, and what to do with those who were sub-par. Some of the grand court preachers thought the hucksters little more than heathen idolaters deserving only of public humiliation or even death.[32] But these opinions, when they were voiced, were usually confined to the *mallam's* circle of students, who sat in the exclusive precincts of the court, a world away from the market.

Most *mallams*, as consummate journeymen, could not afford to be so rigorous in their condemnation. Perhaps it was because these men were aware that their popularity, their living, depended on a kind of mass approval. They needed to speak to the man who had just stepped from the market into the mosque. Or, as was more likely, to his wife, the person upon whom the majority of the burdens, the million-and-one agonies of life, fell.

For Tremearne, there were not two separate belief systems, these rites substituted animal sacrifices with charms made of parts of the Qu'ran, but they were used to ward off the same spirits. For example the name given to the essential spirit in *bori* belief was called *al baraka* by Tremearne's informants; this is also the name given to the concept of spiritual wisdom and the spirit-soul in Sufism. This reluctance of the people to stray from old ways limited how far a journeyman scholar could go in his condemnation of old practises. A man who depended on popular patronage hectored his audience excessively at his peril. Much better to tread a middle way; a bit of hectoring, and then a bit of gratification with a charm.

The rulers of the city, sequestered in their palaces, also had pragmatic considerations that prevented them from leaving the old ways. Islam had always been mostly the preserve of the elite,[33] but if they could not keep control of the mostly-pagan people their power was likely to be moot. This meant finding a common issue. For example, part of the duties of Muslim rulers was that they were required to keep wizards under control. They did this by continuing the practice of electing a "wizard king" or Sarkin Maiya, who acted as the head of a secret guild. The Sarkin Maiya could be called upon by rulers if rogue wizard activity reached unacceptable levels. After all, society demanded other guilds have their leaders; blacksmiths, weavers, traders, even thieves, why not wizards?

The threat of famine in this semi-arid region also frequently threatened to destabilise society. Even the fear of it was not to be trifled with. The short growing season in the dry savannah grasslands was dependent on rains that were frequently late, or early—both could be as disastrous as completely failing for the farmer. *Mallams* and *bokaye* could be found working together on rain ceremonies observed by Tremearne. He observed *mallams*, presumably leery of the overt challenge to God, contract out the rain-bringing rituals to the Maguzawa adepts, who then enacted it in the name of Allah.

In the time of the Shehu, faith in Islam had waned among the courtly Hausa elite. Several generations before, they had been roundly drubbed in a lengthy series of wars against the pagans, who lived in the forests to the south of the Jos Plateau.[34] What use was a belief if it couldn't protect you from your own enemies? Unless the fickle Sarkis could see a real political effect, they weren't interested.

Enter the Shehu, Othman dan Fodiyo. He rejected both the quietist life of a court scholar and the rugged compromise of the market *mallam*.[35] To him and his followers it was totally appalling that jealousy, envy and murderous caprice could be not only accepted, but expected—even actively encouraged!—as it was by adepts of *bori*. The belief that anyone could appeal to the spirits of tree, earth and rock to destroy another man was anathema. The idea that a leader could—and should—be removed for little or no good reason was a shocking state of affairs that led to terrible waste.[36] To dan Fodiyo, the fear of God should be the only thing that concerned the righteous man.

As a youngster, dan Fodiyo learned about *tawhid*, the divine unity, and *tafsir*, the interpretations of the Qu'ran, from a number of different teachers.[37]

He was also well versed in the *Hadith*, the way of the Prophet, the set of principles forged in Medieval Arabia that, if followed correctly, make life most pleasing to God. He was also an expert in the Maliki school of Sharia, Islamic law. Of the four schools derived from the Hadith, this was the first that reached Sub Saharan West Africa, brought over the great desert by caravan traders who interacted with his ancestors hundreds of years before. Another large part of his education would have been learning the stories of the Prophet's life, and how he and his small band of companions defeated the heathen polytheists of Arabia, and liberated the holy places in Mecca.

Dan Fodiyo was born into a Sufi brotherhood. These brotherhoods, or *tariqa*, believed in saints, spirits, mysticism and in rituals like *dhikr*, where a congregation will recite prayers in unison until it becomes rhythmic chanting that can induce a sort of trance. The object of this practice is a spiritual unity with one's brothers and then, hopefully, with Allah. The code of the brotherhoods forbid sins like drinking, smoking, fornication and lying, and they consider themselves purists.[38] But at the time of the Shehu's education there were some, far away at the centre of the Islamic world, that were beginning to think differently.

Unlike some of his mentors, dan Fodiyo himself did not achieve the pinnacle of Islamic practise by completing the great overland Hajj pilgrimage to Mecca. In his early twenties, when under the tutelage of a mentor in Agadez, (an ancient town now in the modern day Republic of Niger) he set out on the journey, but was sent back because he did not have his father's permission to go.[39] Had he continued, he would have found Mecca in the hands of the radical followers of the eighteenth-century Islamic puritan Muhammad ibn Abd al-Wahhab, who died in 1792, when dan Fodiyo was thirty-eight years old. They were seeking to purify the faith from practices they believed had begun to infiltrate Islam in the eighteenth century, such as saint worship and belief in spirits. The supporters of Abd al-Wahhab wanted to eliminate innovation in the religion, called *bid'a*, polytheism, or *shirk*, to return the religion to its basic principles, the way of life of the Prophet Mohammed and the original community of Muslims, known as the "pious predecessors"—al salaf al-salih.[40]

Dan Fodiyo would have become familiar with the salafist ideas of the Wahhabis, as they became known later, as he was introduced to their uncompromising approach by a Tuareg sheikh who had spent time in Arabia.[41] Some historical accounts say he agreed with many parts of the Wahhabi approach to sin, but unlike the Wahhabis, dan Fodiyo was not completely without compromise. These accounts say dan Fodiyo, who was born into the Qadiriyyah brotherhood, eschewed the harsh edge to his preaching, particularly in his belief that the sinner deserved pity rather than punishment.[42] Salafists today who want to claim dan Fodiyo as one of their own, say this is not true. Over the course of his life, they claim, he became aware of the imperative to reject the Sufi brotherhoods and more fully embrace Wahhabi principles of the *salaf*.[43]

Certainly a Salafist like Abd al-Wahhab might have seen some some contradiction between their idea of purity and the beliefs of the Sufi brotherhoods. But other histories of the Shehu say that he hovered somewhere in between the two traditions. They say that coming from a background heavily accented with mysticism, dan Fodiyo accepted that spirits, or *djinns*, were real. The notion of djinns and prophetic ideas do run through much of what has been written about him. It seems though spirits were real to dan Fodiyo at least for a great part of his life, he believed there was only one way to deal with them, and that was through dedication to Islam, signified by total commitment to prayer and submission to Allah. Any Muslim who sought protection any other way was skirting with apostasy. Worse was anyone who participated in deals with the spirits, they were blasphemers and less than human.

The true power of the Sufi brotherhoods however, is that as an institution they bridge both realms of spiritual and political power. Members became a natural elite, that feeling of brotherhood became a political force. Membership of the Sufi sects such as the Qadiriyya, and later the Tijaniyya, meant something in this harsh landscape—both political and physical. It drew people toward it. In order to make way in these brotherhoods the power of your conviction was important, as was demonstrated by the ability to perform long periods of seclusion, where it was possible to get closer to God through solitude.[44]

To many who listened to him, his way must have seemed very attractive. Here was a pious man whose words gave as much comfort as any herb or charm. The message was simple: only Allah should be feared, and all that was needed was to follow a very small number of principles and you would be rewarded in paradise. The constant fear of spirits was diversionary, irreligious and constituted the way to hell.

According to Fulani tradition, his education in interpreting the meaning of the Qur'an would have not only been in Arabic, but in Fulfulde. The act of translation may have led to a deeper understanding and grasp of exegesis.[45] This was probably a good reason many of the most sought-after court theologians and *mallams* were Fulani. This fluency in theological debate in Arabic and Fulfulde, and thence from Fulfulde to Hausa, would greatly aid the Shehu, and his like-minded reformers, in their grasp and wielding of religious power.[46] It made transmitting their message easier, and made their brotherhood more accessible.

He spoke simply about how basic principles of Islam could salve the mind, protect the body, and prepare the soul for the ultimate reward, paradise in the next life. Most of his sermons, according to his son Mohammed Bello, were on one of five subjects; how to perfectly follow the sharia, the law of God; the importance of the *Sunnah*, the way of God; he warned against being a bad pupil, that is to say being too demanding of a teacher; he spoke of how to prevent evil, how to avoid and guard against evil customs (including how to perform ablutions and properly stay clean); he also lectured on the disasters that would befall them if they eschewed sharia.[47]

He taught that the way of righteousness was to reject what he called "the forces of destruction". These were self conceit, vanity, jealousy envy, covetousness, ostentation, vain glory seeking wealth for display, evil desire and evil thinking against Muslims, all things that were every day accepted by the people who feared *bori*.[48]

Despite the warnings against false and idolatrous teachers who claimed to be reformers, many of dan Fodiyo's supporters believed him to be a man of destiny who, it was prophesied, would change the world. From a very young age there had been an air of the uncanny about him. In infancy, it was said by his biographers, he showed a preternatural familiarity with djinns, the Islamic name for spirits that flowed, unseen, through the world borne on little gusts of wind.[49]

His followers believed him to be the fulfilment of a prophecy, which said a *Mujaddid*, or reformer of the faith, would emerge from *bilad al-sudan*—the land of the blacks. This would presage the coming of the Mahdi, and the beginning of the end times. It was well accepted by many, including the Shehu and his followers, that the end of the world was at hand.[50] It had been foretold in Arabic tradition that the Mahdi would soon reveal himself in the lands to the west of Arabia and then the world would enter the millennium, the period before the day of final judgement. Other wise men and women had prophesied the Shehu's coming. In his history of the time, the Shehu's son Bello wrote one of these prophecies down: "A holy man shall appear in the community of the Soudan. He shall renew the faith, he shall revive the religion and establish the service of God. Those that believe in him shall follow him. He shall be known in all parts of the world." Although this must seem very vague to most reader's eyes today, the elements of the prophecy, according to his followers, were coming into alignment.[51]

According to some accounts, the Shehu himself believed that he was in fact the *Mujaddid*, the reformer sent before the Mahdi. All through his life he had received visions, waking reveries in which he conversed with the Prophet Mohammed and the twelth-century Sufi mystic and founder of the Sufi Qadiriyya sect 'Abd al-Qadir al-Jilani. He believed these to be rewards from God for his piety and confirmation of his position as reformer of the faith.[52]

Ten years before he left Degel to perform his Hijra, the Shehu had received a vision of great significance. In it, al-Jilani passed a robe and a turban around a collected group of saints, the Prophet's companions in his lifetime, before dressing the Shehu in the garments. These were embroidered with the *shahada*, the declaration of the Muslim creed: "There is no God but God, and Mohammed is the prophet of God". Al-Jilani then unsheathed a sword and handed it to the saints, who passed it around before al-Jilani handed this too to dan Fodiyo. This, proclaimed al-Jilani, was the Sword of Truth which should be one day "unsheathed against the enemies of God".[53] This version of dan Fodiyo's life has been called into question, the fragments of text on which it is based could be later forgeries, made at a time when people wanted to reassert the Shehu's Sufi roots.[54]

But it is known that his followers whispered the Shehu might even be the Mahdi. He denied it with a modesty one could almost describe as aggressive, lambasting the people who repeated the rumour as liars.[55] He maintained enough mystery to inspire many, but not too much so as to see himself get carried away with it as the man in Hasanalusi's cautionary tale quoted by Bello. Biographers wrote that he won over whole audiences with a smile.[56] The precocious boy had become a preacher of some prowess and renown.

Another important difference between the Shehu and the Hausas who sought shelter in spirit rites was that he was a Fulani.

Nomadic people themselves can often be known by many names, a reflection of their wide-ranging wanderings, and their aloofness from other cultures. To the Hausa speaker, they are the Fulani. To the Kanuri speaker they are Fellata. Among themselves they are Pullo. They can be found in almost every corner of West Africa. In Francophone West Africa, they are known as the Peul.

Their own names for themselves are also diverse, and meaningful. Those who adhere to the cattle herding way of life are known as *yiilotoobe* or "the wandering ones", but are also known as *bororo'en*, "cattle" or "bush Fulani". Fulani who have ceased their wandering, pastoral lifestyles, are called the *huya'en* or *toroobe*, the "town Fulani".[57]

To this day, the life of the "cattle Fulani" revolve around the migrations of their longhorn cows; from wet season to dry season pastures, from high to low ground. Depending on the clan, and what kind of cattle they have, the migrations can be long, consisting of many hundreds, if not thousands, of miles across modern international borders. Or they can be shorter distances, tramping across a modern state boundary, or not even that far.

The precise origin of the Fulani is clouded by myth and mystery, but by the middle ages they were a large presence on the Senegambian plain. As the great West African empires of Mali, Songhai and Kanem rose and fell the Fulani spread further and further eastwards.[58] Over time, large family dynasties grew, developing large herds which were then split and subdivided as the families grew bigger and spread further. As they migrated to find more pastures, families would take on the names of the places they originated. Many centuries of migration history are captured in these names.[59] Two of the major Fulani clans are the *Jallonkawa* who originate in Futa Jallon, the highlands of modern day Guinea; another prominent clan is the *Toronkawa*, from Futa Toro, the pastureland along the banks of the river Senegal, in what is now the Gambia.

The Fulani lived austere, nomadic lives with their animals. Soon after coming of age, boys put aside a quite playful and relatively carefree youth, and take on their responsibilities of adulthood.[60] While out on migration the Fulani expects to suffer great hardship, exposure to the elements, to disease, to violence, to the harsh words of those who, according to the Fulani's own story of their people, were weak, ignorant, lesser beings. The arduous nature of a nomadic life is made possible by four aspects of Fulani culture; Islam, the aspiration to freedom, and the twin concepts of honour and shame.[61]

Freedom for the Fulani can mean two things. Firstly it is the freedom from the dominion of other people. The Fulfulde word *pere* has no direct translation into English, but someone who has *pere* is someone over whom other people have no influence. It is a highly desirable quality. The other sort of freedom in Fulani life is freedom from needs. People who are subject to, even made slaves of, their needs could hardly even be considered fully to be people.[62] A Fulani who was not in control of his needs would be said to lack *puulaku*, that is "the qualities necessary to be called a Fulani", roughly the equivalent of the European notion of "chivalry". If someone has shown himself to lack *puulaku* then he is said to suffer *semtude*, or a crushing, all consuming, shame.[63] The place that, in Pullo culture, a Fulani man can most easily feel free and at ease—free, that is, of situations that might expose him to shame—is away from the influence of others, in the bush, with his cows.[64]

Cattle were—and remain to this day—the centre of life for the Fulani. They are the store and measure of their wealth, and a direct link remains between a large healthy herd and a man's status. Also much of a man's identity is connected to his cows, and how well he knows them reveals how successful a Fulani he is. An admirable Fulani herder will know each of his cows by name. When a true Fulani calls his cows, they come to him.[65]

But by the late eighteenth century the Fulani were not simply transhumance nomads. Many had settled, become *toroobe*, had intermarried with other groups and as wealthy people, they and their descendants took up official positions in the emirates and began to exert influence on politics. This was done mostly by the large numbers of Fulani Islamic scholars. But for these *toroobe* Fulani, the same set of rules about shame and chivalry, freedom and Islam, still applied—even if it was only in the abstract, as an aspiration.

Although many of the Fulani were Muslims (something about their nomadic lives, with its need for brotherhood—and also the great solitudes of living beyond the city, made it easy for them to accept Islam), pagan Fulani also existed. One ceremony, written down by Bello, described a pagan initiation rite. Fulani elders would tie "certain objects" (likely votive offerings or masks) onto the heads of the initiate children. The initiates would then watch as a cow was sacrificed and butchered before a fire. As the boys tried to reach the meat set down by the fire, they were beaten savagely by older, initiated, men. Then they would swear allegiance to the fire, claiming it as mother and father. Initiates would then dance closer and closer around the flames until they were standing on the embers. They would even sit down, Bello wrote, and emerge from the glowing coals unharmed.[66]

Muslim Fulani, disgusted by these heathen practices, fought against them. In 1776 *mallams* in the Fulani heartland of Futa Jallon succeeded in a fifty-year struggle to overturn pagan rulers and form an Islamic state. At around the same time, Muslims of the *Toronkawa* clan in the other enclave of Futa Toro, were successful in doing the same—after a much shorter Jihad.[67]

The Shehu had lived most of his life in Degel, which by the turn of the nineteenth century was a quite substantial village. The Shehu's clan had probably lived there in some form or another for several hundred years before his time. The village would have been made up of family compounds, each with several round huts, one for each of a man's wives, around a central open area. The walls would have been made of mud bricks, and on the huts were conical thatched roofs. The communal areas were screened with fences of dry maize and guinea corn stalks, where the women prepared food, pounding cereals and cooking, with animals including goats and a favourite calf tethered in the yard.[68] The Shehu's family would have owned cows, no doubt, but they were probably looked after by a younger cousin. The Shehu himself made his living from his preaching, and also from spinning rope, an occupation that was more symbolic of his humility and humble nature than to actually make ends meet.[69]

Geographically, Degel had everything migrating Fulani cattle herders needed; it was on a plateau where there would be plenty of wet season grazing available, away from cattle pests and parasites; and when the dry season came, the Rima River was not far away, down in the valley below. Most importantly it was on land that stood on the edge of the influence of the Hausa city states like Gobir.

Most of the Hausa thought the Fulani were "contumacious aliens who refused to accept the established customs of the country".[70] They felt—perhaps not without justification—that the Fulani looked down on them. They also envied their wealth in cattle. As a result livestock rustling was common and officials levied a tax on the herdsmen called *jangali*, which was to be paid in cows. For their part the Fulani cattle herders, keen to avoid what they saw as harassment and the inevitable shame that would come of being belittled by people they thought beneath them, usually did what they could to avoid the towns of the Hausa altogether.

But the political power the Fulani could wield was about to be demonstrated in the Hausa city state of Gobir, among the people the Fulani called the *Habe;* "those who are not us". It would be led by distant cousins of the successful *Toronkawa* jihadists in Futa Toro, a generation previously: Othman dan Fodiyo, his family and followers.

When the Community had been young, and the Shehu in his mid thirties, he had come to Alakawa, the capital of Gobir to meet Sarki Bawa.

Bawa was a warrior-king of Gobir, veteran of many battles with Tuareg raiders from the north and other wars with neighbouring Hausa rulers, among whom there were frequent squabbles over territory and tribute. He was known as *Jan Gwarzo*—the powerful man—for his fighting prowess. Many believed that Bawa intended to eliminate the Shehu; if he could not force him to submit, he would kill him. But in the end, when he set out again for Degel, it was the Shehu who had the upper hand.

The Shehu won five concessions from Sarkin Bawa. The community was granted the freedom to call people to God and convert them, the followers were free to display the trappings of their faith, to wear turbans and for their women to be veiled. All Muslims who had been harassed or imprisoned before this would be freed, and lastly and most importantly, the followers of the Shehu were to be free of the hated *jangali* cattle tax. These concessions gave the Shehu's community a great deal of autonomy. In fact it has been said that it made them a de facto separate state.[71]

During these early years of the community's development Gobir tried to bend the Shehu to their will. They tried to co-opt him by making overtures, such as putting Yunfa, Bawa's nephew, in pupillage under the Shehu. But these attempts were always followed by antagonism and threats when they were unable to turn the stubborn head of the Fulani holy man.

After giving the Shehu his concessions, Bawa, who was an old man of seventy, had a prophecy of his own. Gobir's days were numbered and he, Bawa Jan Gwarzo, might be the last independent Sarki to rule Gobir.[72] He was not out by much, only two short generations.

When Bawa died, he was succeeded by his brother Yakuba, who ruled for four years before being succeeded by Bawa's second brother Nafata, who tried to bend the recalcitrant Shehu to his will. Nafata stripped the community of the special privileges granted by his brother. Muslims were no longer allowed to wear turbans, or pray freely. They were even barred from preaching to or trying to convert pagans. The exemption from *jangali* was revoked. The community now could not escape stringent taxes on their herds, and this had wider implications because of the unjust nature of government in Gobir.[73]

The old judicial framework of Islamic laws were overseen by the court's most trusted civil servant, the *Galadima*—one of the Sarki's eunuchs.[74] But access to the court, and therefore access to justice, was only possible through patronage and favour. In effect, the nobility around the Sarki could do what they pleased, as only they could get to the Galadima, and he was likely to be well disposed to them in every case. In such circumstances, local fief-lords could set the *jangali*, collected as tribute for passing through their lands, at whatever level they wanted. It soon became little more than licenced cattle rustling.

The removal of the concessions heralded the beginning of a campaign of harassment which was aimed not only at the Muslims of the Shehu's community but at all other professed Muslims, and at Fulani cattle herders in general. Nafata only ruled as Sarki for two years before dying. He was succeeded by his son Yunfa, who at one time, as part of an attempt by Bawa to court the Shehu, had been a pupil at Degel. Yunfa even came to see the Shehu, travelling on foot as an act of humility, to try to dissuade him from his unrelenting position against their authority.

But the Shehu remained unwavering. He was convinced of the *Habe*'s inability to reform. By most accounts Yunfa was a hot-head whose actions bordered on the psychotic.[75] Backing down would not live up to the Fulani way, to live a free life away from the influence of other people. He could not abide the restrictions placed on the community—it offended both his Fulani sense of *puulaku*—honour—and his moral code as a Muslim. To back down would be to squander the political power that the community, his brotherhood, had built.

When it came, however, the spark that touched off the conflict was not of either the Shehu's or Yunfa's ordering, but probably the inevitable consequence of a febrile and tense situation.[76] One of Yunfa's commanders attacked and subdued another community of Muslims living in a village called Gimbana, to the south west of Degel. This group had seen the resistance put up by the Shehu's community and were inspired. Yunfa's men rounded up the Muslims and drove them to the capital, where they were to be sold into slavery. Unfortunately for the Sarki's men, their route home took them up the Rima river valley, right past Degel. Horsemen, loyal to the Shehu, but led by his brother Abdullahi, attacked the Sarki's men, cutting them down with arrow fire and driving the survivors off. They rescued the Muslims bound for the slave-ports, but the peace was broken. When his men reached Alakawa, brandishing the arrows of the Fulani, the furious Sarki Yunfa commanded that the Shehu pay for this aggression.

According to the accounts that favour the mystical side of the Shehu, it was around this time that dan Fodiyo received another vision. A decade after he had been handed the Sword of Truth, the twelfth-century Sufi mystic al-Jilani was again in the Shehu's visions. This time al-Jilani came to the Shehu and declared it was time to fulfil his destiny. It was time to unsheath his sword. He then commanded that the faithful remove themselves from the land of the sinners and wage holy war upon them, saying: "Verily to make ready weapons is Sunnah [the way of righteousness]".[77]

Whether the Shehu was convinced by a vision or not, he certainly decided that to wage war against the Hausa, despite their own profession to Islam, was just and right. They were not Muslims he said, but backsliders and apostates.

The Shehu put this in a message which he sent to all the Hausa kings: "That to make war on the heathen king who does not say 'There is no God but Allah' on account of the custom of his town, and who makes no profession of Islam, is obligatory by assent; and that to take the government from him is obligatory by assent".[78]

For the first few years the war went well for the Community. After initial military successes the Shehu was elected *Emir al Mu'minin*, leader of the Muslims, an important title hitherto held by the Mai of Bornu. Dan Fodiyo wrote to the Hausa Sarkis that they should declare their support for the Islamic state that they were founding in God's name. The victories they had won were evidence of Allah's divine approval for their cause. Several refused and were deposed by the Fulanis. Others like the Sarkin Zazzau (modern day Zaria) converted to their cause, but the people under him rebelled. Despite a few lost battles, the men loyal to the Shehu, who never himself entered the field of battle due to his advanced age, were enjoying their conquests. In autumn 1808, four years after the Hijra, the Shehu's forces led by Bello, fell on the walled city of Alakawa. Sarki Yunfa and all his men were slain. "The heathen were downcast and their backbone broken," wrote Bello, "Very many of them repented and became Muslims." The news was sent to the Shehu, but Bello writes that by the time the human messengers arrived, dan Fodiyo was already aware of the victory: "Some people relate that the Jinns went to Shehu with the news of the battle... Others say that God revealed this matter to the Shehu."[79]

Later that year the forces loyal to the Shehu turned on the remaining power in the region. They advanced on Bornu, still one of the great Muslim empires of West Africa, taking control of town after town, rolling the influence of Bornu right back to the swampy fringes of Lake Chad. The Mai of Bornu, who believed he still ought to hold the title of "Leader of the Muslims" fled into exile and the empire's capital, Ngazargamu, fell to the Fulani Jihad.

The Mai went to Kanem, Bornu's cousins to the northeast of Lake Chad, for help. Despite enmity between the two following a civil war that had seen Bornu split from Kanem, help was dispatched. The man they sent was remarkable, one of the toughest warriors and most accomplished theological minds on the continent. His name was Sheikh Aminu el-Kanemi and instead of marshaling a counter offensive, he sat down and wrote a letter.

"Greetings and friendship," it began. "The cause of my writing to you is that when God brought me to Bornu I found that the fire of discord had broken out between your followers and the people of this country. When I enquired why, some said the reason was in religion, others that it was to be found in tyranny."

Fulani herdsmen living in Bornu told him the war was to correct "heathen practices", but that explanation did not satisfy him. "Will you therefore tell me your reasons for going to war and enslaving our people?" he asked the Shehu. El-Kanemi summarised the accusation: "Because you are told our chiefs go up to places and there slaughter animals for the purpose of giving meat as alms, because you are told our women go unveiled, and because you are told our judges are said to be corrupt and oppressive. This practice of the chiefs that you have heard of is a sin... But it is not right to say that they are heathen. It were better to command them to mend their ways than to make war on them."

Moreover, the Fulanis themselves were guilty of crimes, el-Kanemi said, "You are destroying books; you scatter them in the roads, you are throwing them in the dirt." Oaths were broken and "they slaughter men and capture women and children."[80] El-Kanemi saved his most withering attack for last. Far from being a religious reformist, the Shehu must be desirous of something else entirely, namely worldly power. The letter ended: "I wish to inform you we are on the Shehu's side, if the Shehu is for truth. If he is departing from the truth, then we will leave him and follow the truth."

Between Bornu in the east and Gwandu in the west, where the Shehu lived at this point, it could take two months to travel. When the jihadists received the letter they were furious. They replied severally and at length. Most of the surviving correspondence was written on the Shehu's behalf by his son Muhammad Bello. But dan Fodiyo also wrote letters to el-Kanemi.

El-Kanemi should not listen to illiterate people, Bello bristled; "Our only reason for fighting" he wrote "was to ward off their attacks upon our lives and our faith and our families. When they commenced to trouble us they drove us from our homes... Verily the Shehu revealed to us the truth. We saw this truth and followed it." Later he states; "their heathenism is proved to us in that they make sacrifices to stones and large trees, and make trouble to the Muslim faith and prevent men from becoming Muslims".

The withdrawal of the agreements given to their community by Sarki Bawa was harassment and the oppression continued until the Fulani fought back. "They prevented us from practising our faith... they oppressed us," Bello said. The incident with the books was easily explainable, Bello wrote, it had been a minor squabble over "the spoils of war" and he had personally picked up all the pages. If anyone had been guilty, he said, he most surely would have been a low type, and would certainly have been punished.

Bello warned: if Bornu helped the Hausas against them "Your prayers, your giving of tithes, your fasting and your building of mosques shall not prevent us fighting you." Bello might well be angry, for el-Kanemi had questioned the key assertion of the Fulani revolt, that backsliding was tantamount to apostasy; that disobedience was unbelief.

Over the next few years the war drew to a stalemate with both armies raiding villages in the forests and plains to the east and south of Lake Chad. El-Kanemi consolidated Bornu's strength and the Mai returned to rule under his stern stewardship. The jihadists just didn't have the wherewithal to take over Bornu. The Shehu had given the captains of the Jihad their flags, denoting governorship of a territory won by conquest. Only one, who had been designated Bornu, missed out.

The war had also taken its toll on the support for the Jihad. In the early days the Shehu's reformist ideas garnered support from non-Fulani peasants, no doubt keen to see Islamic laws that would curtail the corrupt practises of the Hausa courts. But the practicalities of waging such a long conflict surely dented this enthusiasm. During the conflict there was a continual battle for food and other resources needed to feed the war effort. The Shehu's men would denude every place they stayed of everything the peasants had, swiftly turning them against the community.[81]

The correspondence between Bello and el-Kanemi continued—some were conciliatory, full of poetry, many were lost in transit. Impolitely, el-Kanemi's men killed one of Bello's messengers. In his correspondence Bello continued to emphasise that the fight was started in response to the Hausa Sarkis who had oppressed them: "We are not conquering people for mischief's sake," he wrote, "Indeed when our enemy drove us from our homes at the outset of our cause, then we rose up and drove off their armies in self defence."

But at the same time the Shehu himself wrote to el-Kanemi. In his letter the reasons are less temporal: "We wish you to know our way of life," he wrote, "Our way of life is that of the people of the faith. It is our people who have found the truth and we follow it." Peace could be established between them if the Shehu of Bornu "repent and turn to God, and leave all those customs which are contrary to the law."

These were the two ideals of the Jihad of Othman dan Fodiyo: to repair the faith and to resist the oppression of the heathen. But even before the Shehu died in 1817 the new Fulani-led power was undeniably falling short of his ideals. The order that he ushered in would last for generations, testament to the laws he and his sons set down in their attempts to root the Emirates in Islamic law. It would be a hundred years until the British arrived and supplanted the order by force,[82] but the dynasty would be plagued by insecurity and rebellion.

The justness of rule in any part of the empire was dependent on its individual officials. And although the whole persisted, the centre seemed powerless to impress itself on the regions. Before he died, the Shehu penned a long reproachful poem called *Tabat Hakika*—"Be Sure of That", in which he upbraids officials who were apparently repeating the crimes of the *Habe* rulers, corruptly defrauding people of their land and property, corruptly selling offices and preventing access to justice.[83]

Also amongst his worries were the morals of the men who had won the war. During the campaigns, the forces of the Shehu had taken many slaves, upon which not only the agricultural future of the empire rested, but also the character and future quality of Islamic scholarship, as the Fulani could not be expected to keep up standards of learning the Shehu demanded if they had to expend all their energy doing what their *Habe* slaves could do.[84]

Among these slaves were large numbers of young girls and women, whom the Muslim warriors used as they pleased, despite the condemnation from the Shehu in his poetry. In one of these poems called *Wallahi wallahi*, the only one written in Hausa—presumably for widespread dissemination—he strenuously denies taking power for worldly power's sake and bitterly blames his subordinates: "As for me I have not sent anyone [to do forced labour for me] but it is the governors of the towns/Who have sent you for their own ends I swear by God."

2

DISPUTED TERRITORY

Although dan Fodiyo had failed in his dream of creating a dynasty of spiritual leaders and a purified faith, it hardly mattered to his successors. They had created a Caliphate that made them wealthy and powerful. By writing the history of their overturning of the *Habe* rulers, they created a foundation myth: of a saintly spiritual leader, of a noble race, of their purity of spirit.

This world was about to come into contact with another empire, one that held greater dreams of a new moral order.

Europeans had been sailing to the Bight of Benin to trade for centuries, but the interior of the continent remained a mystery to them. As Europe's economies expanded they dreamed of opening new markets for their products. In Great Britain's case this was principally woven cotton from the mill towns of the north of England, for which they also required large amounts of land where cotton could be grown.

In London, the new men of the mercantile elite established clubs and societies to lobby and fund exploration trips. The Royal Geographical Society and others were formed to fill in the gaps on the map, to push the influence of the European countries, and their associated colonial trade companies, ever outward into the terra incognita. As the eighteenth century became the nineteenth, many of these men were also activists for a new moral vision. They were Christians, in part motivated by a political question that would go hand in hand with the expansion of their trade—the cause of abolitionism and the end of the slave trade.

Many expeditions were arranged and explorers contracted to investigate the blank spaces of the Sahara, to "discover" the source of the Niger, and to contact and establish links with people who, some erroneously believed, lived on the banks of a massive inland sea at the heart of West Africa,[1] or beyond the 'Mountains of Kong' a high range that was erroneously believed to cut off the land fringing the Sahara from the dense forests of the coastal regions.[2] Most of these explorations were failures, the explorers either contracted diseases or simply disappeared. The accounts of those who made it back were sometimes of little use. Their rugged, determined—arrogant—nature meant that they made little effort to make real contact with the baffling people they encountered there, who they invariably thought beneath them. Most of their observations are worse than useless.

However, there was one man whose account we will turn to now. He was the only survivor of a mission that had set out in 1850 into Africa's interior. His travels have, in a strange and unexpected way, influenced modern day Nigeria.

* * *

After twelve days travelling south from the capital of Bornu the party of travellers to which Heinrich Barth had attached himself was struggling. With every step, the thick, blue-black mud caked itself around the bare feet of the spearmen who walked alongside his camels and horses. The clart weighed down their legs and made walking heavy and exhausting. The riders and their animals had it no easier. It was the beginning of the rainy season and frequent heavy downpours had left Barth's gear wet and heavy. The camel that bore his luggage was not well suited to the weather or the slippery, claggy mud, and it loblollied about, threatening to throw its load. With every sucking step it became more difficult.

The landscape they were moving through was stunning, but the European traveller derived no pleasure from it. A mountain of solid black rock loomed over them, with sheer sides and a flat top; the igneous core of an ancient volcano. In the distance the purple scar of a further range could be seen above green foothills. On the ground around them herons and flamingoes waded in the pans of rainwater that lay on the clay soil. When it wasn't raining, the still water of the pools reflected the bright blue June sky. The storms had washed the sky clean of the miserable Saharan harmattan dust. As the day got hotter little white clouds, which stretched off into the distance as far as the eye could see, slowly bloomed and then, heavy with water, let it lash the ground with a whip of a downpour. At night, silent lightning threatened in the distance.

Beyond the hardship of travelling, there was a deeper melancholy about the place that, even through his exhaustion, Barth could not ignore. "The country which we now entered bore but too evident proofs of the unfortunate condition to which it is reduced, forming a thick forest, through which nevertheless here and there, the traces of former cultivation and the mouldering remains of huts are to be seen" he later wrote in his book *Travels in Africa*, the account of his journey from Tripoli to Timbuktu via Hausaland, Bornu, Adamawa, Bagirmi and back.[3] Forests, providing cover for bands of robbers, were studded with ruined empty villages. Huts were burned and scattered, granaries burst open—what remained was wet and rotting. Raiding parties had carried everyone off into slavery, or slaughtered them.

"We halted a short time in order that the whole caravan might form closely together" Barth wrote of the 10th of June 1851, still in the first year of a journey that would last six. "For we had now the most dangerous day's march before us, where stragglers are generally slain or carried into slavery by lurking enemies."[4]

It was a strange party of travellers. Barth and his two servants had set out from Kukawa with a company of messengers from Omar, Shehu of Bornu. They were accompanied by twenty-five warriors, armed with long spears and hippopotamus-hide shields. This escort was provided by the other Muslim power-figure in the region, the *Lamido* of Adamawa. It was he that the messengers were heading to meet. In other circumstances these men might have been at each others' throats, but an uneasy truce had been called. Restitution was the purpose of the messengers' mission to meet the Lamido of Adamawa.

There were others in the party. Barth mentions first a number of traders, looking for safety in numbers, who fell in with them along the way. They drove their asses laden with plates of salt bound for sale to the Fulani herders of Adamawa. He also writes about another, more wretched, group among the band, at least for part of the way; a few young men and women, naked except for leather aprons, huddled among themselves, flinching in trepidation of the men around them.

It was not only these near-naked youths who were afraid. Even though Barth was armed with four muskets and two pistols,[5] and despite the presence of the spearmen, he was still scared. So were the emissaries of Bornu. As they travelled into the land between the two Muslim settlements, these highborn men mounted the best horses in their caravan, put away their bows and took tight hold of their spears, a more useful weapon in an ambush.[6]

The land they travelled through was contested, neither the authority of the Shehu of Bornu nor the Lamido of Adamawa was absolute. Barth remarks that the British Empire and its powerful female sovereign were only a rumour here.[7]

They pressed on. "The forest was partly filled up by a dense jungle of of reed grass, of such a height as to cover horse and rider," Barth wrote, "the forest became very thick, and for a whole hour we followed the immense footprints of an elephant, which had found it convenient to keep along the beaten path to the great annoyance of succeeding travellers, who had, in consequence, to stumble over the deep holes made by the impressions of its feet."[8]

Barth saw the signs of desolation all around:

> The pagan countries, in general, seem to be inhabited not in distinct villages or towns where the dwellings stand loosely together, but in single farms and hamlets or clusters of huts each of which contains an entire family, spreading over a wide expanse of the country, each man's fields lying close around his dwelling. The fields however of Molghoy had a very sad and dismal aspect, although they were shaded and beautifully adorned by numerous karage-trees. Though the rainy season has long set in, none of these fine fields were sown this year but still presented the old furrows of former years; and all around was silent and inert, bearing evident signs of if not desolation, at least of oppression."[9]

The emissaries from the Shehu of Bornu were on their way to settle a dispute between their master and the Fulani leader of Adamawa, Mohammed Lawal. This dispute had arisen because *Kashella* Ali Ladan, one of the Shehu's warlords—now also with them among the party of travellers—had led a plundering army though this very land, burning villages and making slaves of men, women and children as he went. The Kashella had thought it his right to do so; these were pagans, unbelievers who could be sold, according to the law. The Lamido of Adamawa, however, objected. Lawal believed the villages fell under his control. He had converted them to Islam, those villages paid tribute to *him* and *he* held the rights to them. The huddled naked young men and women, were some of the "unfortunate creatures" Ladan had taken. They were being taken back to their villages. The surviving ones, at least. Many had no doubt been already sold to traders heading to the Fezzan, or perished along the way.[10]

Barth was never able to say for sure where exactly the danger came from as he travelled south toward his own, quite separate, goal. Some of the burned villages they passed through, he was informed, were under the suzerain of Kashella Ladan's master in Bornu (now modern day Borno state in Nigeria). Who exactly had ransacked those villages was never made clear. In this patchwork of forests and small subsistence farms, both the Shehu of Bornu and the Lamido of Adamawa employed raiding parties to reave the country on horseback. But other bands of robbers also roamed, led by men of no particular affiliation but to themselves. It was hunting and gathering, not of animals and berries, but of men, their produce and their women and children.

Not every hamlet or homestead could be protected by the lords to whom many of the villages paid tribute. Sometimes they just slipped out of the protective pockets of the powerful and became easy pickings for the raiders. Indeed, these raids were the way in which the reach of each power's influence was decided.

Others refused to pay any tribute at all, and pagans were capable of fighting back. A rumour was that just one of the many groups of stubborn polytheists in this region could field an army of 30,000 men.[11] This made the messengers from the Shehu and the Adamawan guards very apprehensive; "Suddenly the spirit of our little troop was roused; some naked pagans were discovered in the bushes near the stream, and so long as it was uncertain whether or not they were accompanied by a greater number, my companions were in a state of fright."[12] One of Lawal's men had to convince the Bornuese warlord that the naked pagans were loyal to his master, in a desperate attempt to stop the warlord from killing them on the spot. The situation could easily become violent, their small band could not afford that. There was not a friendly walled city within a week's journey. If things turned against them, they wouldn't get far before being hacked down and butchered in the mud, emir's guard, muskets, pistols, or no.

Despite the danger, Barth made copious observations in his journals, noting the presence of crop species; cotton, corn, and the poor quality of the "elephant dung" rice. He described a glade they came across that had been turned into an outdoor blacksmith's workshop, where he hailed the craftsman and questioned him about his techniques. He passed through villages pledged to first Bornu, then to the governor of Adamawa, without being able to tell initially which was which. Barth writes of his belief that the pagans simply took Islamic vows "outwardly" to rid themselves of the oppression of the raiders.[13] In the marshes of Adamawa, where the Kashella of Bornu had no power, Barth observes with some delight the warlord is reduced to "politeness and artifice". The reaction the pagans have to Barth, on the other hand, thrills him.[14] Once they realised he was a representative of neither local "Mohammedan" power, they welcomed him with a sort of baffled curiosity that Barth couldn't help but identify with.

He made notes about the new languages he was hearing for the first time, and the unfamiliar social practises he encountered on the way. He remarked on the nakedness of women and their facial adornments and piercings like the arrow-shaped lip plugs and tattoos of the people of the Marghi region (traditions continued in spite of their professed religion).[15] Rather flirtatiously he even gives gifts to some young women he seems particularly taken with, although their reaction seems rather too standoffish for his liking: "They thanked me insufficiently" he says with characteristic dyspepsia.[16] After spying an enormous fish drying on the reed roof of a hut, he and a companion break off from the group to investigate where it came from, and discover a lake where fishermen pull 20-inch beasts from the waters with their hands.[17] "Adamawa is a promising country of colonies," he wrote appreciatively.[18]

Despite the seemingly ever-present peril, which he wanted to impress heavily on his reader, Barth was clearly in his element.

Heinrich Barth was a singular and driven individual. In the etched frontispiece in the first book published of the rather ill-fated six-year expedition, Barth can be seen in the lower left hand corner. He has the look of a Hollywood B-movie actor, a matinee idol from the Golden Age, known perhaps for his portrayal of ranchers and railroad tycoons in studio westerns. He has a touch of Hemingway, before Hemingway.

He was a consummate traveller, as comfortable on his beloved camel Bu-Sefi as he was on a horse, and he could keep going on either for long, arduous days over tough country. When he travelled he dressed in an indigo bernus robe, red tobe waistcoat and a tagelmust-style Saharan turban. The unfixed dye in the indigo cloth wrapped around his face and neck was so deep a blue that the fabric shone bronze. It stained his skin like the Tuareg caravan riders, such that he resembled a "blue man of the desert". He shed his European name and travelled among the Muslims as "Abdel Karim", although unlike other travellers he made no attempt to disguise his Christian faith. On several occasions people took him for a pagan. He corrected them that he worshipped the one God, as they did.[19] On his travels he was known by many nicknames; perhaps most tellingly the Kanuri in Bornu called him "the overbearing one".[20] In the ten short years between the end of his expedition and his death aged forty-four, he would cement his image as a Victorian patrician of the first order by growing one of the most impressive and bushy moustaches of the era. Barth was the kind of man to whom the nineteenth century belonged.

Born in 1821, Barth was a member of a social group that was just coming into its own; he was the child of a self-made man. His father Johann had raised himself from poverty to become a wealthy trader at the port of Hamburg and was able to obtain a good educations for his children. As a boy, Barth possessed a remarkable degree of self-discipline.[21] His upbringing had been stern, in the strict Lutheran Protestant manner, and he evinced a taste for hard work and privation. At school he was unpopular and thought of as very odd; indeed he eschewed company and subjected himself to rigorous physical and mental extremes in order to toughen himself up. These included taking cold baths in winter and doing long, hard bouts of physical exertion in extreme conditions.

Barth also possessed an amazing linguistic ability. He became fluent in English at fourteen and in Arabic by his early twenties. When he broke off his university education, at the age of eighteen or nineteen, he taught himself Italian and visited the Grand Tour destinations of Venice, Florence, Rome, Pompeii and Sicily. In the three months his party took to trek across the Sahara, Barth learnt Hausa from one of their servants. Then, in the saddle as he rode from Katsina to the capital of Bornu, he learnt Kanuri. The governors and emirs and other officials he encountered along the way seem quite delighted to meet him, and he spent long hours discussing matters with them. Not something that could be said of previous explorers.

Barth had studied law and, before his expeditions, had thought he might become a teacher. But travelling seemed to take over his whole being. This mission he created for himself, with the aid of the British Foreign Office and the exploration societies of the day, seems the most perfect expression of a Victorian ideal; "I have an immense force inside me," he wrote to his father in 1842, "the most altruistic striving towards the great and the true and the beautiful. To be of use to mankind, to inspire and motivate them..."[22] The civilising zeal of the Victorian-era missionary was deep inside him.

In 1850 he set out from Tripoli with exploration leader James Richardson and geologist and astronomer Adolf Overweg across the Sahara with a salt caravan to the city of Zinder. They would be joined later by engineer Henry Vogel. They and their sponsors believed the abolitionist cause could be advanced by promotion of other forms of trade with Great Britain—the two went hand in hand. The Germans, Barth, Overweg and Vogel were persuaded to act for Great Britain at least partly out of their abolitionist beliefs. Barth travelled first to Katsina and Kano, then east to Bornu, where he then turned south to Adamawa. He then headed east again into what is now Chad, before heading back west, through Sokoto to Timbuktu. From there he returned, through Kano again and back to Bornu before crossing the desert back to Europe. For much of the mission he was separated from his European colleagues.

The expedition started to go wrong as they approached the end of their voyage across the Sahara. The travellers were robbed by a gang of desert bandits and most of the gifts with which they planned to buy influence with the kings across the desert were stolen. At Zinder, the travellers split up, seeking to fulfil their individual mission objectives as best they could until meeting a resupply caravan due to arrive in Bornu later. Richardson, the expedition leader, died before it arrived and the scientific instruments entrusted to Barth broke. From that point the scientific parts of the mission were, as far as Barth was concerned, almost forgotten.

Barth's mission was to get the leaders of the land to agree to open up to direct trade with Europeans. A secondary mission, during the Adamawa section of his journey, was to locate and collect information on a mighty river that was said to flow south-west, from what was known then as "The Tchad" and thought to be a mighty inland sea, to the Niger river. It was in search of this second great river that Captain Clapperton had died, twenty-four years before.

The surviving members of Clapperton's expedition, and Clapperton's diaries, had described the new Caliphate of Sokoto, and around the Tchad were the ancient Caliphates of Kanem and Bornu. But neither overland journey, south from the Mediterranean coast across the Sahara, nor north from the trading posts of the Niger Delta through the forests, was feasible for large-scale use by Great Britain. Both were too arduous for Europeans, who were prone to die of disease very easily in the tropics. They would have been dependent on shaky alliances with local chiefs the British saw as unreliable. There had to be another way, ideally using methods that played to Great Britain's strength; naval power. Another route into the interior of Africa, one that might be navigable all the way from the Bight of Benin to what we now call Lake Chad, would have opened up the country to Britain's ships, trade and, as many like Barth hoped, the abolitionist cause. This was the sort of Africa the burgeoning British Empire could manage; water-based trade routes to ancient and "noble" empires.

But Barth had some bad news for the sponsors of his expedition back in London. He had discovered this second mighty river, the "Benuwe" as he spelled it in his communication to his sponsors, rose in the mountains far away to the south-east of Lake Chad, and the mighty inland sea was more a swamp. From Bornu to the river was an arduous journey through muddy forests that would take several weeks. All hope was not entirely lost, he thought; "There will be a great facility for Europeans to enter that country" he wrote to the government of Prime Minister Lord John Russell in May 1851. "By-and-by, I am sure, a southern road will be opened into the heart of Central Africa, but the time has not yet come."[23]

He did not know it as he suffered through the journey to Yola, the capital of Adamawa, but Barth would be the only European survivor of the mission. Richardson died before the party could meet again, Barth's companion

Overweg also died of a fever in Bornu shortly after Barth's return from Adamawa. The engineer Vogel would be murdered in unknown circumstances some time after Barth's returned to Great Britain. Although Barth enjoyed much personal triumph and acclaim on his completed journey, in most of its stated aims the mission was a failure. Barth had a good personal relationship with Lord Palmerston, Lord Russell's successor as Prime Minister, but fell out with the Royal Geographic Society. The knowledge Barth brought back would not be used for some time. After his return, British politics was consumed by the repercussions of the Crimean War. Her Majesty's government would wait several political generations before returning to the tough and unforgiving region through which Barth had slogged with such exertion. It is hard to resist the idea the rigours of his journey contributed to his early death.

For all the conviction he had in the improving nature of his altruism, Barth also unquestionably shared that other delusion of the Victorian European; the superiority of white peoples over what he called "the negroid races". All through his travels he never lost his stiff, racist, European bearing. Barth could at one moment be noting down very sensitive observations, evidently listening keenly to stories he was told, and the next state boldly and unequivocally that they were the work of lesser beings than Europeans. Even though he wrote about the place at length, there is no sense in all of his journals that inland West Africa reached into him and affected that cast-iron belief in the improving mission of white civilisation.[24]

The European notion of "tribe" also coloured how he understood what he was seeing. To Barth, the explorers who came before him and the early anthropologists who came after, African society was made up of homogeneous or near-homogeneous ethnic and racial units. These tribal groups dictated not only physique but character traits and even the capacity to rule fittingly or justly. These ideas were derived from an idealised version of progress that placed Europe at one end of a developmental line, and Africa on the other. The historiography that led to these assumptions was influenced by Europe's own supposed historical journey, from clan, to tribe to nation.[25]

Barth's own worldview stuck closely to the precepts of the Prussian class system, dominated by overbearing, martial, aristocrats. He was an unapologetic anti-Semite to boot. These ideas, which would come together in the succeeding century as the political movement of Fascism, led Barth to arrive at terrible conclusions from his otherwise very interesting observations.

He believed that the quality of character necessary for apt governance was related to racial characteristics and the "purity" of "blood". Where he saw admirable qualities, particularly of leadership, he attributed it to breeding—their blood was presumably inherited from one of the "noble races" of Africans. Where authority had begun to crumble, Barth blamed "corruption", meaning the dilution of the pure blood line. When Barth meets the Sultan of Sokoto—dan Fodiyo's grandson Aliyu—Barth notes that he has very dark skin, somewhat contrary to the supposed Fulani type. After all, Barth concludes, his mother was a concubine, a slave. Barth thinks it therefore unsurprising that Fulani rule over the Hausa city states had begun to wilt; how could such a person expect to have the strength of character necessary to maintain a just rule?[26]

As absurd and offensivè as his conclusions sound to us today, it is from this man that we get one of the best outsider's account of what society was like in the place that would become northern Nigeria, just before the British came.

It is difficult to say when they set off what the expedition expected of the place to which they were heading. It had been a generation since any European visitor had been there and back with news of the country. It is possible that in the early stage of the expedition, the planners of the trip had a rosy view of the abilities of the descendants of Othman dan Fodiyo to maintain order over the new Sokoto Empire. Their hope was that this was a peaceful region; Richardson, the expedition leader, had previously travelled as far as Ghat, in the Fezzan region of the Sahara, unarmed and initially they did not intend to take any weapons with them this time either. Indeed they only changed their minds after the British and German governments insisted they carry rifles with them.[27] This optimism could have come from Richardson's belief in the mission's provenance from God—he was a devout Evangelical Christian—but it is also possible they anticipated the region was stable, ruled by governors who could guarantee they might travel unmolested. Richardson's notes on the purpose of the mission refer to the need to get access to the "most important kingdoms". Did he believe that "kingship" in this part of the world was the same as European sovereign command of a territory?[28]

Their last information about the area was from the notebooks and diaries of Captain Clapperton's first expedition and the accounts from a survivor of the second expedition, Richard Lander. They described the rule of Sokoto as growing in its establishment of a territory under the central control of the system of governance set up by the Shehu's successor, his son Bello.[29] It is possible they expected to find a continuous system of rule that stretched all the way across Hausaland and further, which would guarantee some sort of stability. Along the way Barth procured letters of safe conduct from the Sultan of Air which he believed would protect him from molestation. Is it possible that they believed the rule of the Fulani, thought by Barth to be a "noble African race" and therefore naturally endowed with great leadership, would be better established now over twenty years since the last time a European set foot there?

In reality, as Barth came to realise, the region was anything but secure. "Sokoto is fast crumbling" Barth wrote.[30] While Clapperton had little to fear while travelling in the lands ruled by Sokoto, Barth and his train had to take huge detours through swampy country to get from one city to another.[31] It quickly became clear to Barth that most of the area was only nominally under the control of a Fulani emirate.

Three generations after the man he calls "the reformer Dan Fodiyo" established the Islamic state, it was under pressure from several directions. To the north, the Sultan of Sokoto was supposed to have suzerain over the crucial trans-Saharan caravan way-point of Air, but he could not mediate decisively between warring factions of the town's leaders. As a result the caravan routes were virtually unprotected and open to plunder by raiding parties, these raiders operating under the direction of the competing groups.

In the west of the country a large pagan army called the *Gobirawa*, the pagan Maguzawa left undefeated after the 1803 Jihad, roamed the lands between Kano and Sokoto. They harassed travellers and torched Sokoto's satellite towns, putting their inhabitants to death. The Hausa city of Kebbi was also in revolt against the rule of Sokoto, its forces roamed inside the boundaries of the area that Bello had considered settled just a few years after dan Fodiyo's death, effectively dividing the empire in two.[32]

Nor could the Sultan count on his kinsmen's loyalty either. Rebellious and bellicose Fulani lords like Buhari, Emir of Hadeja, were in open rebellion against Sokoto. When Buhari was a child, dan Fodiyo had prophesised that he would be trouble, as a man he had made good on those predictions.[33] He rejected Sokoto in the hope of taking power himself. In Kano, Barth heard of the executions of men from Hadeja in the public square, their only crime being from a rebellious region. The men were picked out because their manners and speech betrayed where they were from.

There were revolutionaries too. A breakaway community had grown up in an area to the east of Kano, the powerhouse of the regional economy, amid an area of mountainous and inhospitable land, which later became known as Ningi. Barth did not encounter this sect, he only heard of their attacks on the

Sultan's messengers travelling between cities, but Vogel the engineer did encounter them. He had to fend them off with his rifle when they attacked a group with whom he was travelling in 1855.

Further to the east, dan Fodiyo's forces had been unable to recover what remained of the Kanem and Bornu empires. They had advanced up to its borders and gone no further. There, in the capital Kukawa, the descendants of the Safayyad dynasty—one of Africa's oldest Muslim ruling lineages, was itself waning, sporadically unable to protect the villages that Barth was travelling through on his way to Adamawa. Before the end of the century Kanem-Bornu too would be toppled by a warlord at the head of a battle-hardened, bloodthirsty, slaving horde who swept in from the Sudan.

From early on in his journey Barth makes observations on the nature of power and resistance among the people he meets. What can his observations tell us about this place? Waiting for the expedition's baggage to arrive, he went on a small expedition around Tripoli, investigating some of the ancient ruins like Leptis Magna, and older mysterious rock paintings. Tripoli was at this time under the command of the Ottoman Turks, who maintained garrisons in the hills around Tripoli to protect against incursions by Berber raiders. Although the Berbers were militarily no match for the men Barth called "the Osmailis", there was a great deal of dissatisfaction among them.

Indeed, in a Berber village he found the residents were very upset by the presence of the colonial power. After spending a long time complaining about the daily injustices of their occupation, the villagers brought Barth to the real effect of their subjugation by the Ottomans; the very presence was corruption that caused their crops to fail. "While passing a number of saffron plantations, which provide the productiveness of their country, they maintained that the present production of saffron is as nothing compared to what it was before it came into the impious hands of the Osmailis." To the Berbers, Barth noted, the Ottoman "predomination had caused even the laws of nature to deteriorate."[34] The saffron grower's response to the power of the Ottomans was not recorded by Barth, but they were by no means the only people who believed the spirit must be purified in order to stave off political, physical and spiritual corruption.

"It is a remarkable fact" Barth wrote, "that while the Mohammedan religion in general is manifestly sinking to corruption along the coast, there are ascetic sects rising up in the interior which unite its last zealous followers by a religious band".[35] The first of these groups he encountered were the Tinylkum, a puritan sect led by a man named el-Madani, a charismatic preacher who had begun a community based around a religious school near Misrata. El-Madani "endowed it with a certain extent of landed property, from the produce of which he fed many pilgrims." Adherents of the Tinylkum had converted their brotherhood into real power, they used their connections and influence to run the trading caravan with whom Barth and his companions travelled with on his journey across the desert. They helped protect Barth's party from robbers, for a time, using nothing but the power of their own reputation for piety. Their members begged Barth and his friends to convert to Islam in order to save their lives, and it was only when they refused that the Tinylkum could no longer protect them. Barth was very grateful for their company and was careful to point out that they were on the whole not given to violent courses of action.

There was another group, however, for whom mere spiritual cleansing was not enough. The Anislimen—the "devout men", a sect of Tuareg Islamic scholars. Barth said they, by "their ambition, intrigues and warlike proceedings, exercise great influence upon the whole affairs of the country", they "placed themselves in a sort of opposition to the powerful chief of Tin-tellust" and acted as a threatening force of marauding brigands who harassed caravans in the desert around Agadez.[36] At that time there was a struggle between the holders of the Sultanate in Agadez and the descendants of those who had been removed by the Fulani Jihad some generations before.

The Anislimen declared the Sultan of Air was a usurper and his control of the Saharan trade was corrupt. As they themselves were the holders of spiritual purity they should be the righteous leaders of the region. In order to redraw society and seize the trans-Saharan trade, their piety required them to withdraw from the grasp of the impure. Outside society they turned their anger on the caravans that supported it, plundering them to maintain their own and impoverish their enemies.

If Barth had continued looking around he would have found this familiar story repeated everywhere. To the east of Kano, in the emirate of Bauchi, the *mallams* of Ningi were also one such group. A brotherhood of sixteen *mallams* had left the bounds of Kano society and set up their own. They followed a man called Hamza, who secluded himself for long periods of prayer in an attempt to commune with the divine God and be given the secrets of "the way".[37] A history of the *mallams* says that they were initially given permission to live in Ningi by the emir of Bauchi, who at the same time warned their hosts that they were dangerous. And indeed they were. The *mallam*-state of Ningi was a millennial brotherhood, with a charismatic leader who claimed his coming had been foretold. As the brotherhood grew, so did the claims of Hamza's power; it was said he could wrap his tongue around his head like a turban and resurrect the dead. He would have his men bring him baskets full of dead ants, whereupon he would use his magic to bring them back to life, telling his followers, "Even if the Fulani kill you, that is how I will return your lives to you."[38]

In the centres of state power at the time, if your political enemies could not be executed, they were exiled. In such a vast and varied country geography alone could provide an existential challenge to society. Environmental factors like terrain, land quality, famine or flood, or even simply the sheer distance between the seats of government, could prevent the domination of a territory by a single polity. When political factors were included, any member of society could easily find themselves outside the "frontier" of society, in "the bush"—or what might be called a kind of "no mans land",[39] facing a stark choice, make society anew, or die.

The great majority of these movements were short lived. They arose out of feuds between men, transgressions of custom or law that ended in banishments, or attempts to escape oppression or taxation.[40] But just as quickly as a new society could emerge, it might be reabsorbed. Or it could collapse and disperse. The "no man's land" was rarely just that—"frontiersmen" as the anthropologist Igor Kopytoff calls them, had to deal with local people whose occupation of the land predated the coming of the newcomers who saw it as a fresh start.[41] But also new, thriving societies could be born this way too, as Othman dan Fodiyo proved. The Shehu's Jihad had begun successfully. It had, to an extent, remade society. It had grown quickly, but now it had begun to fracture.

Barth was carrying a letter with him for part of his journey, one written by the Sultan of Air to the Sultan of Sokoto. Barth read it before he delivered it. The Sultan of Air details all the alliances between his enemies seeking to remove him, Sokoto's vassal, from his position in a leal court. The Anislimen are "marauders", in league with other pretenders to his throne, he says. The Sultan ends his letter with a simple metaphor, pleading his liege lord to come to his rescue: "You know what the hand holds, it holds only with the aid of the fingers; for without the fingers the hand can seize nothing."

This system of tribute was what bound order together in this region.

The world that Barth travelled through was one in which he recognised offices of state, offices he equated with medieval European titles and feudal relationships. All through the account of his trip he refers to these leaders as "governors", with connotations for a European at the time of a system of governance reliant on the power derived from territorial sovereignty and absolute authority derived from the rule of law.

But here leaders justified their legitimacy to rule—as opposed to the legitimacy of a competitor—not from a secular constitution or agreement, but from a personal endorsement from the Sultan who handed each a flag upon being granted the title of emir. Emirs were title holders within a religious scheme, envisaged as a seat of scholarship.

For a man to be a successful emir, he had to claim possession of righteousness as outlined by the norms of the Islamic brotherhoods that were prevalent across West Africa. In these brotherhoods charisma often ran together with piety in ideals of leadership; the charisma of the individual, his ability to make and maintain a brotherhood, was of prime importance to whether he was considered pious.[42]

Dan Fodiyo's charisma had been instrumental in bringing people together, briefly.[43] But after his death in 1817, his son Sultan Bello resurrected the courtly system of the pre-Jihad era, with a number of different positions and regional heads with titles like *Yerima*, *Galadima*, and *Magajin*, which all represented offices in the court of the *Habe* rulers. This was also the return of the system whereby the title-holders of each emirate controlled access to the emir, and the system of justice. Regional title holders had places at court, as "gatekeepers" for their regions. Tribute, effectively a form of tax, paid in goods and slaves, flowed through them.

However, many of the new nobility decided to station themselves almost permanently at the court in Sokoto, where they built large houses.[44] These positions were filled by Fulanis and were not necessarily hereditary. Appointments were given to men whose abilities the Shehu had relied on to run the war. These were rewards for loyalty, but given to ambitious men, capable in the ways of war and a title was no guarantee of continuing loyalty. As titles were bestowed at the behest of the Sultan or a regional emir, their ability to maintain them depended on their own ability to strike deals and out manoeuvre their rivals. Many were constantly grasping for any advantage they could find.

In Katsina, Barth was restrained from continuing on his way with his caravan by the local Fulani governor. Barth had letters from the emir of Agadez, recommending him as a person of honour and supposedly granting him free passage to the Sultan of Sokoto under the guaranteed protection of the regional governors. But the governor of Katsina, whose praise-singing flunkies styled as "the greatest man in Negroland", refused to let Barth leave until he gave him presents that satisfied his host. Barth had nothing to give him but a pair of scissors, some razors, Epsom salts and laudanum. These he supplemented with some not particularly fine clothes he bought in the market in Katsina (to pay for these he had to borrow money from one of the governor's courtiers). Not satisfied with receiving gifts before his liege-lord the Sultan, the governor also asked for some specific things the next time Barth came through. "He wanted, besides, two things from me which I could not favour him with, things of a very different character, and the most desired by the princes of Negroland. One of these was a *maganin-alguwa*, medicine to increase conjugal vigour, the other some rockets—as a *maganin-yaki*, a medicine of war, in order to frighten his enemies."[45] Barth tries to persuade the governor that such gifts would be impossible, "as we were afraid that if we gave such a thing to one prince, his neighbour might become fiercely hostile to us". The governor of Katsina is evidently well aware of the ramifications of what he is doing; extorting things from the visitor before he could reach the Sultan would have been an egregious twisting of the tribute chain. He was very keen for Barth to keep their encounter a secret from any of his fellow lords—most particularly the Sultan; "He begged me most urgently not to tell anybody that I had made him the presents here, adding, that he afterwards say that he had received them from me from Kano."

Barth, with his official letters of conduct, believed himself to be above the claim of lower officials. However, the governor, styled by Barth not as "emir, son of emir" but as "broker, son of broker", constructs a situation to which Barth, and everything he represents (to use a phrase every Nigerian will be familiar with from the modern media) can be converted to his own use.

The second and third generations of administrators were nothing like the vision of Islamic scholars the Shehu had in mind.[46] Trying to keep the veneer of religious propriety while at the same time participating in the worldly intrigues of rule, coveting the "medicines of war" as the governor of Katsina demanded, had taken its toll.

In some places, the Fulani yoke was thrown off all too easily. The operating theory of governance at work in the courts loyal to the Sultans of Sokoto and the Shehus of Bornu is best summed up by the words of the fifteenth-century Muslim theologian al-Maghili, the author of a treatise on the recommended conduct for princes: "Kingdoms are held by the sword, not by delays. Can fear be thrust back, except by causing fear? Allow only the nearest of your friends to bring you food and drink and bed and clothes. Do not part with your coat of mail and weapons and let no one approach you save men of trust and virtue."

But what counted as trust and virtue was not always clear; in one case, the *Habe* Sultan of Gobir pledged to support the Sultan of Sokoto after Yunfa was slain in the sacking of Alakawa only to turn on his new master in Sokoto after the leaders of the *Habe* Gobirawa mockingly sent him a set of butchers' knives. If he was nothing but the servant of the cattle herding Fulani, they implied, he had better get down to the lowly job of slaughtering their cows for them.[47]

The place that Barth described in his accounts is not one "country", but a political landscape constantly in flux, with new frontiers opening up as personal relations between leaders developed and then broke down. There was a structure of power, administered in Sokoto by the Sultan and his viziers, but the place that Barth describes is one where this central control counted for little. The occupants of walled cities maintained control over the immediately surrounding areas by force, but their ability to protect that land, and the farmers that lived on it, waxed and waned. Each emirate was nominally under the suzerain of the Sultan, but rebellion against that system was common. If an ambitious emir succeeded a loyal one, the power of the centre could not hold him in place; the only way to return what had been carved out of the suzerain was to wait for him to die, or send troops against him and depose him.

Power came from the size of your walls and the masses of your horsemen, but it also could be derived from your charisma, and ability to play the system of tribute while at the same time evading its responsibilities.

There were great swathes of the land nominally in the area under the control of Sokoto, or Bornu or Adamawa that were not actually controlled by anyone. People living in these areas, or living where a city or emirate had withdrawn its protection, were on their own, subject to raiding by the forces loyal to other emirs, rebel lords, or to non-aligned bands of brigands who roamed the country.

Whatever form of power was operating in this part of the world, it did not resemble Hobbes' Leviathan, the benign state that binds everyone together and prevents the war of "all against all", but nor did it resemble that anarchy either. It was a place that powerful men had begun to look around at the resources they had and work out how they could be converted to their own use and maintain their hold on power.

In his diaries, Barth says the land was a "disputed territory".[48] He believed that the authority established in the area by the "jihadi reformer" dan Fodiyo had begun to crumble. But he was partly mistaken. Before the Fulani uprising competing kings warred and quarrelled, the frontiers of the society were constantly redrawn. In the fifty years since the Jihad of dan Fodiyo there had been clashes with resisting pagan forces, the on-going friction with the Bornu empire, rebellious Fulani lords who disputed the authority of dan Fodiyo's successors, and the taxes they levied. Insecurity was chronic.[49] There never was a "territory" the way Barth might understand it, only the dispute.

As Barth slogged through the black mud toward Adamawa, he did not yet know Dorogu's story, but the evidence of this slave raiding was all around him. He gave voice to his melancholy feeling about the disputed frontiers he observed, and the effect on the lives of the people he met: "Indeed it is really lamentable to see the national wellbeing and humble happiness of these pagan communities trodden down so mercilessly by their Mohammedan neighbours... The tempest which had threatened us the whole afternoon discharged itself in the distance."[50]

Barth was not the only visitor to find the mud of the valley he travelled through worthy of comment. There is a story that the mud gave a village its name. This story is almost certainly not literally true—it is more than likely a kind of jokey folk-history. But according to the tale, it was the sucking sound feet made in the wet clart that put the onomatopoeic word in the settlers' mouths. The sound was "Chibok-chibok-chibok"; that of feet stalking through mud.[51]

3

MODES OF DEALING

It would be fifty years before another, very singular individual came to the land above the confluence of the Niger and the Benue, to capitalise on the information Barth collected.

For much of the period known as the "Scramble for Africa", European powers concentrated on the prizes in the south and east of the continent, the Congo region and the Nile basin. Before the 1890s, this rendered much of West Africa something of a side show to the main competition. The French, Germans and the British had divided up the region based on existing trade companies arrangements. This meant that the Sokoto and Bornu kingdoms were packaged as the Niger River Company's "sphere", north of the British Southern Nigerian Protectorate, between the two rivers, the Niger and the Benue. There was some squabbling and intrigue over the drawing of the boundary between the British sphere and German Cameroon to the east, French influenced Dahomey in the west, and French North Africa, but neither the Germans nor the French wanted to become entangled in a real shooting war with Britain. Although African colonies—especially Egypt—had a strong hold on the French public imagination, those in power thought it "madness" to bait the British over them; it was barely eighty years after the conference of Vienna had balanced Europe after the years of Napoleonic Wars.[1]

In reality, the whole concept of the Niger Company's British sphere of influence was a sham.[2] Fewer than 100 civilian staff backed by 200 British officers at the head of 2000 West African troops controlled an area that never exceeded a few hundred metres either side of the Niger. The Company at the time was mostly based in the Southern Protectorate, at Akassa, in the Niger Delta, where it traded palm oil for British-woven cloth, medicines and guns. The company had not extended their operations even as far as the middle Niger, let alone a firm presence in the north.

The man who would change all that was Captain Frederick Lugard, DSO.

* * *

In February 1906 Sir Frederick Lugard, stationed in his hill-top cantonment at Zungeru, was desperately trying to organise the few troops he had at his disposal to quell a rebellion that had suddenly flared in a place he had, until that moment, considered to be successfully "pacified".

Three years before he had embarked on a campaign to remove the rulers of northern Nigeria, waging a military campaign against the emirs of the Sokoto caliphate, the descendants of Othman dan Fodiyo. The rational for this was they were unrepentant slavers, capturing non-Muslim communities in large number and trading them among themselves or indenturing them into labour on their fields. Lugard first ordered the removal of some vassal emirs accused of corruption, before putting together a military expedition made up of European officers and "native" troops of the West African Frontier Force that marched on Kano and then Sokoto. Sultan Attahiru fled. He was chased by the British led forces and eventually killed in a final battle, a total mismatch where horsemen were cut down by machine-guns. Lugard replaced the emirs with men who he believed would be his allies.

The first indication that something had gone wrong in his new protectorate of Northern Nigeria was a telegraph that reached him late in the evening of February 15th. It had come from the capital of the Gwandu emirate, the end of the telegraph line, 200 miles at least from Zungeru. The news from the north was grim; an insurrection had erupted in a small village just outside Sokoto, the seat of the Sultan's power. The villagers of a place called Satiru had attacked and overwhelmed a company of the West African Frontier Force, smashing through their protective square formation, killing them all. Three Europeans were known to have been killed, hacked to death with farming tools.

Most concerning of all to the High Commissioner, the leader of this insurrection may have named himself as the Mahdi, Islam's hidden redeemer, intimately connected with the apocalyptic vision of the day of judgement. If his claim caught on, Lugard feared, the conflagration could be terrible. It was only twenty years since General Gordon had been beheaded in Khartoum by the followers of a man who called himself Mahdi. Lugard had staked his reputation on preventing this very thing from happening. If this was allowed to get out of hand, a catastrophe loomed.

But as he paced the mosquito-screened veranda which served as his office, scratching together a military task force, the restive Muslim villagers hundreds of miles away were not his only concern. There were other people to worry about, and they lived thousands of miles away, in London. This was the moment that would confirm if his policy of indirect rule, through the "native" emirate system, was going to work. If it didn't, his enemies in the British government would surely seize their opportunity and destroy his career.

He desperately needed to hear from Sokoto, from the court of the Sultan. The news would have a critical impact on the future of what Lugard considered one of the British Empire's most promising colonies. It was an imperial endeavour which he had nurtured into being through sheer force of will. Without news, he was acting blind. The whole northern region, which over the past three years he believed he had settled by installing replacement leaders, chosen personally by him, could at that very moment be in open revolt—and he wouldn't know.

Things were not looking good. More telegraphs came in, reaching him from Bauchi, where other "fanatical preachers" had openly called for the slaughter of unbelievers. The resident reported that the word in the marketplace was the Mahdi would reveal himself at a place called Bima Hill, at least 250 miles to the east of Zungeru. Lugard knew Bima Hill was a location of mystical power and special legend among the Fulani.

It held a special resonance for Lugard now too. It was where his troops had cut down Attahiru, the former Sultan of Sokoto, who had fled to the east with a party of followers following his removal at Lugard's order three years before.

Lugard's man in Bauchi assured him that one of these new fanatics had been caught, at least. He had been tried in the native court of the emir and executed. But two others preaching insurrection had evaded capture. They had slipped away, heading eastwards.

Lugard had very little to work with. He had just ordered the rump of the WAFF regiment to march east finally to suppress the warriors in the forested lowlands of the middle Benue. With their regular raids, the Munchi (as they were known in Hausa) had been a constant source of irritation for years. They had just sacked a telegraph station and kidnapped the engineers. It would be days before his troops reached their destination where they would receive orders to turn around immediately and head north-west.

Most of the rest of his troops were stationed in Hadeja, previously a location of unrest and rebellion against Sokoto, and with the word Mahdi floating in the air, he dare not move them from there now. Both the Resident Officers of Sokoto and Gwandu had just left their posts, leaving him without intelligence from the places closest to the action. If this self-styled Mahdi took his opportunity and marched on Kano, which Lugard thought likely, both the resident officer and his deputy there were down with the blackwater fever. It couldn't have come at a worse time.

With West Africa Frontier Force reinforcements in sufficient number at least 500 miles away, a great deal now rested in the hands of the new Sultan of Sokoto, a man whom Lugard had elevated to power just two years before. Now was the moment that would prove if they had selected the right man for the job.

It was not an easy thing—picking a leader. Lugard's own preferred method was something of a gamble. The temptation, certainly of a less confident governor as he, might be to choose a pliant man. But that was not Lugard's way; "I am myself much opposed to the selection of a weak man who may become the puppet of the Resident [British officer] and be without influence, and unable to control his subordinate chiefs," he wrote in his annual Colonial Office report for 1905–06. "In Northern Nigeria it is absolutely essential that the native rulers shall be men of strong character, for it is through and by their aid that the government desires to administer the country, and in every case I have endeavoured to select the candidate whose character was most marked by personal dignity and decision."[3] But what would happen if they were too strong-willed?

He waited for six days without news. In those six days, the mission of a whole lifetime hung in the balance.

Frederick Lugard's involvement in Nigeria had begun over a decade before, under a cloak of secrecy. The then thirty-six-year-old former captain in the British army had made himself "infamous in every land" while working on the other side of the continent, for the Imperial British East Africa Company in what is now known as Uganda.[4]

His mission there had been to prevent a war between the quarrelsome factions competing for control of Buganda, the richest kingdom of Central Africa, and ensure that "white interests" remained served. Almost as soon as he arrived at Kampala, the hill next to the Bugandan royal city, a second order arrived telling him to withdraw immediately; the company had run out of money. Outraged and unsure what to do, Lugard stayed on for a time. Rather than keeping the peace, his presence and the treaties he extorted from the eighteen-year old king, provoked a war.

In order to win decisively the battle that he played a key part in starting, Lugard's two fearsome Maxim guns (which hurled death at 500 rounds a minute) turned the fight into a massacre.[5] The French, who backed the Catholic Wa-Fransa faction, were outraged. Paris newspapers accused him of atrocities: Lugard and the Wa-Ingleza had murdered Catholics indiscriminately, including members of the Catholic missionary order the White Fathers, they said.

Lugard wrote in his diaries of the furore "My maxim is do not go to war and shoot down natives if it can possibly be avoided, but if you do start, give them a lesson they will never forget."[6]

In 1892, as Lugard travelled home to London, summoned by Gladstone's (somewhat) anti-imperialist Liberal government to explain himself, the East Africa Company was broke and on the verge of withdrawing from the region. While everyone waited for an official inquiry into the massacre to come to a conclusion Lugard went on a speaking tour of the country, laid on by the Foreign Minister (and imperial hawk) Lord Rosebery. In town halls and churches up and down the land he preached that not only was his military action not a massacre, it was the righteous defence of thousands of Christian converts. If the British deserted these people newly touched by the civilising grace of Christianity, he said, they would no doubt be enslaved by Muslims. The hawks' case was that the cause of British involvement in Uganda was not only an economic necessity, as Uganda provided many commodities the imperial economy needed, but a moral imperative to prevent Christian souls from slavery. Perhaps unsurprisingly, Lugard's speeches didn't dwell on his shooting of Catholic missionaries.[7]

Lugard touched a resonant note with those who came to see him or read of his talks; he was modest, not bombastic, gentlemanly and possessed of that quality the British middle class found most desirable—the stiff upper lip.[8]

Lugard was a thin man whose moustache dominated his sallow face (even more so than that other Frederick with a famous moustache, that near-contemporary proponent of *The Will To Power*, Friedrich Nietzsche). He could almost have been drawn directly from the pages of Rudyard Kipling. Lugard's parents had both been missionaries in India, where he was brought up. His youthful heroes were David Livingstone and General Gordon. A career soldier, he was a veteran of India, Afghanistan, and Burma. From his very first days in Africa he was convinced of the need to prevent, by force if necessary, the continued enslavement of Christian converts—or potential Christian converts—by African or Arabian Muslims. Writing in his diary on the way from Mombassa to Kampala, he states his belief; "the time for the total abolition of slavery has hardly come yet, but it is fast approaching, and when the Arabs etc have learned our modes of dealing, our trade and our prejudice against slavery then they will understand and see it is to their advantage. Moreover the company will (or should) be feared, and able to to enforce its wishes, instead of going the yambo yambo 'I scratch your back, you scratch mine' principle."[9]

His other great impetus was admiration for the British imperial man-of-action; men who had a will to make something of themselves, men who could—as they saw it—civilise the world. These were men who—as Kipling described in *The Man Who Would be King*—fantasised about becoming something of a benign dictator in a savage world. Despite his dour manners, he possessed a capacity for melodramatic fantasy that was tragic in its bathos. It is said he came to Africa in an attempt to find adventure "and, if possible, death"[10] after being rejected by his first love. In Uganda he had dreamed of marshaling a force of men and sailing down the Nile to seize Khartoum and avenge Gordon, slain five years earlier by the rampaging army of Muhammad Ahmad, the man who declared himself the Mahdi.[11]

Since the 1885 fall of Khartoum and Gordon's beheading, fanatical "Mahdism" had become a British obsession. The very word "Mahdist" stirred up fearful jitters anew in the colonial officer, able to make even the most irrepressible imperialist flinch. As Lugard would discover, just that word could change a "no" to a "yes" in Whitehall offices. "The fate of Gordon," as Queen Victoria had told her ministers, "is not and will not be forgotten in Europe!"[12]

The Liberal establishment, however, were horrified by what Lugard had done in Uganda. They loathed him, considered him arrogant, aloof and mentally unstable. Gladstone, the Prime Minister, thought him a part of a jingoistic cabal who had taken over the Foreign Office. Sir William Harcourt, to whom Lugard would write his reports to the Colonial Office when he became High Commissioner in northern Nigeria, said he was "a man so swollen with his own importance ... that he has quite lost his head". Others said he was a "lunatic" and aimed to "be a second Gordon".[13]

But despite their misgivings, the overwhelming public response to Lugard and Lord Rosebery's campaign to "save" the Christian Ugandans from slavers forced the anti-Imperialist Liberal government's hand. Instead of pulling out of Uganda, the commercial interest was nationalised. The British Government, with its deep pockets and unlimited manpower, stepped in to save, if not quite the earthly bodies of the Ugandan natives, then the interests of the adventurous privateers of the Imperial British East Africa Company.

The Liberals may have thought him mad, but Lugard's will and his achievements had caught the eye of Sir George Goldie, head of the British Niger Company. Talks over who controlled what in West Africa had collapsed and opened up a space to establish a claim to the land between the British sphere and the kingdom of Dahomey, which was considered French. Treaties were needed. In order to get them, someone had to go there and cajole, bribe or force local chiefs to sign contracts giving the British exclusive rights. Lugard was the very man for it, but news of his participation needed to be kept from the French.

In 1894 Lugard left London incognito for the Niger Company's base in Akassa. From there he steamed up the Niger and set out for the Bourgu region with a caravan of Hausa soldiers and porters bearing gifts, to extract what was called a "treaty of friendship" from the King of Nikki before the French could arrive from the other direction. The French later claimed Lugard's treaties were frauds, extorted from the king by a treacherous adviser, the *Liman*. They put a gunboat into the River Niger and fired the starting pistol on a new race to claim territory. But this was not Lugard's concern. His contract with Goldie was fulfilled; he was heading home.

Lugard had been dissatisfied by the way the Goldie's Niger Company behaved in the Southern Protectorate. He had been appalled by the poor state of the troops Goldie had hired for Lugard's mission and was very critical of the day-to-day prospects for "the natives" around the coastal stations. The company's policy was to flood the creek-towns and trading stations with gin, which Lugard discerned was solely to make the locals pliable. Brass middlemen were then unfairly charged duty through the nose.[14] Goods the Brassmen of the Nembe creek bought were routinely seized from their canoes by protectorate customs officials on the assumption they had been stolen, or bought with smuggled gin.

The Brassmen, already angered by being shut out of direct trade with the British by Goldie's company, rose up and sacked the company station at Akassa just days after Lugard left it. Although he was disgusted by the reports of the Brassmen's display of barbarity that accompanied the attack (some of the prisoners taken during the attack, the Akassa company kru-boys, were said to have been eaten), their anger did not seem to surprise Lugard. "[T]here is a most unfair differential treatment," he said about the motivation for the uprising, "and of course the Brass middlemen look on the seizures as mere spoilation". The people of Brass "are treated very arbitrarily," he added "whereas in the old days of competitive traders they were feted, and given champagne and ate with the European traders who competed for their custom."[15] Lugard's austere Christianity led him to believe that gin should be banned from the Protectorate, to keep the peace as well as protect the souls of savages.

Now the offence had been committed, however, Lugard advocated the most stringent prosecution of the insurrectionists—to teach them a lesson they would never forget. Even the smallest bit of empathy he felt for the Brassmen's predicament did not change his mind as to the policy prescription he thought right. But that task was not his to carry out. He had completed his mission and left the Royal Niger Company station, heading to London to make his report.

This would just be the beginning for Lugard in Nigeria. In 1898, the British Government, perhaps influenced by Lugard's machinating in London, gave him the mission of creating a better force of soldiers for the Protectorate. He returned and started the army from first principles, hiring freed slaves and pagans for his new West African Frontier Force. He trained them how to fight the British Empire way, forming a square, one row of rifles after another, the Maxim guns in the centre.

Two years after that, the government bought out Goldie's company at a ruinously high price. Just as in Uganda, the company's interest had been nationalised. Lugard became the first High Commissioner, the head of the British government administration. Here he could do things the way he saw fit. Here, at last, was the opportunity "the man who would be king" fantasised about. In his sights was the promising territory north of the confluence of the Niger and Benue rivers, its vast tracts of land and its economy based on the slavery of a large population of saveable pagan souls. In Lugard's eyes, the emirs were ripe, hostile to the British and in need of "pacifying", in the same way he described the East African Muslims in his diary on the way to Kampala.

It is difficult to know what the Sultan and his people actually thought of Lugard when in 1900 his messenger, a Kanuri man from Bornu called Kyari (who the Sokoto court did not know spoke and understood Fulfulde), arrived at the palace with a letter. The proclamation said the territory previously "vested" in the Royal Niger Company was to be "assumed" as a possession of the Queen. The messenger himself reported that the Sultan read the letter himself before saying that he would never read another letter from a white man, and that if they were to come, he would fight them. Kyari was then bundled out of town.[16] Lugard later wrote that this mystified him. To his mind there was nothing contentious in the letter, there must have been a misunderstanding!

In further letters to the court of the Sultan, Lugard was to spin a narrative, a justifying righteous fantasy, around the presence of the British in northern

Nigeria. The Emirs personified corrupt leadership, Lugard said, based on the undeniable reticence the rulers of Sokoto showed to curtailing their slaving activities. The new Governor of Nigeria shrewdly told Sokoto in 1901; "I desire to inform you who are head of the Mohammedans ... That the Emirs of Bida and Kontagora have during many years acted as oppressors of the people and shown themselves unfit to rule."[17] Lugard deposed them and in their place put people who would agree to deal with him. Whether he knew about Barth's observations about how power was won in this place is debatable, but he was certainly adept at using the same methods. The Sultan did not reply to missives sent to Sokoto for several months. When letters did come they seem to have been, at best, misunderstood or, more likely, manipulated by Lugard, who was machinating the Sultan's own removal.[18]

One letter from the Sultan discovered in the archives by the colonial historian D. J. Muffett was translated from Arabic thus: "Our entire salutations and cordial greetings, and thereafter, for your information, indeed we stood upon your letter and we understood your words, but for our part, our Lord is Allah, our creator, our ruler, and in truth we are bound by what our Prophet Muhammad—Peace be upon him—brought to us. As our God says (in the Qur'an) 'Whatever the Prophet brings to you, and receive, even until the end.' Therefore we will not change it for anything until all is finished. Do not send anything after this."

However, the official letter that appeared in the colonial reports sent to London read: "From us to you. I do not consent that any one from you should ever dwell with us. I will never agree with you. I will have nothing ever to do with you. Between us and you there are no dealings except as between Mussulmans and Unbelievers (Kafiri)—War, as God almighty has enjoined on us. There is no power or strength save in God on high." This, a much harsher sounding message than the first, was taken by Lugard to be an unequivocal declaration of war by Sokoto. After his trawling of the archives and lining up translations with dates of messages received, Muffett believed that it is likely Lugard wilfully misconstrued the messages, or at best misunderstood them, and that the "declaration of war" was only so because Lugard wanted it to be. It was the murder of Captain Moloney, one of Lugard's officers, in Keffi two years after the proclamation was sent that provided him with what he had been waiting for: "casus belli" against the rulers of Sokoto.[19]

Whether or not the Fulani were quite as bellicose as Lugard required them to be can be debated. One thing that is quite certain is that the Fulani court feared the forced removal of slavery. It presented a great threat to Sokoto and the hierarchical way of life at which the Fulani aristocracy sat atop. The system that freed the nobility from agricultural work and allowed them to live the rarefied courtly life, separated from the mass of the people free—in theory—to read Qur'anic texts and dedicate their lives to scholarly pursuits, was dependent on others doing the work. Removal of such slave labour would mean an end to the aristocrat's grip on society, an end to the world as they knew it. Their connection to the system of tribute, the hands that grasped the fruit, was being severed.

This was connected to another type of "end", one hinted at in the letter that Muffett considers more reliably translated. What is meant by; "'... Whatever the Prophet brings to you, and receive, even until the end.' Therefore we will not change it for anything until all is finished"? Until what end? What "all" is finished?

It was not only the end of their rule they believed might be imminent, but the end of the world. Eschatology, legends of the end times, within Islam at this time suggests what is being referred to is more than just a personal end. This is significant, and should not be considered merely a throwaway reference.

Among the heads of the Caliphate, the titleholders and nobility, the clerics, judges and officials of its civil service to the members of their armed forces, to the multitudes of court hangers on, to the traders, servants and the common folk in the towns and in the rural areas, most would have been familiar with—or even adamant believers in—the coming end of the world.[20] What is more, without the colonialists necessarily knowing it, there was a particular resonance between this belief and the coming of the British Empire; many thought that the coming of the Christians might herald the coming day of ultimate judgement.

Islamic eschatology, derived mostly from the Hadith but also from the Qur'an, holds that there will come a time when Yajuj and Majuj, the forces of chaos and corruption (Gog and Magog in Hebrew) will be let loose. Originally Yajuj and Majuj were said to be symbolic forces of flaming fire and surging water. At other times in the tradition they became grotesque, flat-faced, hairy generals of Hell—thought to be associated with the Mongol hordes of the middle ages. In the Qur'an the barrier that holds them back is the sharia, the discipline of the righteous way of life, and once that is gone the forces of chaos will create a dark time where God's approved order is turned over.

In some iterations of legend the wall holding them back is made of iron and molten copper and built by an ancient hero across a valley, somewhere in the east. When it is torn down, this chaos and corruption will also free the

Mahdi—"the rightly guided one"—from where he has been hidden. He will resemble the Prophet Muhammad and wherever he goes he will bring about a "golden time", mirroring the flowering of peace said to have been enjoyed by the early community of Muslims under Muhammad.

But the Yajuj and Majuj, the forces of hell, will still be stalking the land reaping lost souls, creating a horde of unbelievers who have turned away from Allah. At the heart of this will come the Deceiver, with bulging eye, red skin and the word "kafir"—unbeliever—branded on his forehead. He, if he truly has a gender, is *al-Masih ad-Dajjal*, the anti-Christ. What follows will be a chaotic time of perverted spirituality, where the unholy and impure are rewarded as the virtuous, where true spirituality will be indistinguishable from false. With his one eye unable to discern true depth, visually or spiritually, the deceiver will pervert all forms of justice.

This tumult will be brought to an end by the reappearance of Isa (Jesus). He will come again to the world to engage Dajjal in mortal battle. Isa, the tradition says, will defeat the Antichrist and lead all the righteous to paradise. Time will then end.[21] That is the general story according to the Islamic tradition.

But belief in the Mahdi does not have a single thread, it is woven out of many. In Sokoto alone there were many differing debates on the nature of the Mahdi, when he would come, how he would be announced, where it would happen, what the nature of Yajuj and Majuj was, and on and on. The prevailing belief was that in line with the Arabian prophesy, the Mahdi would emerge on a mountaintop. But for those in the Sokoto Caliphate this was said to be was Bima Hill in present day Gombe state, east of the seat of the Sultan. Fulani legend adds to the Arabian and Syrian traditions a ghostly angel on a white horse, waving a standard and charging down the mountain; the flag is white for good news, blood red for bad.[22] Auspicious white vultures also appear in some tellings.

As the white men arrived, from not only Britain, but France to the north and Germany to the east, many associated them with Yajuj and Majuj. A poet wrote of the advance of the British on Zaria:

Gog and Magog are coming, they approach,
they are small people with big ears,
they are those who cause destruction at the ends of the earth,
when they approach a town, its crops will not sprout.
The fertility of the world will be taken away,
the place that gave seventy bushels will not give seven,

the anti-Christ is coming, he will come and have authority over the world,
the Mahdi and Isa, they are coming,
In order to straighten out the tangle.[23]

But there is one element that is common in all strains of Mahdism, that is the prevalence of chaotic or poor governance in the period immediately before the arrival of the Mahdi. After all, how could the end of the world come if everything was stable and prosperous?[24] In Sokoto, this led to there being generally two different kinds of Mahdist belief, the one held by aristocrats and the other held by commoners. In the aristocratic belief, imminence of the coming of the Mahdi was inversely proportional to the proximity of real power; those who held it believed in the eventual coming of the Mahdi, but it was not as imminent for them as it was for those who did not hold power.

Fervency in Mahdist belief also peaks around the end of the Islamic century—in alignment with prophecies that the conditions for the coming of the Mahdi exist every 100 years.[25] The thirteenth Islamic century ended in 1883, at the time of the rising of Muhammad Ahmad, the man who did for General Gordon in the Sudan. There had been several cases of people emigrating eastwards in the 1880s to join these Mahdist armies.

One of the people who made the move eastwards was Hayatu, a great grandson of Othman dan Fodiyo. His father Said had been passed over by the kingmakers in the succession to the Sultan of Sokoto, ending Hayatu's own prospects of advancement. In 1878 he left Sokoto with a band of followers, seeking space to make his way in a new society. His emigration was a move of dynamic religious significance, known in Fulani culture as *perol*.[26] He gathered followers as he travelled. He reached Yola at the eastern edge of the Caliphate, in Adamawa, where Barth had travelled thirty years before, then headed north to Bogo, now in northern Cameroon. From here he preached against the corrupted government of Sokoto and plotted its downfall. It was there in 1883 that he pledged allegiance to Muhammad Ahmad, the man who had proclaimed himself to be the Mahdi in Sudan two years before. Muhammad reciprocated, making Hayatu the representative of his movement in the area, and claimant-in-waiting to the Sultanate of Sokoto, once the army of Muhammad Ahmad turned westwards.

Hayatu had left Sokoto with thiry other similarly disaffected clerics. Over time, this party named *al-Ansar*, "The Helpers", grew. Others followed him eastwards and in Yola and Bogo he gained followers due to the acquiescence of local leaders. These local leaders may have shared Hayatu's Mahdist sentiments; it was also possible that they believed it would be imprudent to go head to head against this band of fanatics and their firebrand leader. Much better to avoid direct conflict and see if they could be bent to their will. They were right to be concerned, Hayatu had joined forces with the warlord Rabeh, an emissary of the Mahdi. Rabeh was vicious, bloodthirsty and cruel, his ravages of the country were all but unstoppable. He swept down at the head of a marauding army, conquering, sacking, slaving and putting to the sword the kingdoms of Baghirmi and Bornu in the late 1890s.[27]

But in 1898 the alliance between Rabeh and Hayatu broke down. Hayatu was killed by Rabeh's men. By now Rabeh sat in control of a large swathe of territory that included Bornu and parts of Adamawa. His tyrannical rule over the area lasted seven years, by the end of it the old order in Bornu was all but destroyed, thousands had been sold into slavery including young children, and countless others murdered in terrible ways.

By 1900, the French moved against Rabeh and the warlord's horsemen. Rabeh's army had slaughtered villagers, scattered populations before them and leaving their corpses for the vultures, they had buckled the empire of Bornu's defences, but they were no match for the well-drilled colonial troops armed with machine guns. Rabeh and his son were killed. Rabeh's decapitated head was put atop a spike and paraded around the land.

The remaining members of Hayatu's al-Ansar were scattered into the wilderness. They hid in the rugged terrain, or melted back into the populations from where they had come, but the allegiances they had inspired persisted through this. Rekindled, they organised in secret. The remnants of this group were behind uprisings in the German parts of West Africa in 1906, the same year as the Satiru insurrection.

Although enacted in the name of the Mahdi, what happened at Satiru was a significantly different kind of movement. Where al-Ansar was led by rebel aristocrats who had to migrate away to another political space to create and nurture their following, the Mahdists at Satiru did not believe emigration was necessary. They wanted to overturn corrupt government and call forth a new divine era of justice, though their anger was focused on the Caliphate's ethnic roots.[28] Their "revolutionary Mahdism" drew upon anger among minority groups and rebel Hausa at the Fulani overlords who levied exorbitant taxes on agriculturalists and lived on the fruits of a corrupt and oppressive government. The commonfolk slogged out their lives on the land, working in *gandu*, a system of feudal-like labour where slaves toiled for their landowning masters.[29]

Like Hamza and the *Mallams* of Ningi eighty years before, the leaders of the Satiru revolt were not Fulani, and wanted not only to be free of Fulani taxes, but tear down Fulani rule. It was also aimed at the colonial power who had imposed their own, even more corrupted Fulani leaders upon them. One of the remaining Fulani emirates not headed by a Lugard-appointed Emir—Gwandu, the second emirate established in the Jihad—was working in support of the insurrectionists for this reason.

Satiru was not only a home to outcast clerics from the emirate capitals of Sokoto and their followers, many others among the Satiru rebels were runaway slaves from the farms of the Fulani fief-lords. They were led by a half blind *mallam* named dan Mafako—"The Blind One"—who held people in sway with magic powers. He preached that when Isa came among them, he would rid the world of corrupt government. No exile to the east was necessary. A cunning and ruthless man, he had convinced followers of his magic powers using ventriloquism and seemed to converse with the elemental spirits and djinns. After their initial victory, the Satiru Mahdists sacked neighbouring villages. The fanatical cult members were purging the area of people who might oppose their fanaticism and who lacked their taste for blood now their moment had come.[30] Dan Mafako gave followers a drink made of powdered herbs and water that had the charcoal of written Qur'anic verses dissolved in it, as mentioned above. The mixture, dan Mafako said, would render them invulnerable to bullets. After drinking the concoction, projectiles fired at them would splash off, like drops of water.[31]

Lugard feared that the the leaders of Sokoto would rally to this half-blind Mahdist, or at the very least be powerless to stop their people from joining the revolt. This was not without reason. Three years before, when the captains of the British Expeditionary Force and their West African troops marched through northern Nigeria to unseat Sultan Attahiru, he and his followers fled eastwards, to Bima Hill. The move had scared the British who assumed it was a move of religious and Mahdist significance, with the hope of rallying people to him in an anti-colonial uprising.[32] Could it be about to happen again? Lugard was also aware of the danger of another Rabeh. He could not allow a new power to carve out territory from his newly won protectorate.

With the added knowledge that the revolt was as much against the Fulani aristocracy, this fear seems misplaced. Sokoto wanted rid of dan Mafako and the Satiru insurrectionists perhaps as much as Lugard, but they were incapable of achieving the job themselves, it seemed. When the Sultan sent 3,000 mounted horsemen to the village in the days after the first British casualties were inflicted, the cavalry were routed by the villagers, still only armed with hoes and scythes. A cleric in Sokoto observed: "We have been conquered [by the British], we have been made to pay tax, we have been made to do various things, and now they want us to fight their wars for them. Let them go fight themselves."[33]

It is not clear from the records that Lugard was completely ignorant of the nature of the Satiru uprising. In communications with his resident officers they inform him that most of the Satiru Mahdists are runaway slaves, implicitly hostile to the Fulani establishment. But if he was aware of what the implications of this were, Lugard removed the references to runaway slaves in his communications with London, emphasising instead the need for a bold action. They must send an unambiguous message to the subordinated rulers of the Empire's new protectorate. The colonial authority would need to rely on them in the future; insurgency would not be tolerated.

To this end, Lugard ordered his captains and their troops to "annihilate" Satiru, erase it from the face of the earth. This they did.

"They killed every living thing before them" a secret inquiry set up into the massacre found later. Fields, it was said, were "running with blood". Men were impaled on stakes, an ancient torture in Sokoto where live victims were lowered onto wooden spikes so that their rectums were pierced. Gravity carried the point through their torso, shredding their organs until the spike protruded, stretching then breaking the skin at the neck. Womens' breasts were sliced off.[34] In all, an estimated 2,000 were slaughtered by the West African Frontier Force of European officers and pagan troopers. Thousands of other surviving women and children were taken by the Fulanis as slaves.

Dan Mafako somehow escaped with the help of a teenage boy. He was caught soon after and during his trial he asked for water. The boy cried "don't give it to him!" When asked why, he said dan Mafako would use the water to turn into an insect and fly away. The blind wizard was executed without delay.[35]

The Sultan declared anyone returning to the village would be cursed, and sowed the ground with salt. It is today an unremarkable patch of land at the edge of a forest reserve.

The truth of this massacre was suppressed from the British public. But it was so disturbing that even the fatefully un-squeamish Winston Churchill (then at the Colonial Office) could not bear it, and asked pointed questions of Lugard and his supporters in London. Lugard was removed from Nigeria and replaced. He faced his own exile to the east as Governor of Hong Kong, for the time being.

Satiru marked the end of the first period of the encounter between the colonialists and the rulers of Sokoto. The first test of indirect rule had come and the result had gone in Lugard's favour. The principle of indirect rule, where a colony could be governed by local elites in a way that did not contradict the interests of the British Empire, had proved to be sound. When these two worlds first encountered each other there had been fear and misunderstanding. After Satiru, things settled down to a level of mutual distrust. But for the old aristocracy, their world was about to change forever.

Following his military campaign, Lugard set about trying to make inroads into what was to him an occluded, arcane and ignorant society. If the colony were to be usefully exploited for the benefit of the Empire, Lugard concluded, northern Nigeria had to be properly prepared. It would need to be brought—as the British saw it—into the modern world. This would not only make the Northern Nigerian Protectorate more understandable to the officers who would become its colonial residents, but also the people the British had to work with must be brought up to understand them.

At the same time, colonial power was also wary of pulling people away from their "native" identities. The British shied away from the idea of changing society *too* much. It would be no good stripping away everything, if the administration relied on the old structures and offices for their system of "indirect rule".

The most obvious place these contradictory aims collided was in the colonial education policy.

From early on the administration had been educating freed slaves at an institution in Kaduna, with some success, and the British wanted to widen this education out to include the sons of prominent men. Not only would they "dispel the ignorance" of the ruling class, as Lugard wrote in a Colonial Office report, they would make the sons of emirs and other leading members of society into ideal administrators for the future colony.

But the emirs resisted the spread of schools. The old order feared the British would obliterate their culture, erasing it with Christianity. In order to assuage these fears Lugard promised to keep missionaries and their schools out of the north. This was not through any ambivalence to Christianity on Lugard's part, but out of expediency. He needed the emirs on his side.[36] From the time that Lugard exerted control over the emirs, until today, the implementation of education policy has been characterised by tension. Tension between cultures, and between different policies set out to reform a society that the British considered backward and ignorant.

The British may have thought them backward, but the emirs thought themselves to be part of a long and proud tradition of Islamic learning dating back, in the case of the scholarly communities of the Bornu emirate, to the eleventh century. These were known as centres of Islamic study not only across West Africa but also across the wider Islamic world. The courtly elite studied and were well versed in science and mathematics. Barth found his gift of a book of Euclid went down very well in Sokoto, as the Sultan's previous copy had been lost in a fire.

Not everyone was conversant with ancient Greek mathematicians, of course. Islamic schools were organised in several levels, the elementary *macarantan allo*, where children learned the Qur'an in their neighbourhoods from a local imam. This was followed by the *macarantan ilmi*, where older youths are taught Qur'anic exegesis, and law. Learning was done in Arabic, but also in *Ajami*, Hausa written in Arabic script, which was a special and important part of the scholarly identity. Each of the larger northern cities were known for different kinds of learning: Kano for the study of Islamic jurisprudence, Sokoto for mysticism, Zaria and Katsina for Arabic grammar and Bornu in the memorisation of the Qur'an.[37]

Children who embarked on this education, known as *Almajirai*, were supposed to be entering into a long period of apprenticeship under a master that could last for many years. Education at any higher level than *macarantan allo* was exclusively for boys, as girls' education usually stopped at the stage of learning the basics of Islamic ritual practice, after which it was expected that they would be married.

Teaching was flexible to allow the students time to work between lessons on farms or with their masters. In times of real hardship, in the last part of the dry season when stores of food are low, they would help their master by begging for alms. The hardship and hunger endured by the students was part of their education. In Hausa culture, having suffered hardship speaks to a good upbringing; it gives the student—the seeker of religious knowledge—the knowledge of being humble before God.

Another key way that imams made a living was through the patronage of wealthy local figures. Scholars were considered knowledgeable about the deepest mysteries of life, were thought to know the workings of the universe and could influence them with scripts from the Qur'an or charms and amulets. The wealthy men of the area would support a "prayer economy" in much the same way as medieval Normans patronised monasteries, the power of having many students of God's word praying for your soul was very desirable.[38]

Hans Vischer's education plan of 1909 emphasised caution and sensitivity to Islamic heritage. Lessons were in Hausa, and students who were the sons of the highborn were allowed to live with their wives and servants and keep the social standing of their class. The course taught a selective syllabus that steered clear of controversial subjects. This separate educational plan for Northern Nigeria was based in Vischer's desire to preserve as best as possible what he saw as the natural characteristics of race and ethnicity. At the time it was thought that it was being sensitive to the cultural mores of "the natives", but it also aimed to prevent them from becoming—as the British had found uncomfortable in India—a "babu" class of educated clerks who had ideas above their station.[39]

This was different from the way education was being managed in the southern protectorate, which operated a wholly imported version of the British school syllabus. This difference in approach in effect created a two-track system, unbalanced, with larger numbers of people receiving an education in the south.

After a few years, the British administration changed tack. When Lugard returned from the Far East in 1912, his vision was to unify the country under a single colonial administration of Nigeria. Lugard was to become its first Governor-General. Nothing that would impede this vision could be allowed to continue. A multi-stream education policy would leave the northern province on a irrevocably different course from the southern provinces. Vischer's system which aimed to educate while preserving what the coloniser thought of as the "natural characteristics" of the African race was replaced with one that emphasised English as the lingua franca of a future Nigerian colony.[40]

But efforts to homogenise education did not succeed in the north. The two-track system, one teaching Western "boko" learning, the other culturally Islamic schooling, persisted. The few who received "boko" education in schools were the children of the compliant emirs, who owed their grip on the offices of power to British colonisers. There were other ways in which the modernising policy was not consistently applied. In the years before independence, for example, the British created government-sanctioned Arabic teaching colleges. These offered advanced education in Islamic jurisprudence and Arabic. Ostensibly these institutions were there to preserve learning in Arabic and develop those who had showed proficiency in Islamic thought, who had not necessarily had a Western education, in order to provide judges for Islamic courts, necessary for the continuation of the Muslim way of life in the north.[41]

It was only when the prospect of independence loomed that the significance of this became apparent. The northern leadership grasped that they risked losing out in an independent Nigeria. Shorn of its privileged connection to the colonial power the northern elite could lose control of the administration of the new republic, simply because the aristocracy's reluctance to promote widespread Western education meant they did not have enough young people with the right sort of education to take the reins of a civil service that would be country-wide, and not simply regional.

Education became the signifier of an important social change among the northern elite. The people who most valued the preserving of culture, the old elite who valued ties to the Arabic world, who were educated in *Ajami* and who had ruled the emirates form the traditional titles of the emir's court, were about to be disempowered. The Nigerians who would take over the northern region were the ones who had come through the Western schools, who were working in the modern civil service, who spoke English.

Nowhere was this shift embodied than in the person of Sir Ahmadu Bello, KBE. Bello, a descendant of Othman dan Fodiyo, had his early education at the foot of a *mallam* where he learned the Qur'an. But he also attended Sokoto's "modern school" and received a western education.

In his late 20s he had been a candidate for Sultan, but was passed over for the title by the kingmakers. He had dabbled too much in the worldly sphere of politics for their liking, and the Sokoto establishment went instead for a less controversial candidate.

He was given instead the title *Sardauna*, a word that means something like "brave one with the sword", or "brave road-opener" and was traditionally the captain of the palace bodyguard.[42] He went to Britain with a university scholarship to study politics and government, and when he returned, instead of assuming a role in the old power structure of the Sokoto Caliphate he emerged as a canny leader of the new political world of northern Nigeria. He was the leader of the north's first political party, and when independence came, he was made Premier of the northern region.

His leadership style was influenced by the old; he always appeared in traditional garb, long flowing robes and a turban were his hallmarks. He was a very religious man who insisted on strict observance of prayer times and proper conduct among his colleagues. At the same time, he also represented the future of Nigeria, namely secular political parties participating in a parliamentary system that owed its heritage to the democracy of the English-speaking world. The contradictions were unresolved in his own person; for example despite his traditional clothing and manifest piety, Ahmadu Bello did not read Arabic.[43]

Bello was the bridge of the old world to the new. But independence from Britain broke this link to the past and made permanent the shift in who held power in the north.

This new northern elite was one that was empowered by the recent colonial past, and had come to terms with it. Bello even said that Lugard's victory and his removal of Sultan Attahiru had been "God's will".[44]

PART 2

4

HEART ROT

A friend told me that growing up in the city of Zaria in the 1960s, as he walked to school every morning the *Almajirai* children, the students of the local imam who learned the Qur'an by heart, would mock him and his classmates with a song. It went like this:

'Yan makarantan boko-ko,
Ba karatu, ba sallah
Sai yawan zagin mallam.

Translated from Hausa, it means: "Children of Western education schools (*makarantan boko*), no learning, no worship, but always insulting the teacher." Following Western education, the song said, was synonymous with disrespect for the correct authority, and therefore showed a general lack of the basic values that held society together. My friend says they taunted him and his siblings and classmates with the confident manner of people who were rejecting something out of hand without looking twice, secure in their belief that what they were rejecting was immoral.

My friend's family were wealthy and outward looking, enough to see the importance of getting their children a Western education, but they were by no means impious. The kids doing the taunting? "These were the street kids, the toughies in my neighbourhood", my friend said. They would play together in the dusty street after school, but there would always be a division between them.

In later life he became a successful banker. He has property in London and travels internationally on a frequent basis. It is possible the boys who taunted him may never have left northern Nigeria in the whole of their lives. When we were talking I asked him if he ever sees them, now they're adults, and he looked at me slightly puzzled as if to say "why would I?" but he said; "maybe if I am back there I might."

I wondered if their taunting could also have been the bitterness that comes of poverty, causing the boys to proudly reject what they could never afford, or were prevented from having.

Since my friend's childhood attitudes to education among Nigeria's poor in the main have changed. Now if you go even to the very furthest villages, kilometres from the nearest tarmacked road, and ask what they want for their children, one of the first things people will say is "education".

* * *

Like all Nigerian parents trying to educate their children, Hadiza Umar has had trouble finding a decent school. She has all the same worries as other parents about her children's education, but as she's a consultant for an NGO working in the education sector, she has a good grasp of how deep, how widespread, and just how bad the problems are. As she tells me about the difficulties parents face in securing education for their children I can hear in her voice that tone so many Nigerians have when they talk about the tribulations of their country; one that swings between frustration and acceptance. It comes with a kind of theatrically deadpan delivery—as one might tell a long and incredible story of a day full of ever-descending woeful events, the grip of which you have yet to escape.

Umar has three children, aged seven, four and a seven-month old. After several false starts she has found a school she is happy with for her seven-year-old, but Umar knows she has to constantly monitor it. "I'm looking for a school that has discipline, good morals. And the teachers, I'm very particular about how they associate with the children," she says when we meet in the city of Kaduna, where she lives and works. She has come to see that a school's reputation alone is not enough to properly judge. Umar is one of the relatively few parents in Nigeria who does not approve of corporal punishment, a practice that is well established in its schools. Many elite institutions, Umar feels, do not deserve their good reputations. "Every time I go to a school I pray they have teachers that will impact positively on my children," she says. In her bitter experience of Nigerian education, this cannot be taken for granted.[1]

In the case of her children, Umar is talking about private rather than government run schools, but in terms of whether parents pay fees, these distinctions are moot. Most education in Nigeria has to be paid for by the parents directly in some fashion. Even those whose children are in government-funded institutions have to pay some form of fee. In some cases this money is paid directly to the teacher at the beginning of term, ostensibly so they will turn up at all.

Umar works for an NGO affiliated with a programme funded by the British government that tries to help state and local governments improve the schools they are responsible for. She visits primary and secondary classrooms and sits in lessons, observes and evaluates school management to find out weaknesses and recommend strategies that she hopes will improve things.

She gives me a run-down of some of the most basic problems of providing education. They come from both the governance and administration of schools and the teachers themselves.

Since Nigeria's return to democracy in 1999, the government of Olusegun Obasanjo made publicly lauded efforts to properly fund education. The Universal Basic Education programme and its counterpart at the state level the State Universal Basic Education programmes were meant to provide nine years of free education to every child. Schooling was to be compulsory, and the programme set out not to just provide it, but improve it as well.[2] Education was made a priority, the government said, to keep up with the demand of a growing population and also to give Nigerians what has been called the "dividend of democracy", real improvements in quality of life—flowing directly from the governance brought in by the return of democracy. Education could be seen as a kind of canary in the coal mine of governance, a measure not so much of how much government has achieved, but how and why things go wrong.

The government promised to fund education adequately. In 2011 a presidential task-force charged with investigating why the UBE had not lived up to its lofty promises found that government spent between 5 and 7.5 per cent of its GDP on education at the federal level, and yet the taskforce found that schools' access to funds remained among the "myriad of challenges" the education sector faces to this day.[3]

Budget figures are drawn up without heeding research into precise needs, with no reference to institutions' capacity to effectively spend the money. Communication between areas of governance is poor. To people working in the system, figures can appear arbitrary, untethered to logical funding procedures. In the education sector, respondents to the inquiry by the Presidential Task Force on Education spoke of there being "apparent budgets", the money that the government publicised that it was giving, and the "real budget" the money that appeared at the sharp end of the system. There are gaps between them, and no explanation is ever forthcoming.

Indeed, budgets are secretive affairs, drawn up by a few civil servants. What money does come down to establishments is often late. That money is often absorbed by the huge salary bills of the state education system. This "recurrent" expenditure is prioritised over expenditure on infrastructure and other physical needs. The system of who is responsible for what has become so complex that even attentive civil servants have begun to lose their grip on what is happening and why. Every management system that the government and its servants use, from payroll information to the most basic of record keeping, is laborious, inefficient and unreliable. Nepotism and corruption in the hiring process has also in many cases prevented the education administration hiring the right people, and often management of reform is beyond the capabilities of the people employed to do the job.[4]

These are problems that Umar is familiar with. She told me: "If you go to the state education service, [with a query about a school] it's possible they don't even know about that particular school, especially if it's a rural one. Their attitude is that if it's in a hard to reach place, then 'why should I be bothered to go there', but if they were they would find that the schools are really struggling and suffering."

Even where administration has been judged to be "good" there are terrible difficulties in providing education. Katsina, the northern state where former science teacher Umaru Yar'Adua was governor before becoming president in 2007, is considered among the top implementers of the UBE programme.[5] In the final two years of his eight year term as governor Yar'Adua had begun a building programme, adding second stories to schools in the state capital, trying to double the number of classrooms. But it was not enough.

In the same year Governor Yar'Adua became president, I visited Katsina in the run up to the election, I found school classrooms packed to over capacity with thirty or forty small children, sitting for hours on concrete floors, chanting sentences written on a blackboard—learning them by rote. One school, Kofa Kaura primary in the state capital, had not been part of the building project and had to resort to desperate measures in an attempt to fit all its pupils in to its fifteen classrooms. Half the school attended in the morning the other half in the afternoon, effectively limiting the number of days children could attend school and doubling the teachers daily workload.

Deputy headteacher Suleiman Isa told me: "We are praying for the government to come and build another storey on our school, we don't know why they have not". Space wasn't the only problem. Isa added: "We have been waiting for five years to have desks. We write to them, but they didn't give us. If the children don't have desks their handwriting isn't good and they get dirty. It's hard for them to learn."[6]

But at the state education board, just a few minutes drive form Kofa Kaura Primary, there were stacks of desks, piled under a tree. There were rows and rows of them, their wood slowly peeling and bleaching in the sun.

Teaching in Nigeria is a profession in limbo. It could almost be summed up with the old adage about factory workers in Soviet Russia; they pretend to work, and the state pretends to pay them. Sometimes there isn't even a pretence. Poor and non-existent salaries and bad living conditions in schools are cited as being the primary cause of absenteeism among teachers. The problem is so bad, researchers say, that teachers playing hooky from school is "endemic".[7] Many teachers have to work two jobs to make ends meet, dragging them away from their classrooms. The career path for teaching is broken, good teachers can't get promoted, seniority—no matter what the level of competence—is valued over ability, and living quarters—if they exist at all—are old and decrepit. Many of the government boarding school teachers' quarters for example were built in the colonial era and have not been properly maintained.

In the rural areas, all these problems are more acute. Umar says that often she finds that teachers at rural schools are reluctant to actually live in the communities they are charged with working for. Even the best teachers, she finds, keep their families in their homes in the city and head to the village on Sunday evening. They stay in a loaned room in the village during the school week and return to their homes on Friday. While the state is supposed to be the one paying for teachers, in reality often the burden falls on the shoulders of the local community. They must provide them a place to stay and find ways to feed them. "They might even give a teacher some land and take time to farm it for him in an attempt to encourage him to stay" says Umar.

Past failures have stocked the ranks of education institutions with unqualified people who have become headteachers and trainers of teachers. Most of the teachers in the classroom are extremely mediocre. They are unaware of modern pedagogy and rely on teaching by rote. In one primary school class Umar observed, she sat with the children on the floor throughout the lesson. "The teacher was just talking and talking and after some time my legs started to hurt. After a bit more time the children started to run away. One asked to go to the toilet and never came back. Soon there were not many children left. When I asked the teacher about it, she said 'that's just what happens.'"

But bad teachers are not just those who are passive and incapable. Umar paints a depressing picture of her experience in schools where teachers are in fact malevolent forces in children's lives:

"Sometimes when we visit schools we find that no one is working, just looking out of the window. They could even be doing their things like selling products around the community. They can even send the pupils to sell things for them, or be sending the children to buy their alcohol they want to take. Then they give the bully of the school a whip and ask him to keep class [while they sit about drinking]. I have seen it."

Under these conditions, Umar says, why would anyone become a teacher? Especially the kinds of bright, capable graduates that Nigeria needs to improve its situation. "They would not want to be associated with the kinds of people who have become teachers," she says. The effect of this is far reaching.

Katrina Korb's office in the University of Jos is dominated by high shelves holding blue hardback books, bound theses, their titles embossed in gold, most of them dating back decades. The room has that faint must of old paper and dust that lingers around every Nigerian office. In the corridor outside students shout greetings to each other, their calls echo down the high ceilings of the unlit hallway, the only light comes from the glassless slatted windows. Korb, an American academic who has worked at UniJos since 2007, is the head of the university's psychology department, which shares a building with the social sciences and theatre arts. The department is supposed to be moving to a new science block being built at the other end of the wide open space that is the UniJos campus. I passed it on the way in, and from the moss growing on the bare concrete blocks and the sprouts of lush grass coming up through the floors—fed by the frequent refreshing rain that lashes the high plateau, it's clear that move isn't going to be happening any time soon.

Korb's academic speciality is in educational psychology, the study of how people learn and how education develops students' cognitive abilities. She sees the effect of the lack of good teaching in junior and secondary school every day in her classes.

In a survey of high-scoring foreign students studying at American universities, Korb points out, Nigerian students come in the top three, but that's far away from some of the realities in Nigerian universities, she says. Teaching a recent statistics class Korb was brought face-to-face with the problem: "A number of my students couldn't tell if a number was greater than or less than 0.05. That foundation, which they should have got in fifth or sixth grade, they don't have it, so how can you teach advanced statistical concepts when they don't have the foundation?"[8]

Lessons like maths are either neglected completely, Korb says, or children are forced into complicated concepts too early, and consequently it doesn't catch. "Nigerian teachers would take pride in it," she says, "They would say; 'look we're teaching students young' but from a developmental psychology perspective, I'd say they're not ready to learn those things, they need a stronger foundation in some of these basics before you can teach them more."

It's a situation backed up by other educationalists I spoke to. One lead member of an international donor-funded programme told me she witnessed a secondary school class where the maths teacher wrote an incredibly complicated formula on the black board, and then simply walked out of the classroom. "If any of the students got it, it would have been because of a miracle, not from any teaching," she said.

If that kind of teaching seems familiar it's perhaps because it calls to mind legends of "cantankerous but brilliant" masters from elite boarding schools of Britain, or tales of arcane Oxbridge entrance exams. This is not completely accidental. The education policy of the colonial administration in northern Nigeria had always been to teach the elite to be an elite.

That all changed when Nigeria gained its independence. "All of a sudden," Korb says "you're having to educate masses. You've gone form a system for a small number of people to trying to educate millions and it's just done too quickly and they couldn't catch up." The knock-on chains of cause and effect become absurd. "Soon there are teachers teaching things to primary and secondary children they themselves don't understand." This has been borne out by surveys carried out by Britain's Department for International Development (DFID), which found that the numbers of teachers who could pass the exams they were supposed to be teaching was incredibly low. In a particularly startling example, 19,000 primary and junior secondary teachers in Kwara state, in Nigeria's north central region, were asked to sit a test. Teachers were required, as a bare minimum, to demonstrate an understanding of literacy and numeracy matching the expectations by the curriculum of a nine-year-old child. Only seventy five teachers—less than half of one per cent of those tested, scored a grade that the surveyors said met this minimum standard. Over half of all teachers tested fell "very far short" of the minimum.[9]

Nigerian education also suffers from what might be called a certificate culture. Since the point of education was to certify the student was capable to work in the civil service, the apparatus of the state, the certificate at the end of the course became more important than the process of achieving it. Today this manifests itself in blatant cheating among students and teachers, which Korb has also observed up close.

One of the worst things that can happen to a tree is heart-rot. A fungal infection, its spores make their way in through a gash in the bark and moulder into the heartwood, the centre of the trunk, breaking down the chains of cellulose and fibres. The fungus travels through the tree's xylem and phloem where it metastasises in branches and limbs, fatally weakening them. Nigeria's education problem is heart-rot, eating away the heart of society.

For Korb, the prognosis is poor: "You have teachers who don't understand what they're teaching, teaching mathematics and social sciences and sciences to the people who are going to be doctors and politicians and lawyers and engineers ... it's a declining cycle."

There have always been families who refused Western education out of hand, Umar says. "They say: 'my child is not going to go to a western school because those people don't pray, or they end up being impolite and rude to their parents, or they go about doing the western way and forget about their culture and all that.' They're afraid of cultural change."

Now she meets people who have seen the how the education system has failed over the past sixteen years. Even those people who might once have been persuaded to send their children to a Western school have been put off. "Some say 'we've seen those that go to school, they don't speak well or write well, they don't get a job, so why bother?'"

5

BIG POTATO ON TOP

Between visits to Nigeria, I heard that a friend, Attahiru, had mysteriously decided to leave the company he worked for and set out on his own. He was a skilled and reliable driver and until then I had thought that he was being paid, if not enough, then at least regularly. Perhaps, I thought, he had moved on for other reasons, like returning to his family who lived in Kaduna.

When we met, just before Eid-al-Adha, he told me the full story. A truck he was given to drive broke down, and he found that the sump was completely dry of oil.

"The machine spoil," he said, with a sweep of his hand.[1]

The place the company got its vehicles serviced was a large Indian-run firm of mechanics in Abuja. My friend had been going there for years and knew the office administrator well. Discreetly, he asked when the last time that particular truck had been brought in for a service and an oil change. He was told it had been at least eight months before.

"A truck like that is consuming oil very well," Attahiru said, "at least it should be serviced every at least four, or six weeks, oil checked, if it is consuming oil like this. This one had not been seen for eight months."

He went to the secretary responsible for the vehicles and asked for the records relevant to the truck. According to them, the money had been paid for the servicing as usual, every chit signed off by the person who had been previously responsible for the truck.

"But it had not been done, and the truck spoil," he said.

He knew what had happened. The truck had been entrusted to someone, that person had been given the job based on the recommendation of a senior member of staff. The job opened up opportunities, not to get paid with a normal salary—but to graze on other fruits. A kickback was necessary. In order to make it worth it, the whole servicing budget was taken and it missed the real purpose for which it was meant. The total amount to make sure the truck was well looked after in that time would have probably been less than 100,000 naira, perhaps no more than £500.

"What did you do?" I asked.

"I complained severally, but nothing happened. They put me on 'auxiliary'". Auxiliary means you still work, but all allowances and benefits are stopped; no overtime, no hazardous job pay, no extras, no bonus.

"They were in it *ci-mu-ci*," Attahiru said. Then, seeing my look of puzzlement he added: "50/50, they were in it together."

"Who?"

He said the name of a senior staff member. He shook his head and said "*Hannu da yawa*! ...It means 'he has his hands in everything."

I got my pen out and wrote the two phrases down, shaking my head too. The sun had gone down now and the crickets were loud in the darkness around us.

Then Attahiru said: "When you go to the market, you see vegetable in baskets, like onion, Irish potato?"

I nodded.

"If you just look small you will see some beautiful one on top, big one!" and he held his hands up to show me. "But if you look under very well, you find many small one, spoil one, poor one. That is *Kashin dankali*. It is big ones on top. That is how it is."

Although he said he had left voluntarily, like all things, I wondered if there was something more to it, but I didn't know if I should ask. It was obviously a matter of pride.

* * *

The origin of his trouble, Major Yahaya Shinko said, was the time his superior officers attempted to haze him when he transferred into a new unit of the Nigerian Army.

At six feet four inches, Shinko cuts a tall and upright figure, with a very military bearing. Despite having been kicked out of the army seven years before I met him, he came to meet me dressed in green trousers, black boots and a white T-shirt; the military PT uniform. He talks with a purposeful and direct manner. In his interview he didn't say the words "um" or "err" once. His delivery is the clipped tone of a man used to making himself absolutely clear. He presages his precise recollections with repeated phrases like "at this material time..." He is, one senses, a person who would bring a methodical approach to any job; Shinko gives the impression he is a stickler for the rules.

"When I was newly posted there was a sort of ceremony held for us," he said "there was an old tradition which they maintain, they brought a variety of alcoholic drinks for us to take in the presence of senior colleagues, including my commander."[2]

Shinko, from Kaduna, is a Muslim and refused to celebrate with a drink, as Nigerians call these celebrations to "wash" his new posting. He was the only one of the new intake into the Electrical and Mechanical Engineering Corps to refuse. "I told them I had never drunk alcohol and would never start because I believe that once you start you can hardly stop. That led to me being a target." He had been given an order and refused—in front of senior officers and guests, the alumni of the engineering corps.

"That was the beginning of my problem," Shinko said.

When he then reported to his new post in the southern coastal city of Calabar it was clear that he would not be getting on with his commanding officer. Their relationship was strained from the start.

"He was informed by someone in Lagos that I was not the kind of officer that obeys orders or respects his elders," Shinko said matter-of-factly.

But Shinko was far from being a poor soldier. He had been a member of the elite National Guard, created by the military ruler General Ibrahim Badamosi Babangida (known universally as IBB). The guard operated outside the military establishment, directly under Babangida's command, with a single purpose—to protect Nigeria's ruler from his own military.[3]

When Babangida stepped down following the crisis created by his annulment of the 1993 elections, the National Guard was disbanded by his successors. Most of the senior officers were retired, the soldiers who remained were pressed into the regular army.

Shinko was sent on several courses so he could retrain. As part of his duties with the engineering corps, his new expertise was in weapons procurement and deployment. His role was to liaise with trainers from foreign military and arms manufacturers in France, India and Israel and decide what weapons the Nigerian Army needed. For this he needed to be well versed in the capabilities of the various armoured units of the military, all the different weapons systems they were trained on and how these weapons should be deployed. His training was lengthy and expensive and specialised. He spent time developing valuable relationships that might in the future benefit the army.

Almost as soon as had he completed these courses, he was compulsorily retired out of the army.

On the day it happened, he bumped into his commanding officer in the corridor of his unit's Headquarters in Calabar, in Nigeria's "south-south". The CO asked him if he had received a letter from the Nigerian Army HQ. He told the CO he hadn't, but when he returned to his office, the retirement order was waiting for him.

"And the thing was, my wedding was coming two days after. I called my wife-to-be and told her what I had just received, and said 'If you were marrying me based on my career, the career is no more.'"

To Shinko, this was not just a simple story of the army squeezing a disobedient misfit soldier out of the ranks. His dismissal fitted into a pattern, one that he had observed close up, again and again, for the six years he had been in the military. Now it was finally happening to him.

"In a company, if someone spent money and sponsored you to attend such courses, will his just phase you out? Or if you were to leave voluntarily, he will say no; I have spent a lot of money on you so I will not allow you to go... But because the army is run by some individuals that believe this is their own private company, they can take you out once they don't think you fit their kind of profile. This type of thing has caused some problems in the system."

When he is quizzed on who he believes instigated the problems in the system, Shinko is emphatic and unhesitating in his answer; his old boss, Ibrahim Badamosi Babangida.

Unlike some other transitions involving military power in Nigeria's history, IBB's 1985 ascent to the presidency was through a bloodless palace coup.[4] Officers under General Babangida's command arrested then head of state, General Muhammad Buhari, and placed him and his deputy under house arrest. A number of officers were removed from their posts and retired, but no one was killed.

The change in personnel at the top was initially welcomed. Nigerians had seen Buhari enact harsh anti-corruption programmes that had begun to become painful to some. He detained journalists and political opponents without trial under the powers given him by military decree. Newspaper editorials welcomed the charismatic and outwardly jovial General Babangida as a "redeemer" who could save Nigeria from the economic woes caused by financial mismanagement during the Second Republic.[5] But Babangida would become the person in whom ultimate power rested. He combined the post of President and Commander in Chief, and in that position was "arguably the most powerful of the country's military rulers."[6]

Unlike Buhari, a stiff, somewhat austere Fulani noble, IBB came from a new class of Nigerians. This group's entrance onto a stage previously reserved for northern aristocratic players was enabled by the transformative powers of the military. He was from a minority group in the Middle Belt of Nigeria and his family had been poor; four of his siblings died in infancy.[7] But for Babangida and many of his age-mates, the military revolutionised their prospects. It gave them the tools and resources they needed to catapult themselves into power. IBB's graduating class in 1962 was full of people who would, in one form or another, have material effect on Nigeria's future for decades to come.[8]

Babangida possessed an incredibly persuasive and likeable personality. Contemporaries recall the infectious power of his charm, his ability to communicate with just about anyone and his remarkable memory for names, (including the names of wives and children which he could recall at a moment's notice after years of absence).[9] He was seemingly always smiling, the kind of smile that is synonymous with a kind of special character across West Africa; big and gap-toothed.

But behind the smile was a very cunning mind, superbly able to seemingly keep its owner several paces ahead of anyone else. He was dubbed "Maradona" by the press, in reference to his unpredictable moves. He had an ability to take control of the game and outmanoeuvre not just his enemies but people who were not yet his enemies, but would be. Later he capitalised on this image Nigerians had of him, and dubbed himself "the evil genius".

Babangida had been involved in the 1966 counter-coup, launched by northern officers against the south-eastern cadre who had wrestled power from Nigeria's post-independence First Republic. By his own admission, he played a role in every coup since the 1975 ousting of the post-civil war leader General Yakubu Gowon.[10] It is even thought possible that he was the hidden hand behind the coup that brought Buhari to power, that he connived to put Buhari there for a limited period, always intending to step in when the moment was right. As soon as he emerged from behind the curtain into the office of the Head of State he, more than anyone, knew there would be people out there plotting to remove him.

There were two coups uncovered before they could be enacted during his period of military rule. In both instances the men accused of plotting against

Babangida were executed. The first attempt happened in the same year as IBB's own coup. It was masterminded, according to the prosecutors, by one of Babangida's best friends.

Mamman Vatsa and Babangida had grown up together, joined the army together, served as the commanders of neighbouring units during the civil war, and Babangida had been best man at Vatsa's wedding. When the coup was uncovered, the reasons investigators said the officers had done it were because of jealousies over subordinate officers receiving jobs in the administration, the refusal of the IBB government to accept an IMF loan and the overly lenient release of political opponents imprisoned under Buhari. As motivations for a "do-or-die" plot go, they have been called "amateurish" and unconvincing.[11] This, combined with the ruthlessness which Babangida put down his friend (who at the time was of the same rank and seniority as himself), and the Vatsa family's protestations of his innocence long after his execution, have led some to question the existence of a plot at all. "Many felt it was a ploy by the regime to get rid of his opponents," wrote the historian Eghosa Osaghae in *Crippled Giant*, his account of Nigeria since independence, although it is not entirely clear if Osaghae himself endorses this view.[12]

The coup plotters were executed hours after their sentences were confirmed on 5 March 1986. The executions were recorded on a video camera, and a copy sent to IBB. He watched Vatsa, his boyhood friend, take off his wedding ring and wristwatch, hand them to a soldier and ask for them to be given to his wife... "saying, 'tell her to take care of my children'", Babangida later told a Nigerian reporter in an interview, "I was so touched I couldn't continue watching. I turned away and that night I couldn't sleep. Vatsa was very stubborn."[13] If Vatsa was the victim of a "phantom coup" of Babangida's devising, then it was a cold deed indeed.

The sensitivity Babangida had to the possibility of a coup meant he had to find ways of neutralising his colleagues. The military's ability to spend money was curtailed and restricted.[14] This was true across the whole of the armed forces, but one of the consequences of the Vatsa coup was that Babangida choked the Nigerian Air Force in particular. The coup plot was said to have been unique in Nigeria's history of coups, in that some of the officers involved were pilots. They confessed to planning to bomb the Dodan Barracks in Lagos, then seat of Babangida's power. The NAF's Jaguar fighter jets were gradually auctioned off and the rest of the air fleet, once thought the biggest in Africa was left to crumble.[15] By 1993 the NAF could barely scrape together five serviceable jets.[16] These were Alpha trainers bought by the Second Republic for training pilots.

Babangida would hobble the military in other ways too: he shook up where brigades were stationed, moving key parts of the organisation to far flung parts of the country. This made it harder for officers to communicate with each other, particularly those needed to start a coup. Even meeting to carry out exercises and training would be made deliberately difficult. His tinkering was also immensely practical: he moved the army's heavy gun battery to another location, one that was not within artillery range of the new capital—and presidential villa—then being built in Abuja.

But the prime technique Babangida used to control the military was rooted in psychology and based on arbitrary punishment and lavish reward. His ability to stay on top relied most dependably on being able to tweak the greed gland of his fellow military men.

Babangida created a clique of favoured officers who became wealthy overnight and were given the trappings of absolute power. Babangida's inner circle, dubbed "Babangida's Boys", were elevated to military governors of states and were the absolute expression of autocratic lawlessness. Babangida lead by example, answering to "your excellency" and appearing with great pomp in a flamboyant uniform at official parades. He and his boys travelled everywhere in long motorcades, sirens blaring, forcing other travellers form the road.[17]

But this favour could be removed without warning, leaving the man out in the cold and in very real danger of imprisonment or worse. This set the people in subordinate positions to Babangida to jostling among themselves for favour, in fear of the koboko whip-sting of its removal. This was a man who was not to be underestimated, who had executed his best friend and barely lost a night's sleep, after all. This favour and fear approach spread through the ranks, with minor officers forgetting their military roles to concentrate on the real business at hand, of scaling the ladder upward, enticed by the riches that went with it. This process of bestowing of a position, essentially the gifting of money, became known as "settlement".

Shinko saw this first hand: "To the younger ones their officers are Alpha and Omega, and whatever it is that they ask they will compensated for, even if it is by the president. By refusing to do it then he fears he will be sent out of the presidency and even they may have some tricks to trap him and maybe he will find himself in jail. Once you don't have a link to a highly placed general who is very intimate with the president your fate is sealed."

In order to continue to spread this web of patronage that emanated from Babangida's core group, the government created new officials and domains for those officials to occupy and compete for. To this end he established eleven new states, which would receive disbursements from the oil wealth directly from government.[18] But this logic of "settlement", essentially solving problems with the liberal application of money, would supercharge divisions of ethnicity, religion and regionalism in Nigeria. The word carries with it the implicit threat of violence; if you want to be settled, it follows you must first be disturbed.

Babangida's rule coincided with a period of violence between Muslim and Christian and between regional minorities and larger ethno-political groupings. There were "inter-communal" riots in the late 80s and early 90s across the north, in Ilorin, Kafanchan, Kaduna, Katsina, Funtua, Kano, Zaria, Bauchi and Zangon Kataf. In the most violent of them—in Tafawa Balewa in 1991, at least 1,000 were killed after a fight began over whether the meat sold by a butcher was halal. But the immediate causes of the riots shed little light on the extremity of the violence. These were conflicts over the power bestowed by state governments to those who were considered "indigenous" to their area. The conflict came down to which group of people could say that they owned the land. Being a "settler" implied that they had less rights, fewer positions in the state power hierarchy, and less access to the trappings of power, flowing out from the centre. These conflicts were also coloured by the context of older enmities, their participants spoke in terms of being dominated by Hausa-Fulani majority in the north. Indeed, the second coup that rocked Babangida's administration was struck by its participants as a blow against what the plotters called the Hausa-Fulani domination of the Niger Delta and the Middle Belt.

State creation and ethnic strife were not the only ways military men could access government patronage and make money. In 1990 Babangida sent Nigerian troops to Liberia as part of the Economic Community of West African States' Ceasefire Monitoring Group (Ecomog), which was ostensibly a multinational effort. But, in reality, most of the organisation was down to the Nigerians, who provided 75 per cent of the troops.[19] The Liberian civil war had raged itself into a bloody stalemate and Monrovia was torn between the grip of several rebel factions. Liberian civilians were either starving to death or being killed in the cross-fire as they scavenged for food. The president was besieged in his villa and rebels, who used drugged-up child soldiers, cannibalism and juju to brutalise and terrify everyone, were circling. Into this melee, Ecomog forces were sent to monitor a shaky and even non-existent cease fire. From the moment they landed, under fire on Monrovia beach, they ceased being peacekeepers and became part of the war.[20]

Before the war, Babangida had been a close ally of Liberian President Samuel Doe. The Nigerian president had used Liberia, with its financial system that used the US Dollar, as an offshore banking centre where he could convert soft naira into hard dollars.[21] Nigeria desperately wanted to protect Doe, and failing that (as they did), prevent one particular rebel leader—Charles Taylor—from taking over. The engagement would last six years—outlasting Babangida, the interim government of Ernest Shonekan and stretched into the rule of General Sani Abacha, Babangida's onetime deputy, who would take over in 1993 following another coup.

Nigerian troops arrived in Liberia poorly equipped; some lacked weapons while others lacked boots. Training was an issue, there were accounts of Liberian villages being bombed indiscriminately in aerial bombardments. In another incident, hundreds of civilians were killed when the navy shelled a village.[22] According to Shinko, who served in Liberia, some Nigerian patrols would simply abandon their weapons when they met rebel forces in return for being allowed to live.[23]

They were reportedly paid only $15 a day and this was only sporadically disbursed. They made up the shortfall by looting, earning Ecomog the sobriquet "Every Car Or Moving Object Gone".[24] Nevertheless, the first few years of Nigeria's Liberian adventure consumed the Nigerian treasury's oil windfall—the cash bonanza that fell at their feet during the first Gulf War in 1991. Approximately $4billion went into Ecomog, an estimated three-quarters of which was "converted to the use" of people at the head of the Nigerian military.[25]

Later in the war, it became apparent to other observers in Liberia that Nigerian forces were stealing weapons and selling them to opposing rebel factions at the same time, despite the near certainty that the weapons would also be turned on the Nigerians themselves. When this was reported in a Liberian paper, the Nigerian head of Ecomog threatened to "deal ruthlessly" with anyone "spreading stories that could cause confusion".[26] Nigeria strongly denied supporting the rebel factions in such a way, but, as Stephen Ellis wrote in *The Mask of Anarchy*, a political history of the conflict, the support of the rebels by corrupt means "was to be sure, no less than the truth."

At the same time as Nigeria was defending its hegemonic position as West Africa's heavyweight, Babangida was going through a process of transition to civilian government. The question of how exactly Nigeria should be governed is one that has never been comprehensively answered, left open to interpretation and therefore manipulation, at every stage of Nigeria's history. Even Lugard demurred from trying to seek a solution, explicitly saying in his communications to London that the precise form of government for the province was a question that could be resolved at some indeterminate point in the future. Babangida put a limit on his search for constitutional reform and eventually resolved to hold elections in mid-1993. But did Babangida actually want to hand over power to civilian rule, or rather ensure that the military continued to hold the reins of power in some form?[27]

His public reasoning for extending the transition period and meddling with the rules of who could be, and who could not be, a politician were cloaked in the vestments of a paternalistic desire to nurse Nigeria to a political maturity. The idea was that, by the primaries, two political parties would be formed, one slightly to the right of centre the other slightly to the left. To prevent the parties being split down the old cleavages of north and south or Christian and Muslim, people wishing to participate in politics were asked to form local associations. These would then be assessed and judged by a National Electoral Commission, who would make sure that members understood the democratic process and the proposed federal constitution. Then the associations would be grouped together under two umbrella parties, rationalised by their different outlooks.

The parties and associations did not persist, in fact they fell apart. The logic of their formation as a political arrangement above the connections of ethnic ties did not hold up. What did stick, however, was the logic of the comprador class that Babangida had created.

Although many of the IBB Boys were removed from their positions in the regimes after Babangida, their influence persisted. When civilian rule returned it was these men, empowered by the settlement of military regimes, who would remain at the heart of things. It would be they who would would create the conditions they needed to replicate themselves.

Shinko had some observations about how the military worked: "So it is either that you are related to the commander in chief, or you are from the same tribe, or from the same region, or have the same religion, or have a prominent person behind you that belongs to his political party before you can be considered to hold a particular position," he says. This could easily be applicable to other forms of public life in Nigeria today

The writer Max Siollun noted the effect of these relationships went beyond the military and into the political realm: "These clustered networks of personal loyalty blurred the differentiation between the senior officer corps and senior politicians. Both were part of the same corrupt elite, civilian and military elites became interchangeable."[28]

What began as a security strategy for a military elite became the existential logic of Nigeria's comprador class, the turning of institutions from the functions of government to the business of self-interested enrichment, infected everything. Many of the very same people are in high office today.

In the early 1980s and 90s Nigeria also witnessed an explosion in the level of violent crime. At the same time as Babangida was doling out money as patronage in some areas, in others he implemented drastic economic reforms, called Structural Adjustment, which saw the size of government quickly reduced. The government retired many civil servants from Lagos ministries, or slashed their salaries by 30 per cent. In Nigeria, the input of money from oil revenues into the economy comes through the largest employer—the state. Its reduction had dramatic and negative effect on the economy.

The earlier desertion of agricultural policy, in favour of oil and the rentier state that accompanied it, had seen agriculture collapse. In the 80s and 90s a lack of military government policy to deal with this saw rural livelihoods decline further. Swift urbanisation had been causing cities to grow uncontrollably, with unplanned slums spawning their own satellite towns of further shanties quicker than any government could keep up. Cities like Lagos in the south and the state capitals of Kano and Kaduna as well as some of the other northern cities (although to a lesser degree), became hubs of the informal economy where hustle in small-time service industries could pay. It also presented opportunities—to those who were so inclined—for predatory extortion. Young, unemployed—unemployable?—men forged connections to a myriad of militia, gang or quasi-political and union bodies who in turn were clued-in to the money from the patronage networks of "politics". These young men, known as "area boys" in the south, were known by different names in the north—names like Gombe's *'Yan Kalare*, implicated in at least seventy political murders, or Bauchi's *Sara Suka*—the "Cut and Stab". They, and a myriad of unnamed gangs of street toughs competed at the bottom of the pile.

It had long been a practise of some northern governors to run "rehabilitation" programmes for groups of armed robbers. These were thinly disguised ways of bringing such men-of-violence under the wing of people who could use their particular set of talents during elections. In 2007 a vigilante in Bauchi showed me a letter held by an armed robber he had apprehended in the commission of a robbery. It was addressed "to-whom-it-may-concern", from a commissioner in the neighbouring state government confirming the man was employed as a "forest ranger", officially sanctioned to be in the wilderness. The vigilante I spoke with said the letter was meant to cover the robber if his presence "in the bush" was questioned. The rehabilitation programmes, the vigilante said, were flimsy, public relations events where armed robbers were effectively pardoned after they swore on a copy of the Qur'an never to rob again. Some even used the programme as an alibi for cover as they went on robbery operations, he said.

Since the 1980s the figure of the armed robber looms large in Nigeria. They are usually folk devils (although some achieve "heroic" status too), and are a real risk to life and property. For people who live in the mostly un-policed suburbs of large towns, the fear of word getting round that you have something of value to take is ever present. As more people moved to larger and larger unplanned urban areas, policing, always at a low capacity, became stretched past breaking point.

At the same time those with the right connections were being enriched. They separated themselves from the urban poor and concentrated themselves in the exclusive Government Reserved Areas, where they built big houses behind high walls. This was not entirely new, the GRAs were the same expression of power as their historical antecedents, the precincts of the emirate aristocracy, but these were not the same few royal families; they were a new breed.

Instead of separating themselves from the *talakawa*, the poor, in the way the emirs had done, relying on traditional offices of power like gatekeepers, palace guards and a deeply rooted sense of deference, this new class protected itself from the precarious nature of their position by co-opting the federal institutions of protection. They used the enforcers of the state's monopoly on violence: the police.

When the military government withdrew, the state had many official security agencies that were supposed to take up the role of keeping law and order, not least the police and their paramilitary brigade the Police Mobile Force or Mopol. Most people's day-to-day encounter with the police is at a checkpoint where the police will shake you down for a bribe. To put it kindly the police are faced with urban populations that are almost impossible to adequately police, they lack the necessary training and facilities, pay or security. When they patrol the streets, it is from the back of flying pick-ups, sirens blaring. When they stop it is to bark orders or mete out a beating—which is also their only interrogation method. To ride on the back of a police patrol vehicle one thing is immediately apparent: nobody looks at you.

But the life of a police officer is also incredibly precarious, hence they develop strategies to minimise the amount of risk they take. One of the most effective is to withdraw from policing the sprawling, labyrinthine, dangerous slums where people live, and concentrate on protecting the homes and businesses of the elite. In Nigeria today it is common to see wealthy people, beneficiaries of the system that disburses wealth as a form of patronage, with an armed police guard at their house, or driving their car. They are provided by their superior officers who contract them out like security guards.

The elite captured the police using the same reward and punishment tactics as the military had been subjected to. Junior officers must play a complicated double edged game of "follow my leader" with senior officers who are trying to "remain relevant" within the institution, that is to say advance and accumulate power and—hopefully—wealth. Within the police there are geographical areas that are preferred by different officers, centres and peripheries, which offer different levels of intensity of the game that officers must involve themselves in.[29]

In the police there are multitude of punishments for officers who fall on the wrong end of their superior's plans. One of these punishments is known as "Yobe-for-complaint". Unwilling, recalcitrant, and incompetent officers, unable to play the game of jostling for position might very well find themselves sent out to one of the worst areas to be a policeman, such as an overwhelmingly rural state in Nigeria's north-east where the prospects of making money are poor, like Yobe, which has lately been a hotbed of Boko Haram violence. There they can be safely forgotten about and left to rot.[30]

This withdrawal from policing some areas in favour of wealthier beats focused the institutions of law and order on the needs of a wealthy few rather than a wider application of their purpose. Often it is said that the Nigerian policing system doesn't function. This is wrong. It does; just in the interests of a few people.

What was left by this withdrawal is not chaos. Although whole areas are without the effective presence of the police, communities respond by entrusting their safety to self-organising groups of vigilantes.

Yakubu is a massive guy. He enters the room hunched, shoulders rolled over and I'm immediately aware that he is a powerfully built man. When we shake hands it felt like he handed me a brick. He is wearing a pair of bug-eye wraparound sunglasses, which he puts up on his bald head.

We meet in the office of an organisation set up to coordinate the activities of vigilante groups. It is run by a former Navy officer, Captain Umar Abubakar, who travels the country training vigilantes in an attempt to regularise their work and regulate them. This training, in some places sponsored by the Britain's DFID, is mostly aimed at preventing vigilante groups dispensing what is commonly called "jungle justice", the summary execution of suspected armed robbers who fall into their grasp.

As we sit on Captain Abubakar's couch, Yakubu explains to me how he came to be a vigilante and what the job entails. His voice is rough like sandpaper. He rolls his r's and some words he drags out to emphasise his point. As we talk, Captain Umar sits at a desk across the room; he is listening but working on something else.

Yakubu is the commander of vigilantes for his local government area in Kaduna city, and he's been in volunteering to do it since 1999. A builder by trade, he still works on sites occasionally, but the life of a vigilante takes up most of his time. He commands a dozen or so men and women who wear a brown uniform with a maroon beret and yellow badges sewn, wonkily, on their chests and arms.

The basis for the security offered by the vigilante groups comes from the socially interconnected nature of Nigerian society; in their community, people's histories are known. Historically, strangers were rare in communities and would have to report themselves to the emirate officials, who would want to know exactly what their business was and where they were staying. Even though this practice died out long ago with the advent of large scale urbanisation and the mass resettlement of Nigerians from other parts of the country by the British, people's origin and social connections are still very important in establishing if an individual can become a vigilante, or if they are—in fact—a robber.

"If any of them do anything bad we know his house, we know his father, we know his parents. We can go and pick him, not like the other security agents. This one," he indicates an imaginary policeman in front of him "was transferred, they don't know where he," nodding at an imaginary robber "come from, they don't know where to get you. But we do. There is no escape."[31]

The selection process for being a vigilante relies on this knowledge too. Yakubu says anyone wanting to become "one of his boys" must submit referees, and he will chase them up. They have to include a local government head, a district head, someone who has owned property in the applicants' place of origin for at least twenty years and the applicant's father, grandfather or uncle. These references are necessary to convince businesses in the areas that the vigilantes won't turn robber when they get into positions of responsibility. He won't go into how much they charge businesses for their protection, saying only: "There is no salary for this work, no allowance." He says, "it is just in the morning that people come and volunteer, they say take this" he mimes handing over a wedge of cash "...we appreciate your service."

People certainly do appreciate the vigilantes who spend their nights patrolling the dark or standing at a cross roads, lit only by a torch and the flickering flame of a burning tyre. They carry a metal hoop, which they frequently strike like a bell, letting the people know that someone is still awake, watching over them. The night is not to be trifled with, and a vigilante's work might also take them out into the space outside the city, into "the bush". This is a psychologically charged place, one where strange things can happen, and strange beasts and spirits still live. The vigilante's nemesis, the armed robber, is a ruthless individual, bloodthirsty and unencumbered by morals or qualms. To the vigilante and policeman alike they are irredeemably evil and use powerful charms and medicines to give themselves evil power, and smoke marijuana (known as Indian hemp) to dull the senses.

The vigilante have their own forms of protection. I ask Yakubu, does he have a charm?

"I have charm yes, but I cannot tell you, how can I? I worked for it, I went and got it. It is mine."

But he does say that some of his boys hold pieces of the Bible or Qur'an in their pockets when they go out on operation to protect them.[32] "There is some among our boys who if he-", he said indicating the imaginary armed robber in front of him "hold a knife you cannot run away. Even if you try and chok him with the knife" he mimed a stabbing "he knows that the knife will not enter him and so he will not fear you." Yakubu held my gaze, "There is someone that because of gun, he will not fear to come close to you because you have gun. And don't be surprised—if God wishes—if you try and shoot him... he can disappear. If it is God's will, the way he wants it."

He says that the belief in the importance of the work they are doing is important to God: "You must have your belief that you are out to do this thing, not to cheat any one, not to do anything but to save your community." His gravelly voice rasps out the word save. "So God will assist you."

He is proud of his record that in fifteen years of vigilantism, none of his boys has ever been killed. The same cannot be said for the robbers they catch. In the past vigilante groups would dispense a quick execution to people who they seized. After many training seminars, they now know that they are supposed to hand over the people they arrest to the police along with evidence. Although he strenuously denied it, I get the feeling that this has not been stopped entirely. But in cases where the vigilantes seize someone and are not yet sure what they have done, they have some techniques for finding out.

"We have what we call *theatre* and we have *workshop*," says Yakubu, without any real hint of what is coming next. "We have different standard, and that if it touch your life, *all* will be revealed."

I am puzzled, "what do you mean?" I ask.

I am told that "workshop" is a special rope that when they tie up suspects' hands in a certain way, whereby the cord begins to feel like it is cutting into the flesh. Yakubu snaps his fingers several times to rate the pain. "That rope will be entering you! You will feel it will cut your hand into two, so if you want that rope to release you will say 'oh this is what I know this is what I don't know.'"

I glance up at Captain Umar Abubakar, thinking he might be concerned that Yakubu is telling me about things that perhaps Umar would like to train him not to do, but the Captain is shuffling papers around his desk as he listens impassively.

"What is theatre?" I ask.

Yakubu's pride in his technique is evident: "I am suspecting you are an armed robber, I have the way that if I torture you now you will tell me the truth."

"Torture?" I say.

"Yeah, torture. What I will do is I will break a needle and hold your finger, this big one, and be choking it." He holds his thumb tightly in between the thumb and index finger of his other hand, revealing the whorls of his thumb pad. He made the action of pushing the needle into it, his grip so tight the finger was swollen pink, "...and before I reach 20 times you will say something."

Before I can say anything he continues: "If you have not said something, I will now take you and put rope on your wrists, you understand me?"

I still don't say anything.

"We have syringe and we put it inside your prick and before it reach half way," he mimes putting the long needle of a syringe up my urethra, "you will say nonono, let me tell you truth. That is *theatre*." He sits back and looks at me, "anything with your private part, it is not a joke. You will prefer for someone to remove his head." He touches his thumbs together and splays his fingers around his neck in a strangulation motion, and laughs heartily.

Eventually I say: "The people you protect, they know you do this?"

"They know."

"And they approve?"

"That is why they assist us," he says, "we don't have salary, we live by assistance. That is how we live."

6

STOMACH INFRASTRUCTURE

"All politicians lie," Abdullahi Ladan tells me.[1] For a self-confessed political animal, he seems fed up with politics. "When I got to this, the middle of my life—I found that all of the politicians tell lies. That is what led me to think, let me step down from this politics."

Ladan is not a politician himself, but he has worked for many of them over the years. Although he holds no elected office, in his area of Kaduna he carries a lot of weight. In his political career, Ladan has been a deal maker, a kind of "Mr Fixit" for Kaduna state. He is now in middle age and has a family, but he is still best known as a youth leader. His group, the Arewa Integrity Forum, has been around since the early 1990s.

"People respect me, I have politics in my blood," he says. The source of this respect is his family heritage, his uncle was well-connected in the northern region after independence. His brother is the chief Imam at Kaduna's biggest mosque.

His office is a room in his modest home in a southern district of Kaduna. The walls are covered in pictures of Ladan standing with luminaries from the Nigerian security world, the defence minister, the heads of armed services and with his boss, the former intelligence chief, Aliyu Mohammed Gusau.

Gusau, a mercurial figure in Nigerian politics, built a reputation for himself as the eyes and ears of Babangida. During the Babangida years and under General Sani Abacha in the nineties, Ladan was an "intelligence consultant". During this time, both regimes maintained extensive webs of spies reporting the activities of student activists, radical lecturers, democracy activists, public intellectuals, politicians and traditional rulers.

In the years since, Ladan has maintained his connections. If there's anyone who knows about the Nigerian route to power, it is him.

"I get the youth jobs," he told me, showing me football team-like photographs of him standing with young men. "Whenever I hear about a position in the police or army, or any security agency, I take it, put one of my boys there."

These same jobless youth are the ones politicians used for political thuggery, smashing up polling units and intimidating voters, carrying out their errands and dirty deeds.

"I'm the type of person," says Abdullahi Ladan, "if I say yes, 40,000 youths say yes."

Ladan says he used his power to save them from the life of thuggery. The boys knew that if they appeal to him, he could get them a valuable position, but it is clear the jobs came as a reward for helping to "deliver" elections.

His clout has saved him before now. During 2011's post-election violence, rioting youths passed through his street on the way to sack the residence of an official from the ruling People's Democratic Party (PDP). They left Ladan's house untouched.

We talk about the methods politicians use to rig elections; rigging before the vote, by manipulating the voters register, increasing the number to give the riggers slack to work with; during the vote, by paying the opposition's agents to look away, boxes are stuffed with pre-thumbprinted ballots; and after the vote, at the collation centre, with the connivance of the police, the army and the election regulator.

But now, Ladan says all that is over.

"Anyone who try it in the future will not succeed," he says. "The community is facing serious problem. As we go at each junction you can see people how they are, some people cannot eat three times a square meal, they are supposed to have wife—they cannot, they cannot change their clothes twice. No one can tell you guarantee what is happening now. Society has already changed. Even those I have anointed, they fear what is going to to happen... the ones below them cannot hear."

* * *

Abdulmajid pointed out of the car window toward the long, low, pink building on the far side of the large patch of open ground we were passing on Kano's Zoo Road.

"The bomb went off just by the side there," he said. Abdulmajid quietly regarded the spot where, only a few weeks before, death had been dealt out indiscriminately.[2] A teenage girl had approached the entrance of the brand new shopping complex, where the Indian-owned Shoprite supermarket had only recently opened, and detonated a bomb strapped to her body. She killed three people instantly and injured a dozen more. It was one of two attacks that day, another female suicide bomber attacked a queue of women waiting for water in another southern suburb of Kano, northern Nigeria's most populous city. When we passed, no trace of the attack was visible but as we drove by the place, there was a silence in the car as we looked on without knowing what to say.

Abdulmajid Sa'ad is an aspiring candidate for election to the Nigerian House of Representatives in Abuja, the lower house of the National Assembly in the 2015 general elections. He and his aides were late to meet a group of women in Unguwa Uku—The Three Neighbourhoods, a southern suburb of Kano city. The way was down long streets lined on both sides with ramshackle shops and lock-ups, butchers' stalls and mechanics. Somewhere the party got lost, took a wrong turning off the main road and had to backtrack. There are few street signs in these unplanned neighbourhoods, only bright, digitally printed, advertisements for malaria medication or milled wheat semovita. Here and there, a wonky portrait of a politician painted on a door, or a wall, a slogan sprayed underneath. The two cars in which the group travelled revved over ridges in the road and around the puddles filled with thick orange mud, dodging yellow auto-rickshaws, goats, young women in coloured jilbabs and boys larking around on street corners.

A man stepped out of his gate to collect a stack of firewood, giving a glimpse into his home. Inside there was a courtyard, shaded by a green tamarind tree. Adjoining it would be a number of simple rooms made with bricks of dried mud covered with a render. In a corner, under an awning, a soot-black pot would be resting above an ember. In the yards of more fortunate families a *sallah* ram, bought this year at exorbitant cost, would be standing proudly. Come Eid morning the slaughter knife would spill his blood into the open sewer-drain running through the yard, from where it would flow into a ditch in the street. That courtyard was just one in a many-million-piece, cob-and-concrete jigsaw that sprawled for miles in every direction.

They parked the cars by a rubbish-filled culvert and someone called over a local street tough. A teenager in a day-glo pink T-shirt emblazoned with an image from the 80s movie Pretty in Pink and matching sunglasses approached. If he looked after the cars, they said, he would be paid on their return. He nodded and went to sit in the shadow cast by a mud wall.

The meeting was being held in a children's bedroom, off a small courtyard at the back of a big family compound. The women were wearing bright wrappers and dresses in colours that clashed and complimented, patterns that swirled. They sat on the floor of the small room in two rows, waiting for the man who wanted to be their representative in the lower house of the National Assembly. The women would not have looked out of place at a feast. In fact, Eid al Adha, when Muslims celebrate Abraham's willingness to sacrifice his son on Allah's orders, was just a few days away—but this wasn't a celebration. It was an underground political meeting. The women Abdulmajid was meeting are opinion formers in their community who he believes can help him get on the first rung of the political ladder. I had come along to see Nigerian politics at the grassroots level.

The midday sun had quarried its way into the shadow of the courtyard and exposed all the concrete to its heat. Inside the square room there was little space for the twelve people who gathered to sit there. The women waited quietly as Abdulmajid and his visiting party shucked off their shoes at the door and sat down. Also among the visitors were Baba Ahmadu, Abdulmajid's political agent, Hadiza, Abdulmajid's special adviser in charge of women and Dr Bashir another political organiser Abdulmajid had brought with him.

As Abdulmajid slipped into the shadow of the room and folded his limbs underneath him to sit down, he looked slight. His thin body disappeared inside his pastel green riga, the long collarless kaftan-like shirt with fine embroidery at the neck. He was perhaps the youngest man in the room. In this place, where age and seniority are so important in politics, he looked it. Yet Baba Ahmadu, the elder man, invited Abdulmajid to lead the opening prayer. Despite his youth, he had to be the most important person present.

It was very hot and humid in the room and when the prayer concluded, the host of the meeting—a woman named Rahimatu—handed around half a dozen hand fans. They were like stiff little flags woven out of banana leaves. The women wafted each other, spinning the woven mats around in their hands. Abdulmajid said each of these women represented at least twenty more, currently elsewhere in Ungwar Uku and beyond, in the federal government constituency of Tarauni.

Abdulmajid's voice was quiet and his manner was very reserved. "I am a true Kano man, from Tudun Nafawa," he said, "In fact, my family house is just by the giant rubbish dump there."

Although Abdulmajid had come to seek these women's support, he hardly looked any of them in the eye as he spoke. He spoke just above them, or slightly to the left of them or slightly to the right. I was told later that most of them were divorcees or widows, but that there were a few married women among them. My colleague, the BBC journalist Abdullahi Kaura Abubakar who had introduced me to Abdulmajid, said you could tell the married women because they were "somewhat shy" and didn't speak during the meeting. Abdulmajid had said this meeting—of several married men, meeting other men's wives and single, unattached, women in a private house—would not raise conservative eyebrows unduly, but he had to be careful. He must project the right tone as a prospective candidate. An older man, a more established man, a senator perhaps, would not be able to address a gathering like this.

He sketched a brief story of his life so far to this point; where he had been to school; what he studied at which university. His family are well known in the area: "If you go to that place and ask for the 'House of Brooms', that is my family home, everyone knows my parents and grandparents and great grandparents, so many years back," he said.

The thirty-four-year-old's father built his fortunes as a petroleum sales executive for the Total oil company, travelling around the north managing the movement of one of the most valuable commodities there is. After leaving Total, Abdulmajid's father turned his contacts, acumen and capital to selling imported second hand cars in Kano. Cars, their import stickers still on the windshield, are tightly packed into every space around Abdulmajid's office, a leafy courtyard off Kano's Zoo Road. Due to his success trading in two of northern Nigeria's key commodities Abdulmajid's father is well connected, the family are well known by both Kano's elite and by the ordinary folk of the area. The family wealth was enough to educate their children to the best standard that Nigeria can manage.

Abdulmajid is not the only one of his family to aspire to move into politics. Four years before, in the 2011 election, he had wanted to contest this seat, but he had been asked to step aside in favour of his older sister Sa'ida. She campaigned under the banner of the opposition Action Congress party, only to be defeated by Nasir Baballe Ila, the candidate of the ANPP, the All Nigeria People's Party—another northern opposition group. In 2013, both these opposition parties joined forces to form a grand coalition called the All Progressives Congress, as a unified opposition to the ruling People's Democratic Party in the 2015 elections. Consequently this time there will only be one opposition candidate, instead of two. When I met Abdulmajid the competition is tight, he thinks that there may be a chance the party might decide to dump their incumbent candidate.

Abdulmajid was meeting the women five months before the election, when candidates were at that point officially barred from overtly campaigning by the

Independent National Election Commission. Although this ban doesn't seem to apply to everyone. Billboards made by prospective candidates, some Abdulmajid's competitors, have begun to appear in Kano. Their posters all show the candidates between two opposition heavyweight figures. On one side, the outgoing governor of Kano state Rabiu Kwankwaso, who is coming to the end of his second and final term as governor, and General Muhammadu Buhari the former military head of state and a longstanding opposition candidate. In September 2014 both these men were vying to become the opposition's presidential candidate.

Abdulmajid, lacking the resources to pay for such adverts, is conducting what he calls "underground campaign"; small visits to key local organisers. These are people who can mobilise support for campaign rallies and polls to come. The first hurdle for Abdulmajid is to take the party nomination at the primary. He is counting on these women to be his vocal supporters with their party delegates who will, in principle at least, decide who will get on the party ticket in December.

But if he is to have a chance of being elected, he must also convince the elders of the party that it would be a mistake to continue with the incumbent in this constituency. If he is to make his first step into politics, he must show he is a person of influence here. He must convince the party that he has what Nigerians call "relevance". What the party will be looking for is how he will fit into what is known as the "machinery on ground."

Abdulmajid says his small stature makes people believe he is younger than he actually is. But, he says, if his opponents in politics take that to mean he is a "small boy", unworthy of consideration as a serious person, then they might be underestimating him. He says he has been noticed by members of the APC party leadership. They have partnered with an experienced and canny election agent, Baba Ahmadu. Ahmadu is an experienced political operator (Baba, father in Hausa, is an informal title given to men of seniority). His involvement suggests that the party could be taking Abdulmajid seriously. Before the meeting Ahmadu said: "He is a young man yes, but he has strengths that come from that." These strengths are useful attributes that the party might consider if they might for any reason doubt the incumbent: "The first is that he has no enemies, yet. The second is that he has no reputation for corruption." Did a second—unspoken—"yet" hang in the air?

Abdulmajid told the women in the children's bedroom: "Now is the time I hope Allah will help me, this time around. This might be the right time to contest so that I can represent you, Insha'allah," he said. The women nodded and a murmur of approval and assent went around. Abdulmajid's words were formal, correct, without undue exaggeration or boastfulness. They were being well received.

"My hope in this meeting," he tells the women, "is that we are not here to tell you what we are going to do when we win the election, I am here to know what you want. Because if it is something that can possibly be done, we have elders that can guide us to determine how we can achieve it. I am assuring you as much as possible you will find me trustworthy in attending to the needs of the community."

Abdulmajid wraps up his short speech without fuss: "I am very grateful to you and I pray Allah to make us together here, and there." The collected group of women clap enthusiastically and make appreciative sounds. Baba Ahmadu moves the meeting along. A woman in a tight head cloth is eager to speak. She introduces herself as Zainab and then launches into a rousing oration. Her gold-capped incisor tooth, the fashion among some northern ladies, glints as she speaks.

"You are going to see the best of women! You are going to see the best of women!" she cries sweeping her pointed finger into the air. "Since you are going to go along with us, if you like we can bring fifty women here. If we say we are not with you, we are not with you. We are supporting you so if Allah wills it, no problem, we are taking you to government house." The weighty finger waves in Abdulmajid's direction "So don't forget us!"

This is the most common complaint about Nigerian politicians. During the run-up to elections they come down to places they would never normally go, to seek help and support to get elected. Frequently before, during and after elections the gangs of young men who politicians surround themselves with clash with other groups loyal to other politicians. In the melee people are wounded and their livelihoods ruined. Voters themselves are intimidated. Ordinary people whose lives are dependent on the informal economy endure days of movement restrictions where businesses are forced to close. If violence erupts before or after the elections, the disruption can last for weeks and lead to terrible losses.

All too often, as soon as the politicians are elected, they disappear, leaving their promises hanging in the air. Big pledges, like repairs to roads, new water boreholes, more schools and hospitals, are forgotten. Communities favoured by the candidate, like his own village or areas where people from his ethnic group are concentrated, may see a new road, or electrification programme or an agriculture project. But most people say that they never see or hear from their local representatives after they go to Abuja, and nothing ever seems to change.

Zainab warned Abdulmajid: "The way we are going to support you we expect to you to remember us!" Abdulmajid nods quickly and the women laughed. Zainab continued: "I am saying the truth, if you carry us along, wallahi, each of us can bring twenty votes. Ceremonies are for women! Only good women are mobilisers—like ants!" At this more clapping broke out. One of the women, a thin Fulani wrapped in a skein of dark material sitting with her back against the wall, bent to her side and let out a high-pitched ululating cry.

Zainab had more: "If we say you will wipe away our tears, everyone we can invite will come." She leaned forward and gathered up her words in upturned hands to make a point. "We don't have jobs. We have some who have many children and who don't have any means of sustenance. So if you call us and tell us that you will support us by means of some jobs or businesses, that's all we need." As the clapping broke out again she continued "with that you can get our attention and we will be chanting: 'Only Honourable is the best'! Anywhere you like, we will go."

This is encouraging stuff for Abdulmajid. He attended Bayero University Kano, and was involved in the student's union. When he talks about politics he is brimming with progressive ideas and, at least when talking to journalists, talks about the need for change with passion. He is idealistic, no doubt, but he is also ambitious. As a measure of how serious he is, he has brought people to do his talking for him. Baba Ahmadu swept up the clapping and in his soft voice said: "Here is a woman whose husband will not take any more wives; Hajiya Hadiza,"

Hadiza stood up to speak. She shouted out: "APC CHANG-E! A-P-C CHANG-E!" The women join in for another round of chanting. Hadiza is Abdulmajid's "head of women's campaign". She is the one who arranged today's meeting. She is also a party delegate with a vote to cast at the primary. A lot of Abdulmajid's hopes ride on her.

"I now feel as if I no longer need to make any effort," she told the women, congratulating them for their loyalty, "I can now go and sleep, we have all the votes!" She impressed upon them that their loyalty would be rewarded, she knows the problem with Nigerian politicians, of them disappearing once they get elected. "Everyone knows Hadiza does not talk nonsense, Hadiza does not tolerate betrayal, does not take disgrace. She will never go with anyone who has a tendency for disgracing or betrayal. I have sworn to some candidates in the past, but ate my words because the promise made to me has not been fulfilled. But this candidate," she said pointing to the quiet man in the middle of the room "will attend to all of your complaints." She paused for a breath and then uttered a common Hausa saying: "No man is perfect, everyone is a nine, not up to a ten. I am assuring you he cannot do everything 100 per cent, we might fail in some areas but 85 per cent of our promises we will fulfil, so I am begging you."

Other candidates will be courting these women. They will come with money. Abdulmajid's competitors are well established men, men who have built up capital, both political and financial, while working in positions of government. Abdulmajid was aware of the difficulty ahead. Before we went to the meeting in Ungwar Uku, he said: "I am just coming, I am a new timer, those who have held positions of authority have money to buy votes, to mobilise support. They are more popular, it's not going to be easy."

Among his opponents for the ticket are directors of state agencies or special assistants to the governor, as well as the incumbent member of the House of Representatives. These are powerful people, people whose claims to "relevance" are harder to dismiss.

Abdulmajid says: "These people have money, they had opportunities, they had contracts, they were given privileges by top ranking people. Some of them have what they call 'public relations' with others, so they want to pay them back now. Some will get money direct from their bosses, their political godfathers, who are campaigning along with their boys." When Abdulmajid said his competitors had benefited from "contracts" he is talking about the system under which contracts—to supply the government with goods and services—are doled out by key political personalities to loyal allies. The contract value is inflated, and the excess money divided, or "chopped", between the recipient and the godfather who bestowed it. In Nigerian pidgin the phrase "chop" means to eat. It also means to share out money, usually squeezed out of these government revenues. There are many levels to these contracts, from small to big. They could be for government supplies, like paper or light bulbs. Larger contracts, for bigger players, are found in infrastructure spending, on roads, schools, culverts, state-owned factories that are built and never used, universities bearing the name of a "big-man". Contracts to provide fertiliser or fuel are lucrative in the extreme, mostly because the products are worth more on the black market than they are on the open market, which is frequently unable to provide adequate supply. If you add on top of that the constituency allowance given lawmakers in their very considerable expenses, it is clear that politics—before a bill has been read or a vote has been cast in the parliament—is very big business. Governors, the executive leaders of the federal states have the added benefit of the "Security vote" huge sums in their budgets which can be spent at the governor's sole discretion.

Anything can become a mode of sucking money from the pool. In return for being granted a position from which he can "chop", the recipient is expected to use his influence to win elections to return the man who gave him the position, his "godfather".

There is another factor working against him, one that unsettles Abdulmajid. "They can use anything, like charm or ritual, they do them too," he says. These charms and rituals can range from rich politicians paying large numbers of *Almajirai*—religious students—to pray for them, to other less public ceremonies, incantations and amulets that they buy from spiritualists. "There is huge money for ritualists, for cultists, who supply them, and if you show your displeasure at these things then you can become an outcast."

Abdulmajid's competitors have deep pockets and when they are "on ground" they bring money to distribute among key local organisers to maintain loyalty. Instead of holding an intimate meeting with the candidate like the one Abdulmajid had organised, his opponents' campaign managers would have sent the head of their women's campaign—someone like Hadiza—to share out money with the most influential members of the community. This cash is then disbursed further and at every stage people take their own cut. As the election approaches, the available share of these budgets handed out by the parties to buy support dwindles. Pressure grows to get hold of some of it. Until, on election-day, there might only be 50 naira in it for the recipient at the lowest level. This can lead to squabbles and even fights over who is going to get what.

Abdulmajid is not in a position where he can do this. Without bottomless pockets, Abdulmajid has to find his way into a network. "I cannot fully escape the use of money," he says. "So I will have to find a strong candidate for president or governor and be in his camp, so I can benefit from his resources." To that end he is hoping that the former Vice President Atiku Abubakar, who left the People's Democratic Party in 2006 to become a stalwart of the Action Congress, and who is now a leader in the APC, will take him under his wing. There have been some initial overtures; Abdulmajid has been called to meetings and given some tasks to do. These invitations are symbolic of a bond between them, but they are not solid yet.

Having no money, Abdulmajid must appeal to people in other ways, using other tools, in order to generate a following. Hadiza now bent slightly to speak to the women closer. "Imagine someone who spent so many years suffering and has not died despite the suffering, why will she die now?" she raised up again, shrugging her handbag back further up her shoulder. "We like money, and I that is standing before you likes money more than other persons," all the women laughed, "I like the money that if you give me I will go to my bed and just enjoy myself," and without a pause she said, "and I will give alms to the needy. But-" and here she emphasised "I do not like the kind of money that if you give me even before I leave here, it will finish. We should be fair to ourselves, for Allah's sake, at least for once we should build something."

Finally Baba Ahmadu spoke up. He told the women a story that he thought showed the qualities that Abdulmajid had that would impress these women. He said: "I know Abdulmajid to be someone who is steadfast and hardworking. Whatever he needs to do he will achieve it. He sat with President Goodluck Jonathan! Abdulmajid wanted to contest the leadership of the Nigerian Youth's Organisation. He sat with the president and was asked to withdraw. Goodluck Jonathan arranged it so that he should withdraw, but he withdrew because he is obedient. As small as he is, he sat down with the president. 'Abdulmajid', the president of Nigeria said, 'withdraw and allow so-and-so to contest'. If he did not withdraw, it would have been a slight. So we are proud of that fact."

For Baba Ahmadu, campaigning means constructing a rhetorical platform that emphasises Abdulmajid's close ties to the upper echelons of Nigeria's political elite. It is not important that the women in the meeting do not identify with President Jonathan, a Christian from the Niger Delta who is much maligned in the north. They don't believe Jonathan has their interests at heart, but Baba Ahmadu drops the name regardless. Nor is it important that the reason for the presidential sit-down was to convince Abdulmajid to step down from contesting a position for a preferred candidate. An outsider might say Abdulmajid's withdrawal showed political cowardice, as much as positive deference. But that would be to misunderstand Nigerian politics. What is important is the impression of bigness given by Abdulmajid's association of with the top echelons of politics, the "big men". Through Abdulmajid, his agent is saying, these people will have a direct link to the biggest man of all.

"Abdulmajid is just like a brother to me," Baba Ahmadu said, "and by God's will, we are going to give him good advice so that he does not treat us the way that the present incumbent is treating us." The women all clapped, they looked contented. He concluded: "We are praying that Allah takes us to our homes safely. We are not going to abandon you, we are not going to disappoint you." After a parting prayer, the meeting was over.

The Nigerian primary system is the intra-party election of candidates, where party delegates turn up en masse to vote for the candidates the party will put forward at the election. Under floodlights that illuminate the harmattan haze, the dry Sahara dust that blows down on the north wind and dries your nose and eyes, lines of delegates will file past green boxes with clear plastic sides. At the conclusion of the primaries, held some months before elections, successful candidates in northern Nigeria are presented with their party's flag to indicate that they have the faith of the party elders, or are the departing occupant's approved successor. Pictures of the presentation of the flag are run in newspapers and the candidate is given the title "flagbearer" to be used synonymously with "candidate". This use of flags is a deliberate echo of the nomination of leaders by Othman dan Fodiyo, who gave his emirs flags of the Jihad as they took over more towns, it is a deliberate co-opting of the historical as part of the visual imagery of politics.

The primary election process is a key event in Nigeria's democratic calendar, both at local and national level. It is the first major act of what amounts to a theatrical spectacle. In many races the primaries are where the real "election-or-selection", to use a common phrase, takes place. For the handful of key players at the top of Nigeria's political food chain, that means it is far too important to be left to chance. The delegates are rarely acting solely on their own cognisance, but as part of an orchestrated display of political will.

Who can become a player in Nigeria's politics? Appropriateness for candidacy is dependent on, firstly, what the person under consideration can "deliver" to the elders he is wooing. Can the candidate either provide the grassroots support necessary to deliver their area's votes in a bloc? Or can he bring money to the campaign of his sponsor? Or, equally importantly, has he the muscle to prevent the opposition from rigging things in their favour?

In areas where there is little grassroots support for a candidate and much scepticism about politics, but the candidate is an indispensable part of the political machine, the threat of violence is never far. Since the return of democracy, "political thuggery" has been an endemic problem across Nigeria. Over their careers politicians cultivate large groups of "youth", young men who act on their master's wishes, browbeating people into attending rallies, scattering the rallies of their opponents, breaking up polling stations and filling ballot boxes with "thumb printed" ballots. The longer the career in politics, the more a politician is likely to rely on political thugs to bend his people to his will.

In the process of dividing positions in government, Nigeria's "Ogas-at-the-top" try to put their own favoured candidate into any available role. There will come times when these men cannot agree, but to fight over it could be damaging to both. In the arcane political discourse carried out in Nigerian newspapers, key political players talk about the need for a "consensus candidate" in these situations. Appointments like this, which happen at all levels of political office, are part of the horse trading that characterises Nigerian politics. Who exactly it is who forms the consensus on these candidates is important. These decisions are not made at the ballot box by the electorate, but at late-night meetings in palatial houses in the Government Reserved Areas in state capitals, or in Abuja's exclusive Asokoro district.

This was evident at the national conference of the People's Democratic Party in 2007, which I reported on for the *Daily Trust* newspaper. The primary election was to select a successor to the retiring president Olusegun Obasanjo, but according to the delegates at the conference Obasanjo forced all other state Governors who were eager to contest to stand aside at a late night meeting, leaving his chosen successor, Umaru Yar'Adua. The leadership of several parties of delegates, from the states whose governors had intended to contest, left it until the last minute to arrive and cast their vote. One delegate told me the leaders of their state delegation were still in negotiations with the party elders about how they would be "settled", what they would be given in return for voting the way the President wanted.

"We have our signs and signals so that we know when an agreement has been reached" the delegate told me. At the street currency markets in Abuja's Zone 7 the next day, where Hausa money-men sit at picnic tables below umbrellas and in the shade of mango trees trading naira for crisp foreign notes, the value of the local currency dropped by two to three points against the dollar, so many large sacks of notes were being changed.

Although these women were vocal in their support, it was far from clear at that stage of the election process, whether Abdulmajid had the necessary clout, the "relevance", or the money, to win over the real people who decide who will proceed and take office; Kano's political godfathers.

In the event, Abdulmajid's ambitions were short lived. Along with many other aspirants, he was blocked from contesting by the party and didn't make it to the primary. He says that an open primary was never held. The governor of Kano state, Rabiu Kwankwaso agreed to retain the incumbent office holders and shut out any other competitors.

Before the national APC primaries Governor Kwankwaso had ambitions to become the party's presidential candidate. This ambition, Abdulmajid says, exhausted his campaign funds and when it became clear that he would likely lose out to Muhammadu Buhari at the primary, he realised that he would need even more money to keep his political career afloat. In order to run for a seat in the Senate he asked everyone who owed him for their positions, Kano's incumbent office holders in the National Assembly included, for large cash donations to his campaign. In return he guaranteed the incumbents would all return for another four-year term, without competition.

Abdulmajid heard on the political grapevine that this was a possibility, "in politics nothing stays secret for long," he said.[3] When it came to the process for collecting the form candidates needed to fill in to register their intent to contest, it emerged that the price the candidate had to pay the party simply to pick up the form had been raised to several million naira, an exorbitant price that chased most candidates out of the market.

"The rules are full of loopholes" said Abdulmajid, "you can see that Nigerian politics does not allow good leaders to come through. We were not in the governor's camp, and he muscled out the other candidates."

The move caused much anger and tension within the Kano APC. One of those dissatisfied was Baba Ahmadu, Abdulmajid's party agent. The man who had said Abdulmajid was his brother and how listening to one's elders was a vital characteristic in any candidate, contested the same seat he had been lining up for Abdulmajid, but for another party. He defected to the PDP, at that time the ruling party at the federal level.

The spectacle of the campaign, with posters covering every available surface, frantic rallies and national conferences, disguises that the parties themselves are weak institutions. They are based not on ideology, but on the individual ambitions of political leaders. Many of the most vocal members of the opposition are former members of the ruling party, and defections, like Baba Ahmadu's, are common. But in Ungwar Uku, the opposition APC own the machinery on ground, and there is little prospect of the People's Democratic Party being able to rig the election in their favour. The party primary was the real contest, the actual election process will be, as Abdulmajid said, "simply a formality".

"Machinery on ground means everything," says Abdullahi Idriss, the news editor of the *Daily Trust* newspaper. "You have people who are working for you, the people who you pay to be in every village looking out for your interests, this is one thing; you are 'on ground'. But it is not enough. If you talk about the machinery then you include the security services; the police, the secret service, the army, everyone. Once you have them under your control, then you get the [election regulator] Inec staff. You can even buy the agents of the opposing party in the election. When they are all working for you, then you control the machinery on ground."

Nigerian politics are "politics of the belly", the country runs on "stomach infrastructure".[4] It is not uncommon to see in the newspapers pictures of politicians "donating" gifts to the people; motorcycles to men so that they can earn a living as *achaba* motorcycle taxis, hair salon equipment and sewing machines to women. Governor Kwankwaso's rival for a senate seat, the incumbent PDP senator Bashir Lado, like many politicians across Nigeria, has been disbursing sacks of rice to people in their homes and in markets, earning him the Hausa nickname of *Lado Mai Kayan Mia*—"Lado the food distributor".[5] But these "donations", paid for by money from government budgets, amount to a tiny fraction of the money flowing through political offices.

In Nigeria the role of elections is far more complex than a simple, familiar, caricature of the democratic process; as a method of maintaining accountability in government. Elections here are a focal political moment, but not between the people and an elite who hold power. Rather they are part of a process of horse trading within that elite, where power and money are shared and the elite's grip on the country's resources is maintained.

Every election since independence in 1960, from the Local Governmental Area to the Presidency, has been in part decided by such horse trading; by a network of influential men playing out political games. The players are not necessarily acting in the interest of a political party, and the rules don't adhere to the voters' policy interests. What is at stake is their personal advancement up and down Nigeria's snakes and ladders. Deals are often done across party lines, as these horse-traders know that to get the best deal, one cannot exclude dealing with your enemies.

The power the godfathers wield is the ability to say who may join the political elite, and when they may enjoy the fruits of the prize; access to government funds. Once someone has taken their place at the trough, they have become part of their godfather's "machinery on ground." During elections, members of this elite who have tried to fly too high are scorched and laid low. New, promising, members who otherwise might become troublesome upstarts, are brought into the fold.

It is a dangerous and nasty game, the sole purpose of which is to maintain power, seemingly at the cost of actually governing. Worse, it has affected even those who live underneath this elite. People at the very grassroots have all but given up on the things that can come from effective governance. Instead they scrabble, sometimes literally tussle on the ground, to get their hands on a crumb from the national cake.

After the meeting in Ungwar Uku had broken up, I asked Zainab—the woman who had spoken so passionately—what it was exactly that she wanted

Abdulmajid to do for her. What did she mean by "drying her tears"? Zainab said: "Without money I will vote for APC. We are not people who will vote for 50 naira, we don't want something like 50–50 naira or something small for our vote. We want him to help us in our business." Asked what business she would like to get into, she says she makes and sells liquid soap, air freshener and other cleaning products.

"After he win, if he assist me with some things I can get myself well... Like the chemicals, if he assist me, like; 'whatandwhat you need?' So if I can say: Buy me so-and-so chemicals..." Zainab said in English.

Abdulmajid interrupted with a cough and a clearing of his throat. "How much will it take?"

"Like N30,000 (£120), or N20,000, whatever you can do. We are many, so you cannot say N100,000, N200,000, we are plenty, you cannot do like that. N20,000 or N30,000 is OK."

What about things like roads, hospitals and schools?

Zainab said, "Oh yes we want those things too. I have children, we want him to make schools, roads, boreholes, all things like that." But something about her tone said something different. She spoke of the things that, for most Western economies form the bare minimum of the social contract, as almost a second thought.

After so many years of asking and of being told that these things were coming, they seem further away than ever. Asking for them seemed less of a priority than angling for a small amount of money to get a business going. After all, as Hadiza said to the women; "Imagine someone who spent so many years suffering and has not died despite the suffering, why will she die now?" After so many rounds of this game, where politicians come, promise things they cannot or will not deliver and then disappear, Zainab's goal has become simpler. It is to collect as big a share of what is on offer as possible. She wants to maximise the amount of the national cake that is being divided at election time.

Their dilemma is the sort of thought experiment discussed by economic game theorists; the women may not have faith that the political aspirant in front of them will be able, or inclined, to return and fulfil his promise after the election. Do they therefore fulfil their promise and wait to be rewarded? Or do they give up on that and collect what they can in the short term; "now-now"?

If Abdulmajid was surprised by the terms of the deal she expected, he didn't say so. But I thought I saw some apprehension in his eyes. When I asked him what he thought, he changed the subject; "what I am doing now is just to make the network which I can use once I have won the primary, then I can use the networks I have made to push on to the elections" he said.

We returned to the car. The young street tough sat smoking a large joint with his friends, Molly Ringwald's eyes in halftone black and white staring out from his T-shirt. Abdulmajid put his hand in his pocket and pulled out 200 naira (about 80p) and gave it to Hadiza to pay the boy.

I asked him again about Zainab's expectations. She wouldn't be the only one with such a demand, I said. "Isn't that a lot of chemicals you're going to have to buy?"

He looked at me with a frown and told me, sadly: "We might not be able to accomplish everything."

7

EATING THE CORDS OF SOCIETY

In the late 1980s, the American political scientist Richard Joseph gave a name to the process of corruptly seizing and redistributing resources in a way that enforces an elite's grip on power. He called it "prebendalism", the term itself is borrowed from the Catholic Church, where it refers to the rights that clergy claim to money in cathedral budgets. The word carries with it entitlement to funds that might otherwise, in other official circumstances, be used in the process of governance.

In Nigeria, at the root of this feeling of entitlement is a network of connections based on the identities that underpin government, within society. Leaders of regional, ethnic, religious and language groups are expected by their supporters to glean as much as they can from available sources and share it among their kinsmen. By virtue of a shared identity, leaders are entitled to certain rights from their community, and in turn those leaders can make claims within a wider community of leaders of allied ethnic identities. The corrupt allocation of resources in return for power is all too often built around what Joseph called a "moral tie" between client and patron.[1]

Such relations have become the rational way to protect power in a political landscape that is very diverse, containing many different ethnicities and language groups and where the consequence of losing power is to be frozen out of the proceeds altogether.[2]

Nigerian politics is a quilted blanket of clashing and complimenting patterns. Each of the patterns on these swatches of fabric are derived from complex interactions of tradition, language and ancestry. The history of Nigerian politics since independence is the history of these interest groups dividing up the benefits accruing to the federal republic. In public leaders do deals in the name of their people, only to privately enrich themselves in the process. Increasingly what is supposed to be shared never reaches further than the leader's immediate network; the people he wishes to influence "on ground" and his godfather who placed him where he is.

Nigerian political discourse has morphed and mutated, rolling over many subjects over the past sixty years. It has taken in subjects like the nature of leadership, how many states should there be and "the federal character"—the idea that Nigeria's diversity should be reflected in the employment policies of public institutions. But the single most divisive issue that has arisen is the issue of sharia, the divinely-bestowed principles of acceptable behaviour at the heart of Islamic law.

Currently twelve northern states operate a form of sharia law that sees both civil and criminal matters referred to a sharia court. The controversial *hudud* punishments for adultery and theft are, in theory, applicable. But although there have been several well publicised cases since 1999, nobody has yet been stoned to death for having sex outside wedlock. Very few thieves have had their hands amputated and those who have submitted to it voluntarily.

Christian minorities living in these states are, in theory, not subject to these courts or their decisions, but many communities are bound by the social rules of sharia; women wear veils and often experience some degree of segregation in public, on public transport or in school, for example. Alcohol is only openly available where there are large populations of Christians, and in towns where it is mostly sold in "mammy markets" protected on the precincts of police or army barracks, or in the closed gardens of expensive hotels or clubs. These are the effects that are most noticeable, and that make headlines. In many instances the rules applying to the social realm are sporadically enforced, if at all.[3] Where rules are applied it is done with a high degree of arbitrariness, steeped in political pragmatism executed for short term goals.

The decisions of sharia judges are restricted mostly to the realm of custom and traditional justice, courts who rule on inheritance disputes and divorce; federal high courts come above them above them in the constitutional structure of justice.

And for some in northern Nigeria, this is not enough.

* * *

"They are aliens!" exclaimed Abubakar Rabo, head of the Kano Censorship Board.[4] The interview had started cordially enough, but as Rabo got more and more involved, his voice began to raise in volume, control over his aggravation slipped. He was angry, and let me know it.

It was the autumn of 2007, the Censorship Board had been in the news in the weeks before because Rabo had announced a moratorium on film production in Kano state. A thriving scene of movie producers, dubbed "Kannywood" by the media, had been banned from producing films for six months. Work on all productions based in Kano would have to cease, and any company wanting to produce a movie after the ban was lifted would have to apply for a licence from the board.

Upon hearing that I wanted to meet Rabo. Hasan Karofi, my colleague at the *Daily Trust* newspaper, quickly drafted an official letter and printed it on the newspaper's yellow-headed notepaper. Rabo, he said, was a stickler for such things. And indeed when we were in his office in the Kano area of Hotoro, before Rabo allowed me to ask any questions he made it clear in very formal language that he was only entertaining this interview because he knew my colleague and because we had approached him in the right way. Otherwise, he said, he would not have felt it necessary to explain himself to me. This I presumed was because I was an outsider—a white man, and moreover, one who didn't submit himself to Allah.

The filming ban was instigated following the viral spread of a clip, shot on a mobile phone, of a prominent actress in the Kano film scene having sex with a man who was not her husband. The film, shot by her foreign exchange dealer boyfriend and best described by a friend of mine as "sex from A to Z", was first circulated mobile-to-mobile using Bluetooth connections. Inevitably, as soon as news of its existence spread, someone began burning it onto DVDs for sale. By the end of the second week after the scandal broke the boys who hawked housewares from their carts up and down the city's streets were selling the disks. They hung on a loop of string from their carts, each one marked with a single word in pen, the name of the shamed actress: "Hiyana".

Hiyana herself had gone into hiding. It was barely three years since the last big moral panic over women in the north; an unmarried woman who had been sentenced to death by stoning by a sharia court in Bauchi. The woman, a divorcee named Hajara Ibrahim, had a baby without being married, which a sharia court judge decided was "proof" of adultery. The judge said the four witnesses to the act, the safeguard against spurious conviction claimed to be effective by supporters of sharia law, were not required.[5]

The film had had not been officially released by a production company, but Rabo, a former head of the semi-official Hisbah religious police set up to enforce sharia-compliant behaviour in the ancient city, knew who to blame. Kannywood's lack of moral fibre had led to this scandal, he said, and their lack of morals had put the whole city at risk.

He was clearly furious at the filmmakers. He castigated them, accusing them of all kinds of crimes. Chief among his accusations was that they were outsiders, a kind of fifth column, come to corrupt not only public morals but "Hausa-Fulani" tradition. Of all the things that he was upset about, what angered him most was the thought that these people were traitors to culture.

"In their films they sing and dance at the drop of a hat, that is not our culture!" he raged. The volume of his voice rose. His tone, where it had been formal and stiff, became aggravated and colloquial. His pugnacious manner was accentuated by his eyes that widened to their full extent with every emphatic statement he made, a wagging finger raised in front of his face.

By "Hausa-Fulani", Rabo was invoking the combined names of the two dominant ethnic identities that have held a hegemonic power in the north. But implicitly, what he meant was Islamic tradition, and more precisely, what he was referring to was sharia law. What was needed was for the authorities to re-establish control.

The only question was, which authority?

Without fully realising it, the film-makers had become the centre of a conflict between two politicians who were using their commitment to sharia law to undermine each other. At that time former governor Rabiu Kwankwaso, who was angling to return to office, had regained some popularity during his time out of office in the politics of the street over the man who had ousted him from the Governor's palace in 2003. Governor Ibrahim Shekarau was Rabo's boss.

Kwankwaso used the situation to his advantage. Appealing to the sentiments of pious minded elders, he painted the incumbent governor as someone who had been neglecting the morals of the city. He was turning away from God, the whispers went; how could anyone expect justice?[6] The ban was Shekarau's response. Kannywood got trapped between two politicians, both rushing to claim the mantle of Hausa-Fulani piety.

Looking back, such discussions seem almost quaint, certainly compared to what has happened since.

Derived from the Hadith and the Sunnah, the sayings and the ways of the Prophet, the sharia is the way of living which makes life most pleasing to God. There are four differing schools of thought on how exactly this should be done, and each proposes a slightly different form of law. These four schools were formed in the years after the successors of the Prophet Muhammad drove rapid colonial expansion of Muslim territory, out of Arabia and into North Africa.

The aims of the original Muslim community of Muhammad's followers was to improve their own relationship with God and live in a way that was pleasing to Allah.[7] Muhammad, scholars of Islam say, did not want to make a different form of law, set apart from Bedouin tradition. For generations after the Prophet died, the Hadith and the Sunnah existed only in oral tradition. The sayings and ways of the Prophet, which cover all subjects—from ablutions before praying, to the amount of inheritance a wife receives on the death of her husband—were mixed with the existing oral traditions of Arabic society. Indeed, for several generations after the time of Muhammad the word Sunnah did not denote the actual sayings of the Prophet, but was used to refer to traditional customs. The intention of the first Muslims was not to govern as a state does, but to correct these older ways and, where necessary, eliminate them.[8] It was to set out, once and for all time, what was allowed and what was forbidden in the eyes of God; what was halal and what was haram.

But when the reach of the Islamic dynasties stretched from the seat of the caliph in Baghdad to where the sun set on the West African Maghreb, there arose a need for a form of law that could be taken to all parts of this new world that the Muslims were building which would not become diluted by the new local customs or revised by the leaders of Islam's new territories.

This new codifying of the Sunnah and Hadith was done not by the Caliphs, who ruled their parts of the Islamic empire with the arbitrary tyranny of the Prince, but by Islamic scholars. These were charismatic figures who had created a following for themselves with reputations as learned men. They used their study in Islamic exegesis to align the new parts of the Islamic world with what they saw as Allah's true will, in a uniform manner. It was a difficult task. Several hundred years had passed since the Prophet's death, and the sayings had dissipated into oral tradition. This meant that there were many different versions of them. The scholars who organised these sayings into books, saw it as their job to edit them and recreate what their research led them to believe was an "authentic" text that described what Muhammad would have done in response to any situation.[9]

The purpose of these laws, collected and edited before the first Christian millennium, was to protect Islam from the manipulations of lingering polytheism, the evils of innovation and the tyranny of the worldly rule of princes. They sought to create a uniform society across the growing Islamic empire, as it engulfed new territories and new traditions, so all could live in accordance with God's wishes. They sought to perfect the connection between them and the traditions that Muhammad had indicated were blessed, and steer new followers away from the ones that were forbidden. The purpose was to create a bridge over time; to reassure Muslims that by following these approved rules their lives would be most pleasing to God. That would be true if they were a merchant in the souk, a vizier advising the Caliph or a beggar in the street.

Its most ardent followers say there is no role for the modern concept of the state in sharia law.[10] Although the sharia addresses rulers and guides them on their personal moral duties and the limits of acceptable and just behaviour, it does not establish forms of legislation or regulation in government. It set up the role of judges and courts, but it does not view these as a state institution or establish an art of technocratic state management. Sharia law did not lead to Muslims in the new Islamic empires accepting the sovereign power of the state as a supreme institution, the acceptance of state power that Michel Foucault called "governmentality";[11] rather it vested the judge with the power to apply God's law in the search for spiritual equity.[12]

While northern Nigeria was a British territory, the colonial administrators allowed the emirs to retain their sharia law courts.[13] This was part of Lugard's system of "indirect rule" conceived to keep the commitments of the British colonial administration to an absolute minimum. In the court of every emir there was an *Alkali* (the Hausa for the Arabic *Q'adi* or judge) who would hear cases that were brought by petitioners, just as they had done for centuries before. The only change under the British was the addition of a higher court that heard appeals to these rulings. This system of appeals was created by the British, there is no provision for such a court in Islamic tradition.[14] The Muslim Court of Appeal was in Kaduna, the seat of colonial government in the north, and was convened on an ad hoc basis, with judges selected for each case.

In the period between the end of the Second World War and Independence, as the realisation set in that the withdrawal of colonial rule was inevitable, British lawmakers decided that to best preserve the unity of the country that they had brought together, a new legal code should be introduced for northern Nigeria. This would be based on the system of British law but still have an element of sharia taken into account, and it would not be out of step with the movement to become a modern republic.[15] This new legal code separated off "personal matters", concerning inheritance and land ownership for example, from criminal and civil cases. The sharia court system could only rule on these personal matters. A permanent Sharia Court of Appeal, presided over by the Grand Khadi, was also created.[16]

At the dawn of Nigeria's First Republic, what Nigerians thought of their liberation from British colonial rule very much depended on where they came from and which cultural heritage they claimed. At independence, Nigeria was divided into three; the Northern Region, Western Region and the Eastern Region. Relations between the leaders of these regions and the political groups that they had formed in the pre-Independence period were tense, as they jockeyed for position in order to shape the future of the country and reap the rewards.[17]

Southerners, whose leaders had spearheaded the anti-colonial movement, saw "freedom" as the possibility of self-determination, freedom from both British rule and from the Hausa-Fulani hegemony which had underpinned the British system of indirect rule.

But the leadership in the north felt differently about it.

As much as the withdrawal of the British was welcomed by the Hausa-Fulani and their allies and co-religionists, to the northern elite freedom meant the freedom to install sharia law.[18] As Matthew Hassan Kukah, Archbishop of Sokoto, put it in his seminal work, *Religion, Politics and Power in Northern Nigeria*: "It was a freedom to impose a limitation on freedom."

But the constitution of the new republic placed federal courts, which dealt in a legal code similar to British law, over the sharia courts. To do so was anathema to many northern Muslims, and an assault on their notion of religious freedom. This decision would spark a debate between proponents of divinely-bestowed Muslim law and the man-made politics of modern government that has continued to rankle ever since. Sharia became the fulcrum in the balance between regional and ethnic identity groups, and their battle for control of the state. In successive constitutional discussions, sharia has been a consistent theme. It has become not only a discussion between Muslim and non-Muslim, but between adherents of Islam within the power elite, and outside of it. There has been no permanent agreement and participants have on several occasions in the past turned to violence.

Following independence, in the north the party in power was the National People's Congress, led by the charismatic Ahmadu Bello. As Premier of the northern region, Bello could have become Nigeria's first Prime Minister. Instead he nominated another man for the job. Bello preferred to stay in the north and protect his political network there, rather than get involved in the intrigues of Lagos.[19]

Besides, in the North among Muslims, he was seen as an important figure in the life of faith. After the disappointment of being refused the top position in the religious world, he crafted himself an image as the protector of his ancestor's legacy, the custodian of Caliphal values.[20] Bello went on a big push to convert as many of the remaining "pagan" communities in the Middle Belt and other areas, leading large conversion ceremonies at which whole villages would convert en masse. At one of these it is recorded the town burned all their idols as a symbol of no return.[21]

There were other coercive methods. In order to get a job in government, and all that this brought, it was necessary to be "Hausanized"; in the civil service it was expected you would speak Hausa, dress in the Islamic fashion and be a Muslim. Conformity meant the possibility of advancement and more access to government funds.[22]

Bello himself dressed like his ancestors, in flowing indigo robes and turban. Into the gowns were stitched traditional patterns, of several jagged knife shapes, known as *aska*, over the left breast and a round sweeping spiral on the right known as *tambari*, the king's drum. These patterns were thought to ward off the evil eye.[23] Inside his robes and turban he would also have had sewn amulets of protection, small leather packets containing verses of the Qur'an, the symbolic connection to Hausa tradition and the visual imagery of his ancestor's Jihad, which he used to bolster his political power. He boasted about his achievements in spreading Islam, telling the 1964 World Islamic League Summit he had converted 60,000 "infidels" in only five months.[24] But his dreams of Islamic expansion would be cut short.

In 1966 a cadre of Igbo soldiers from the South East took over the government. They burst into the houses of the Sardauna, Federal Prime Minister Tafawa Balewa and premier of the Western Region Samuel Akintola, and executed them. Other key politicians and military figures were also assassinated. Nigeria was plunged into a long period of fractious military rule, of coups and counter-coups. The country was set on the road to civil war.

In both of Nigeria's periods of military rule, 1966 to 1974 and 1983 to 1999, and especially after the upheaval of the attempted Biafran secession, constitutional debates were mostly squashed. But during the regime of General Olusegun Obasanjo, just before the hand-over to the second democratic republic in Nigeria's history, a conference convened to discuss whether sharia should be accommodated into government and law.

Among proponents of sharia, opinions differed only in their degree of essentialism as far as it concerned Muslim identity: "If we believe in unity and diversity, if we believe in respect and accommodating lawful and legitimate peculiarities of each other, there is no reason a sharia court of appeal should not be established throughout the country" argued Yahaya Gusau, a founder member of Jamaatu Nasrul Islam, a group that funnelled Saudi money into Nigeria to fortify Islamic institutions. Adamu Ciroma, a man who vied for the presidency in the Second Republic and went on to become a central bank governor and finance minister, went further: "If I am not subject to the Sharia, I will regard myself as not having freedom of religion" he said.[25]

Southern politicians were not the only people worried by this. Those who represented the numerous non-Muslim groups living in the north did not believe, or were not mollified by, assertions that the establishment of sharia would only effect or be operative for Muslims. They believed that it would be tantamount to the establishment of Islam as the state religion, and would give Muslims a preferred status; it would be antithetical to the establishment of the modern nation of Nigeria.[26] Many among the northern minority communities must have believed that—as they could see in the cities and towns of the north—once a minority was living in an area where Islamic practices were the norm, there would be heightened pressure to conform.

Not all Muslims were totally in favour of the proposal either. Yoruba Muslims, who often came from families which had both Christian and Muslim members, did not want to have sharia rules imposed on them as it forbade Christians from inheriting anything from Muslims, and vice versa; they saw sharia as a northern thing, an Arab imposition.[27]

There were still enmities among the northern populations that, within living memory, the Hausa-Fulani had raided for slaves. In some places slavery had never really gone away; Kukah quotes a representative from Taraba, north-east Nigeria, who said: "Slavery is still being practised in this country, Sharia condones the practice of concubinism. The area I come from is one in which a lot of people are being regarded as slaves. I have a mandate from this area to come and appeal to the conscience of any man who has respect for the essence of human beings and human rights to do something."[28]

Having sharia as an acknowledged and exclusive basis for the rule of law in the north would be the end of their separate identities, many feared. Without identity, these communities would lose any hope of elbowing their way to a place at the table where they might "chop" with the others.

The proponents of sharia were unmovable on their position that the very notion of a search for a solution, the prospect of compromise was antithetical to true sharia. It was as good as selling out.

No agreement or consensus as to how sharia could be accommodated in the law of Nigeria was reached at the 1978 conference. This period failed to see any resolution of the question of the role of sharia in the country's political and legal institutions, partly because neither side could escape the politics behind the demand for sharia. It appeared sharia was being used as a pawn in a greater struggle for overall control of the apparatus of the state, and the prebendal patronage networks that propped it up.[29]

While the south would never accept what it thought of as "creeping Islamism",[30] Kukah writes that the breakdown in the debate was caused not necessarily by the north's rigid adherence to religious doctrine, but by the northern elite's own fear that consensus would be the end of the political dominance the ruling class exerted over politics.

There was no profit for anyone in compromise.

In the end, General Obasanjo fudged the issue and the issue of state religion was dodged during the Second Republic. The government of Shehu Shagari was beset by crippling corruption and in 1983 Nigeria was plunged back into military rule for fifteen years by a coup. Consideration of the sharia debate was put on hold at the state or constitutional level. Buhari concentrated his efforts on a campaign against the corruption that had infested the Second Republic. Although Buhari was a northern Muslim, a Fulani man, his programmes in office were carried out in the secular character of the Nigerian military. Twenty months later he was replaced by Ibrahim Babangida.

Those who believed that all forms of injustice flow from the the continuing subjugation of Allah's righteous way by man-made corruption were left with a feeling of anger and resentment. Despite there being no discussion on the constitutional level, the next phase of the debate about the place of divine law in Nigeria was well under way. It would not come down from the ranks of the politicians, but up from grassroots movements. After all, this was far from being a simply an elite debate, taking place in the rarefied surroundings of top universities and constitutional conferences. An anecdote Kukah recounts shows this very well. In 1985 a British legal academic was invited to give a talk on the post-independence Nigerian criminal code. The British colonial bureaucracy had left Nigeria with a penal code adapted from Islamic law, but this manipulation stirred feelings that were deeply held. Instead of talking to a hundred law students at the Ahmadu Bello University Zaria as he expected, the academic found himself to be addressing thousands upon thousands of people who had come from far and wide, from schoolteachers to illiterate blacksmiths, all wanting to express their desire that divine law must be freed from the subjugation of man-made laws.[31]

This period of grassroots pressure for sharia was a very active one for Islamic radicals in the north. There was the Katsina-based group called Da'wa, who looked for inspiration to the Egyptian Muslim Brotherhood and their leader Sayyid Qutb, executed by the Egyptian government a decade before.[32] There was also the Yoruba-centric Muslim Students' Society who gained favour in the late 70s among Kano's students during another constitutional debate on sharia held during the second republic.[33] These popular movements were strongly influenced by the Islamic revolution in Iran, which broadcast the message to Muslims that the failure of government was linked to the reaffirmation of radical Islam.[34]

But most dramatic of the sects that sprang up at this time were the 'Yan Tatsine. A charismatic Cameroonian preacher called Muhammadu Marwa, known by everyone in his Kano neighbourhood as Maitatsine, had been building a following among the poor, the *talakawa*. A tall, thin man with very dark skin and a pronounced squint in one eye, he stalked the labyrinthine passageways of old Kano with his followers, embarking on raging speeches and Qur'anic exegesis sessions against Sufi sheikhs and wealthy Muslims. He castigated them for being heathens and commanded his followers cast off the trappings of colonial Europe, forbidding them from using modern technology, torches, watches, medicine, or riding motorbikes. If he saw anyone doing these things he would exclaim in broken Hausa "Allah kai tatsine!" Cursed by Allah! This was the source of his nickname; Maitatsine—"the one who curses". His beliefs were also heretical, he claimed that he was a prophet of God, in direct contradiction of Muhammad's revelation that there would be no more prophets after him. He and his followers even denigrated the Prophet Muhammad: armour worn by one of his followers was found to contain the inscription "There is no person like the worthless Muhammadu Allah".[35] One of Marwa Maitatsine's sayings was "may Allah curse those who disagree with this (our) version!"

By 1980 his followership had been growing in Kano's old town for almost two decades. Unlike other strange sects who went out into the bush to begin their quests for spiritual purity, Maitatsine had come into the old city. In its alleys and passages he found many followers to heed his call. Kano is sometimes known as "the elephant's stomach", testimony to its seemingly unending capacity to accommodate the people who migrate there from rural places when agriculture fails to sustain them. 'Yan Tatsine were overwhelmingly farmers and small-holding peasants who had been made bankrupt, been driven off land, or whose land had been swallowed by desertification. This rolling agrarian crisis had sucked in other forms of trade, blacksmiths, cobblers, and others as people left their villages to find better livelihoods. This wasn't just happening in Nigeria, but across the region, and Kano drew in people from Mali, Burkina Faso, Niger and Chad. In the city they struggled to make a living.[36] They were sustained by donations from wealthy sympathisers and by begging for alms, which was lucrative.[37]

The state government of Kano, headed by Abubakar Rimi, did not know what to do with them. Rimi tried to find some accommodation with the group, inviting them to meetings and to eat and pray with him, although later this lead to accusations of complicity.[38] The group had slowly been taking over the district of Kano's old town, centred around the house where Marwa Maitatsine lived. By 1980 there were perhaps as many as 10,000 in their community.[39] They clashed with neighbours regularly and violence around the edges of the group increased. A devastating clash with the state loomed.

What they believed in was a hotchpotch of heretical ideas, heavily influenced by Marwa Maitatsine's own beliefs and reading of Islam. Primarily, 'Yan Tatsine held that there was no law except that of the Qur'an, but they also refused to accept that Mohammed and Isa (Jesus) were prophets. Consequently they rejected the Hadith and Sunnah as illegitimate. They played down Qur'anic injunctions on the treatment and legitimacy of wealth and overemphasised the Qur'anic condemnation of usury and and the impiety of rich men. They also talked up verses that called for steadfastness and martyrdom. They distinguished themselves from other Muslims with substantial alterations in the daily practices of prayers and the forms those prayers took. These were however, not simply the product of Islamic ignorance. These modifications were purposeful and meant to create a distinct identity for the group as a revolt against orthodox Islam and its support of an unjust social order.[40]

They were also a millenarian group in their beliefs—the end of the world was approaching, Maitatsine said, when a spiritual redeemer would emerge in the form of a warrior, who would lead the righteous forces of Allah in battle against evil.[41] But when it came, the trigger for violence was the death of Maitatsine's son in a street fight between gangs.[42] Demanding justice, followers of Maitatsine clashed with police. The 'Yan Tatsine, believing themselves protected by amulets and special sand Maitatsine had given them, attacked policemen armed with automatic weapons,[43] throwing themselves on the guns in wave after wave. In the five days of violence that convulsed the city at least 4,177 people, sect members and civilians—probably many more—were killed. After the initial clash, the area of Kano where the sect had been living was barricaded by soldiers, who swept through the streets, executing hundreds of people, mostly poor young men, to prevent any of the group getting away.

Muhammadu Marwa Maitatsine was killed in the fighting. After the riot subsided, his body was displayed in public for all to see.

Some of the group escaped and there would be outbursts of violence in the years that followed, in 1982, 1984 and again in 1985. Each was brutally suppressed by the military, who rounded up and stripped people in public in order to "screen" for members. This was based on rumours that the sect marked their people in secret ways, said most often to be a tattoo of a cross or a circle, or both in various places on the body.[44] But there was never any unanimity about these rumours and no real way of telling who was a member or not.

The 'Yan Tatsine revolt was an example of how a charismatic preacher could harness religious zeal and turn the anger of the poor into a social movement.[45] The heretical preacher had made no accommodation with the state and the latter had responded brutally, crushing him and his followers.

At the same time as 'Yan Tatsine were growing in strength, there was another radical group that was very active in Nigeria who were growing and expanding their influence. Like Maitatsine, they began by campaigning against the Sufi orders, to whom most of the Northern Nigerian elite were associated. And like Maitatsine they gained in strength and number rapidly. But unlike the squinting one-eyed heretic of Kano, this group would not come into conflict with the state. Their future would be very different. They were—and still are—Salafists, advocating a return to the most fundamental principles of Islamic law. But they have been much more successful in spreading a radical doctrine and they would go on to be influential, eventually taking over the mainstream of Islamic discourse in Nigeria.

The origins of this new movement can be traced back to almost three decades before the second period of military rule. It was in 1948, in the quiet town of Maru, Sokoto state, that one young reformer was about to make himself known.

The Sultan of Sokoto and his adviser, the Waziri, had both been disturbed to receive a private letter delivered to the palace, the seat of the old Fulani caliphate. The espistle, from a hitherto unknown young man, demanded to know why the Sultan allowed emirs to receive knighthoods and other honours bestowed by the British royal family. This was an indefensible breach of Islamic practice, the letter said. It was especially heinous, the writer continued, as the awards were often named after Christian saints.

In 1948 the authorities in Sokoto were dependent on the legitimacy given them by the colonial power. They felt this letter to be a direct challenge to the status quo. At a time of deepening resentment at British imperial power among northern Nigerians, it could spell trouble. The Sultan and his Waziri set out to investigate who had penned the letter.

They discovered him to be an earnest and studious twenty-six-year-old named Abubakar Gumi, then enrolled at the teacher training college. The British colonial administration had opened the school for training teachers in the new town that had grown up along the road that ran from the busy trading city of Gusau to Sokoto. They had been setting up schools and colleges since Hans Vischer's time, but uptake had hitherto been slow. The aim was to produce northern graduates who could run the civil service, and it was only by the late 1940s, after the Second World War, with the possibility of the withdrawal of the British and independence looming, that institutions like this became popular among the sons of the elite. The Native Authority, the indigenous administration that was backed up by the British, had begun to impress on those at the pinnacle of northern society that it would be better to have a civil service run by indigenes of the north, rather than better-educated southern interlopers.[46]

The Education Training Centre in Maru was also known as the place where a left-wing firebrand and champion of anti-colonialism named Aminu Kano worked. The Sultan decided further investigations were needed into this Gumi. They wanted to discover if there was any argument existing against this young man which the authorities could use quickly to snuff the business out, before it got out of hand.[47]

Gumi, the son of a well-known *mallam* and *Alkali*, was thought by the British head of the college to be a brilliant young student. He had gone to a prestigious school along with the children of the very highest members of Hausa-Fulani society. Quiet, earnest, straight-talking and intelligent, Gumi was the type who would be a good fit for a plum position in the civil service, or as the head of one of the government academies. But he was not motivated to join that caravan. Instead he was studying the process of education in order to become a better *mallam* himself. His mission was to use the techniques of Western education to further the understanding and acceptance of a very strict back-to-basics form of Islam in the mould of the Wahhabi ideas from Saudi Arabia. Pictures of him at this time show a bearded man, his upper lip trimmed close, holding a microphone with a calm expression of absolute conviction, peering over his glasses at an audience with an unflinching gaze.

His approach would be nothing short of revolutionary and he would become a sheikh of extraordinary influence and reach. He believed that Nigerians, despite their professed faith, were in fact very poor Muslims, full of deviant practises and weak ideas about what the Prophet intended life for a Muslim to be. He wanted to find his way in the world as an *Alkali*, an Islamic judge, or an imam so as to further educate Nigerian Muslims in the proper practice of their faith.[48] By the time he was studying at Maru, he was already well versed in Islamic jurisprudence and Islamic practise. According to his autobiography, he had also developed an unfortunate habit of obstinately correcting his elders on their poor knowledge of law or custom without regard for the consequences, even if it resulted in their embarrassment and his ostracism.

Sokoto's spies reported that he had persuaded the Muslims of the teacher training college to shun Friday prayers in the town's main mosque, and instead they held their own prayers among themselves. Worse still, the young man conducted prayers in his own house, where he also gave lectures, at which—it was said by the gossips—he proclaimed himself to be the Mahdi.

The Waziri, the Sultan's right hand man, drafted a warning letter to the young Gumi. It read: "This is a time for keeping silent and staying at home." The letter, written in classical Arabic in the Waziri's own flowing hand continued: "whoever speaks the truth would die."[49]

This was evidently serious stuff.

Gumi later wrote that he was was fortunate to have a good relationship with the British officer in charge of the college, a man named Spicer who had lived a long time in Nigeria and, according to Gumi, spoke Hausa well and understood the culture. When the authorities wrote to the white man with a list of accusations against Gumi, the first thing Spicer did was to summon the young man for a cup of tea, to see if they couldn't sort things out without any "unnecessary unpleasantness".[50]

The reason the group had shunned the prayers at the town was procedural, one which to the non-believer might seem trivial, if not mystifying. But to Gumi and his growing band of followers this was a matter of great importance. The local imam, Gumi said, did not perform the correct ablutions to lead the prayers and nor did he purify himself properly, hence was impure and the prayer invalid. As was common in rural northern Nigeria at that time, people did not perform ablutions with water, but by rubbing dry sand over the skin of their hands, forearms and feet, in a lesser kind of ablution that according to the Hadith should only be done by those who were prevented from using water by illness. Gumi's acolytes considered that this young man had revealed to them a truth that had been hidden, or forgotten, or twisted by the evils of innovation and heathenism. The revealing of this simple truth and the charisma with which it was delivered was enough to bind them to him.

Spicer tried to resolve the matter quietly. But no accommodation could be found. Soon the question of how a local imam performed his ablutions threatened to become a major incident. Rather than lose face against a young and impudent upstart, the Sokoto authorities backed the imam who had been appointed by their emirate. The matter went as far as the council of emirs where it was raised before the Emir of Kano, the head of the Native Authority. At that stage the council, the highest members of the local aristocracy, said Gumi's grasp of the situation was correct, and that was the end of the matter.

"But instead of joy for my victory," Gumi wrote in his autobiography "I was suddenly seized by fear... that it had been discussed by the senior emirs of the entire region meant that it had been quite serious indeed. My little attempt to correct a local mistake here in Maru had been given unintended dimensions."[51]

He did not perceive himself to be in conflict with anyone until it had become very real, with possibily terrible consequences for him. "I was simply being the teacher, interpreting the religion to my students. The law was not mine but God's and its terms had been described in the books... How could anyone get into trouble because he had said correctly what God had revealed?"[53]

It would be a key moment, a turning-point in his life that would set the scene for all that was to come. Later, his mission to correct the accepted Islamic practice would have very real and violent consequences.

A direct consequence of his letter was that Gumi came to the notice of one of the North's most charismatic leaders. His letter challenging the Sultan of Sokoto had attracted the attention of the Premier of the Northern Region, Ahmadu Bello, who wrote him an encouraging letter and met the young man.

Gumi chanced upon the Sardauna again while on the Hajj pilgrimage. "The Sardauna at once made me the Imam and guide for the Hajj. I felt honoured to be asked to lead this group, which included some of the most outstanding personalities in the country."[53] This bestowing of such a trusted leadership role in someone so young, in the company they were in, meant a lot; he had been brought into the fold. From then on, he continued to mix in these circles. Bello and Gumi would become friends. The Sardauna of Sokoto sought Gumi's advice on most religious matters, as he did not read Arabic, as mentioned above.

With the connivance of a colonial officer (Mervyn Hiskett, the historian and linguist) Gumi applied for a post in the new Sharia Court of Appeal, Hiskett adding a few years to his age to make him appear a better candidate. At the interview he found the board were old colleagues and former teachers. They were well disposed to him, despite his abrupt manner.

In 1962, on the retirement of the Grand Khadi, his onetime teacher, Gumi took over the post; he was now at the summit of the Islamic legal system. His view on the meaning of law was uncompromising. He believed the British had deliberately conspired to weaken sharia by leaving out the realm of "civil law" which was the preserve of the magistrate's or customary court. This conspiracy, robbing the courts of the power divined by God, prevented the people from experiencing proper sharia. Worse, deviation from the true sharia was part of a colonial plot to destroy the indigenous culture of northern Nigeria, specifically Islam. "The sharia cannot be compared with any other law made by man, either in scope or orientation," Gumi said,

> The Sharia operates on principles of recognition for the supremacy of God and belief in life after death, when all men shall be brought before God to answer for their actions in this world. For me, this is a significant issue specifically in relation to the English Law which lacks any credible spiritual values. In more than one respect the English Law betrays its European origins, including those pre-Christian influences which characterise it, and which are particularly odd in our cultural setting.[54]

His attitude toward Nigerian Muslims and the sincerity of their faith was unchanged. As a young man he had felt that most of them were ignorant of their true faith. Now he saw that failing extended to Islamic judges too, though he seems not to have set great store in reforming the court system's personnel. When judges retired, Gumi appointed new people where he could, often choosing those with no legal experience, but whom he knew held similar attitudes to himself.[55] But he made no attempt to sweep out judges he thought were ignorant. When erring cases came before him at the Sharia Court of Appeal, they fell into two general categories. There were those which the wrong decision had been made through ignorance of the true law, or those which had been arrived at by corruption, where Gumi suggests but does not accuse directly, that one of the parties had colluded with the judge. But if this apparent evidence of poor practice at the lower sharia courts disturbed Gumi, he does not let on. Retelling these cases in his ghostwritten autobiography, there is no sense of concern that these poor judgements have any negative meaning for the system of sharia. It is a perfect system given by God; that God had put him there to correct the other judges' mistakes was sufficient proof of that.

Gumi says that his appointment in 1960 as the deputy Grand Khadi, assistant to the highest authority on sharia law in the land, came as a great surprise to him but, between the lines of his narrative, with his relationship with the Sardauna Ahmadu Bello and his position among the northern elite, it is possible to see an invisible hand at work.[56] Perhaps not a divinely guided one as Gumi believes, but the unspoken agreement of an old boy's network easing his passage upward.

The Hausa word *sarauta* means something roughly similar to "traditional power", and has a similar meaning to "noblesse oblige", and sums up the aristocracy's attitude to their right to rule.[57] The story of the relationship between Gumi and the Sardauna epitomised how this traditional power worked, protected and replicated itself.

That political power system was based, as Bishop Kukah observed, on a system of aristocratic hierarchy, the assumption of a Hausa-Fulani superiority. Since the days of Mohammed Bello, the son of Othman dan Fodiyo, this aristocratic Hausa-Fulani dynasty had thought of rulership as its right. Society was highly segregated, with the court aristocracy living in the refined quarter of town away from the *talakawa*, who looked up to their liege lords with an almost unquestioning reverence. The British made use of this. But after independence the northern elite sought to maintain its position in the face of many other new hands reaching into the pot.

If his relationship with these traditional beneficiaries was an enabling one for Gumi in terms of his position, his relationship with the Sardauna actually put a hold on him in terms of his theological radicalism. Like many of the Hausa-Fulani aristocracy, Ahmadu Bello was an ardent proponent of Sufi brotherhoods. He had even tried to institute a brotherhood in his ancestor Othman dan Fodiyo's name—the Usmaniyya.[58] Whereas Gumi, who had spent time as the representative for Nigeria's pilgrims in Saudi Arabia, had his ideas formed by the salafist doctrines emanating from the Kingdom. Where Ahmadu Bello wore robes emblazoned with spiritual symbols, the *aska* knives and the *tambari* drum and trusted amulets and charms for protection against the evil eye, Gumi wore simple austere clothes without adornment and ensured all his followers did the same. He would have shunned completely the practice of using charms. Salafists believe that Islam should return to its purest form as practised by the Prophet Muhammad and his first community of Muslims. They hold that people who worshipped the Sufi saints, like the founders of the brotherhoods Ahmad Tijani and Abd-al-Qadir al Jilani, were not Muslims—rather, they were infidels.[59]

From the pages of his autobiography Gumi's unshakeable belief in the cultural superiority of Islam and the superiority of Muslims over other people, is radiantly clear: "The roots of our instability lie deep in the concept of secularism, which eats away at the very cords which should bind us together as a nation," he writes, "by divorcing our government from God we are at once encouraging selfishness and unfounded ambitions. The current system does not acknowledge God, which is why we lack direction. Leaders find it easy to lie and cheat and cover up all by resorting to cheap sentiments."[60] There is no question that the God referred to in this quote is the Muslim Allah, he does not tolerate any other God. Elsewhere he talks about Christianity as being "the white man's religion" and scorns southerners for copying the white man in pursuit of reward from the colonial master.[61]

In the first month of 1966, restrictions on Gumi's radicalism were removed. Gumi was at his friend Ahmadu Bello's house shortly after the coup faction shelled it into oblivion following Bello's execution. According to his own account, Gumi found the corpses of the Sardauna and his wife in their compound and carried their lifeless bodies to safety. He was the one who washed and wrapped their bodies and arranged for their burial.

As much as he grieved for a friend who had been killed—and hated the people who murdered him—Gumi was, in a way, released by the Sardauna's death. He was now free to write and preach widely about his belief that straying from the original tenets of Islam was the cause of much of Nigeria's misfortune,[62] and that Sufi traditions were heretical. Their mode of praying—with arms crossed—was innovation, and the Sufi use of rhythmic trance to make transcendental journeys to the spirit world was nothing short of polytheistic blasphemy.

Gumi was among the first of the Nigerian preachers to use the mass media to disseminate his ideas. He appeared regularly on the radio, a medium of prime importance in Northern Nigeria. He and like minded people wrote regularly for the Hausa language newspaper *Gaskia Tafi Kwabo*—'Truth worth more than a penny'. In 1972 he wrote a controversial book called *The Right Faith According to the Sharia*, which set out clearly that he believed Sufi practices were heretical. Inevitably, he came into conflict with the authorities, who until this point were usually members of a Sufi brotherhood, usually either the Tijaniyya or the Qadiriyya. By declaring them to be heretics Gumi was, to many ears, suggesting that it was a righteous Muslim's duty to kill them. Gumi's followers were enjoined to rid their mosques of *tariqa* members.[63] They set about making new places of worship separate from the old ones.

Gumi claims there were several attempts on his life. One night two soldiers came to warn him that they had been contacted by a group of prominent people who were plotting to kill him. When these two same men turned up in Saudi Arabia at the same time as Gumi was there on one of his frequent visits, he alerted the Saudi authorities and asked for their protection.[64] Secretive cabals of powerful brotherhood members also sent thugs to harass his followers constantly.

By 1978 his followers had acquired a name; The Society for the Removal of Innovation and the Reinstatement of Tradition, *Jama'at Izalat al Bid'a wa Iqamat al Sunna*, sometimes JIBWIS, most often known as Izala. It had also found a home, in the city of Jos, the capital of Plateau state in Nigeria's Middle Belt region, away from the old establishment.

His supporters were in the main middle class northerners: self-made businessmen, civil servants and educated university intellectuals. In time the appeal reached down into the next generations, the middle class children of the 1980s who grew up through the system of Western education and went to university in the north.

They were drawn to Sheikh Gumi because of his reformist zeal, but also because he was opening up new space for a growing class of people in Nigerian society. This arena was both political and economic. Gumi's connections in Saudi Arabia afforded him great access to business circles there.[65] In a time of military rule, religion and politics in the north had a particular affinity.[66]

Izala were not like Maitatsine, they were not a fringe sect at the edge of society. They were gaining more popularity with new middle class city-dwellers, and their reformist ideas were catching on. Izala was attractive to the new class of businessmen and civil servants because the path they offered to a more religiously fulfilling life was simpler, and less costly for the average man. For example, in traditional Hausa culture, once a child was born the family must hold a naming ceremony, which involved the whole village, with the family of the baby required to feed everyone and give them gifts. In a village setting, where the number of people was limited and because only simple food was expected, this was a manageable burden. But to the modern city-dwelling civil servant, such ceremonies could be ruinous. Izala preached that these sort of traditions were not Islamic, and therefore unnecessary. The prospect of not having to fork out so much every time a child was born, which in northern Nigeria could be frequently, was a soothing balm to the heads of the household, particularly in the tight financial times that followed the Structural Adjustment policies of the mid 1980s, which saw many civil servants lose their jobs.

Izala also attracted the political class, as religion is a fine mobiliser of communities in the support of a local politician.[67] Gumi's association with the political class, their patronage of him and his organisation, came early on. Izala was founded during the Second Republic under President Shehu Shagari, and became enmeshed with the political class. Izala were not spared the scrutiny of General Buhari's anti-corruption efforts.[68] Gumi spoke out against Buhari who detained suspected corrupt officials of Shagari's government and targeted

Izala preachers for investigation. But during the military regime of General Babangida, Gumi became one of a few religious figures allowed to broadcast and write freely. Babangida even became a patron of his movement, funding the society's publications, including a commentary on the Qur'an.[69]

Instead of attacking the government, Izala courted it. Gumi saw his role as being a father figure to the young people he wanted to encourage in the right way of faith. This meant encouraging action where it was appropriate to their aims, like *takfir*: denouncing Sufis as unbelievers who, according to the Salafist beliefs of Izala, are "deserving of death".[70] But it also meant restraining the youth where required.

According Abubakar Gumi's son Ahmed, what made his father Sheikh Gumi different from other radicals was that he did not advocate turning on the state: "He was a patron, or even grand patron to the youth [of the Society], so that he can check their excesses, excesses in their literature and how they conduct themselves. If you leave youth to form an organisation they may think of even toppling the government. They don't know their limitations. The subject of his teachings was always leave the government as it is," Ahmed told me.[71] He had become the leader of Izala following his father's death in 1992. Gumi's father did not advocate the withdrawal of the faithful from politics; rather he commanded his supporters to get involved with government. As a consequence, "almost all the major leaders in the north today are associated with Izala," Ahmed Gumi said.

This brought Izala into conflict with the people who refuse to make accommodations for man-made law. The younger Gumi has been threatened with death and attempts have been made on his life. When I met Ahmed Gumi at his house in Kaduna, he was looking over a number of shiny boxes, ticking them off an itinerary—the components of a state of the art surveillance system to protect his house. Armed police guards were not far away.

The advancement of sharia in this new democratic period was also used by politicians as a tool to project themselves in a competitive political atmosphere and as the academic Alex Thurston says, "access power, define public morality and shape the course of sharia implementation".[72]

In the fallout of the 2007 Hiyana scandal, several in the film industry were jailed for defying the censor board. An actor was jailed for making an unlicensed film which featured "Indian-style" dancing. Two actresses were run out of their homes by the Hisbah for being "immoral"—living independently without husbands. The emir of Kano staged public events at which Kannywood films were branded "pornography" and burned in great fires. A film director I interviewed at the time was jailed for two months after a film he released within the moratorium was found in Kano's market.

The eagerness of politicians to pursue sharia did not convince everyone. The jailed director, Hamisu Lamido Iyan-Tama, a larger-than-life character on the Kannywood scene, a virtuoso of film-making energy who works on several productions at once with the verve of Cecil B. DeMille, believed his film was exempt because it was funded by a grant from the American government, and was not officially distributed in the city. But as the newest release from a popular director, the film *Tsintsiya*, a reworking of Romeo and Juliet set against the backdrop of riots in Kano between Christians and Muslims in 2001, inevitably ended up in the Kano market.

When I interviewed him before his arrest in 2007 he was adamant that the censorship board was not taking its decisions for moral or religious reasons. They couldn't be, he said, because he was known to be a very upright and morally correct person in society, his films carried messages of peace and tolerance and unity, featured actors who were dressed modestly and didn't have extraneous dancing and singing of the type that, he thought, made the censors especially angry. His films were lessons in good morals but, he bellowed several times; "There is no teaching without entertainment!" It was a maxim he was sure was lost on his detractors.

The Hiyana furore was a double standard, he said: "No Hausa or any actor would like to see his face making affairs with any lady, this is a kind of deceit. She is an actress, but who is the man? Doesn't he have a business? The man was in foreign exchange why don't they say ban foreign exchange?"[73]

His arrest and the wider use of sharia in Kano were examples of how politics uses religion to settle scores and retain control of their positions, Iyan-Tama told Nigerian journalists in 2008.[74] Furthermore the governor and his group wanted to get rid of him because of his political ambitions. Iyan-Tama had campaigned to become governor in 2003 against Ibrahim Shekarau, and Shekarau and his sharia officials had never forgotten it. His foray into the political sphere had been unsuccessful, but as a popular and charismatic film maker, he was building a following.

A following, whether through films or politics, will always present the authorities with a threat, he said. He told me: "because I make films, many people chop from them, they can eat" and as he saw it, one person coming to him for money, training, guidance, a job, was one less coming to the political godfathers.

His star actor, the leading man in *Tsintsiya*, Baballe Hyatu put it more bluntly. "They are not attacking us for religion, they are attacking us for their selfishness."

After I met Iyan-Tama he was arrested several times and spent a great deal of time trying to clear his name. On his release from jail scores of people paraded with him through the streets. But since then he has stuck to film making, directing and starring in a film about his imprisonment, and hasn't dabbled explicitly in politics again.

In 2010 Rabo, Ibrahim Shekarau's sharia attack-dog, was let go from his position as head of the censorship board. He had been discovered by a vigilante group with a half-naked, underage girl in his car in the middle of the night. He claimed that the situation was entirely innocent and had been blown out of all proportion by his political enemies. He was arrested and wrote a statement, but he then left the country for Saudi Arabia, and the case has never come to court.

To the pious of the north corruption of all kinds is attributable to deviation from God's law. To the uncompromising, political corruption is a natural consequence of devotion to man-made law and the poor state of politics. But in order to continue as a state, to have the table at which the diners eat, compromises have had to be made to accommodate the modern world of politics.

Among many northern Nigerians, who believe that it is important not to deviate from the holy, this creates a feeling of tense resentment. For instance, my colleague Karofi had obviously been thinking about my interview with the head of the censorship board while he was driving away from Rabo's office. After a period of silence he said: "It was like two worlds interviewing each other."

Taken a bit by surprise by this I asked him to go further, tell me what he thought.

"You see, you in the West think that we are going back to the Stone Age by our devotion to our faith. ...On our behalf, we think it is you who are returning to the Stone Age."

To the hard-line of sharia proponents the compromises of politics push them further and further to the edge, their concerns irreconcilable with the project of a Nigerian republic. Over the years, that group has grown, and has become less and less convinced by the need to participate in a greater Nigeria. This group of people have become what the academic Johannes Harnischfeger called a "counter elite". Angrier and angrier at what they see around them they have become more and more strident and implacable in their insistence of the single solution they believe in: an uncompromising application of sharia law.

PART 3

8

THE REST OF US ARE JUST HAWKING PEANUTS

The motorpark in Maraba. People squeeze out of packed minibuses bringing them from the surrounding areas, step onto the oil-stained ochre soil, hail a motorcycle taxi (called an *achaba* in northern Nigeria)[1] and head to work, to the market, to church. Those travelling out of town wait in inter-city taxis for the remaining seats in their car to fill up. The driver will take the wooden destination sign from the roof and set off. As the morning burns away, hawkers weave between the cars, selling biscuits, sachets of water, bananas and cones of peanuts. All around is a cacophonous chorus of defiance; conductors fling open side doors of moving busses to yell out their destinations over the cockerel-cries of motorcycle horns, exalting another day of life.

It was February 2009 and I was at the motorpark looking for *achaba* to talk about an oddball story I was working on; I was looking for motorcycle riders wearing dried vegetables on their heads.

In those days, before anyone outside of Maiduguri had heard of Boko Haram, Nigeria was a rich and reliable source of "odd news". If journalists working for Western news organisations weren't writing about the oil business, or filing stories that moved markets, chances are they were working on a human interest story. Mostly they likely involved the mysterious and the strange, the absurd and usually humorous aspects of life in Africa's most populous nation. Indeed as someone who wrote for a publication that didn't specialise in finance, this sort of story was pretty much my stock-in-trade.

I hoped that by writing odd news stories in such a way as to smuggle in background information about this wonderful and at times bewildering country, I could show people who would never know Nigeria something about this important place. Even stories that didn't hold up, those about magic, curses, juju and the like—if you rubbed them a little, often you found they revealed something true and interesting. It was like the film director Iyan-Tama said: "there is no education without entertainment!"

To say these stories were Western journalists obsessing over the strange "otherness" of Nigeria isn't quite true. After all, it wasn't just the foreigners who found strange tales irresistible to retell. Rarely a week passed in the newsrooms I worked in when my Nigerian colleagues didn't fall about laughing as they discussed some absurd story that had been unearthed. If anything Nigerian newspapers are far more gung-ho with their dedication to mining the comical "weird" vein of journalism, splashing on thinly-sourced stories of shame, magic and taboo that would make the night-editor of any British tabloid newspaper wince and reach for the indigestion syrup.

I didn't know it at the time, but the story I was working on in the motor park would turn out to be one of the most important of these stories, or at least the one that would have arguably the biggest fall-out. The Nigerian Police Force had tightened already existing laws requiring drivers and passengers of motorcycles to wear helmets. In the case of motorcycle taxis, all drivers would have to provide helmets for their passengers. There was an uproar. For sure everyone knew that taking a trip on an *achaba* could be a dangerous thing. Drivers were known to be reckless. Often drunk or high, crashes and serious injury were a frequent occurrence. But nevertheless, many Nigerians didn't like the idea. At the very least everyone had an opinion on it.

Objections ranged from the sartorial—women complained the helmets would spoil their expensive hair weaves—to another sort of safety concern. It was said that *achaba* riders could use the helmets to put passengers under their spell, overpower them with charms placed inside the webbing. Faced with a choice between guarding against physical injury and exposing oneself to the dangers of juju, people were not altogether one hundred per cent sure they wanted to disregard their own spiritual safety in order to protect their corporeal wellbeing. In the run up to the day the law was to be enforced, Nigerian newspapers were full of stories about women being bewitched by *achaba*. Some disappeared into the ether, or fell into catatonic states, whereupon they were forced to do unspeakable things.

Mostly, the law smacked of ulterior motives on the police's part. In Maraba, one of Abuja's "satellite towns", across the state line from the capital in neighbouring Nasarawa state, motorcycle taxi drivers at the motorpark were sure;

the police didn't care about public safety. They were simply opening another avenue of extortion. A motorcycle taxi driver called Monday told me the new rule was going to cost him 10,000 naira (around £40) to buy two helmets. There was no way he could afford this as he made between 300 and 400 naira per day (less than £2).

"The cost of living here is too much," Monday said, "We're not able to buy the helmet, not to talk of feeding ourselves".

Everyone knew what would happen. When the new tough stance came into force, the police would set up flying checkpoints, mobile ambushes, near markets and motorparks and busy thoroughfares. They would swoop down on motorcyclists, flailing sticks and canes as bikes madly accelerated out of the jaws of the trap. *Achaba* not caught out instantly would execute hasty and dangerous escape turns in the hope that there were no police officers, or the wasp-liveried vehicles of the Vehicle Inspection Office, lurking in the bushes behind. In the rush to escape, people would in all likelihood be hurt. The police would seize bikes and hold them for a ransom which few could afford.

People who drive *achaba* are close to the bottom of society. They are men (only men drive *achaba*) without much formal education, possibly without any other skill (or at least not one that they can make money with). Many sleep rough, under bridges or awnings, some sleep actually on their motorbike to guard their only source of income. Most don't usually own the bike themselves, but owe someone else money for it every day. In some cases they have been given these motorbikes by local big men in public displays of wealth and generosity, and to oil the wheels of the "machinery on ground". These big men, local government chairmen, state commissioners, all the way up to state governors, call it "job creation" and in the past have called down local journalists to take pictures of them as they make their hand-outs for the pages of the newspaper.

But in fact the wealthy despise the *achaba*, and the people who ride them. They are blamed not only for all the accidents, and the nefarious activities of spirit cults, but also for armed robberies—often committed on bikes for a sharp get away. They swoop around roundabouts, collecting at traffic junctions where they form a growling beast at rest, then they rush forth like an angry host of bees. Gradually *achaba* were being banned from cities like Abuja, Lagos and Kano by the metropolitan authorities—with the blessings of their wealthier citizens.

Being an *achaba* is to be close to, if not actually at, the last resort. With a trip costing about 70 naira (28 pence) they are mostly used by the poor too. Their existence in large numbers is manifestly a symptom of Nigeria's economic problems. These are men who have not been put to work in factories, or farms, who cannot enter the civil service, who in many cases are even denied the rights of full adulthood within a hierarchical society because many cannot marry. They are men without status. All that the authorities can think to do is say "ban them", as if you can ban such things.

This newly toughened helmet law was, in the minds of most, just another squeeze on the wider population of people already in perilous circumstances. Even if a rider were not caught and fined, the added financial risk to the *achaba* would probably raise fares. This hike in the cost of transport would mean an inflationary rise in other prices, which in turn increased pressure on people's pockets, already stretched to breaking point.

When the regulations came into force, something strange happened. As hardly anyone had any helmets to wear, some *achaba* drivers took to the streets with all sorts on their heads. There were pictures of people wearing paint cans and buckets; but best of all were those spotted by by Mustapha Mohammed, the BBC Hausa Service correspondent in Kano: riders wearing hollowed-out watermelons and calabash, the rustic hemispherical bowls made out of dried pumpkins which, before the advent of plastic, were ubiquitous as liquid vessels.

These *achaba* had set their faces against this barely disguised official extortion. Their resistance was characteristically subversive, with abundant touches of Dadaist surrealism. I am unashamed to say it made good copy. But in truth the protests were neither widespread nor organised. Most Nigerians simply added this new trouble to the long list of things that made their lives difficult, prayed, hoped the police would soon lose interest and carried on.

In one part of the country, however, this cat-and-mouse between police and harassed Nigerian motorists would have much more serious consequences. In Maiduguri, in Nigeria's north east, it would become an unlikely trigger for bloody violence. Enforcement of the helmet law caused an incident that would spark an uprising. This, in turn, would pitch Nigeria into war.

* * *

The door opened and the slight young man entered the office between two plainclothes policemen. They had brought him from the cells at the other end of the station. Hollering from the other men still inside echoed down the concrete hallway.

He was thin, younger than I expected. He looked to be barely more than a teenager. His pink riga was dirty and flecked with small spots of crusty blood. He smelled of the cell, of fear and filth. A policeman pointed to the floor and the prisoner sat down quickly. The officer then slouched in the leather seat by the door.

We were in the office of Maiduguri's Special Armed Robbery Squad. The place is known locally as "The Crack", ostensibly because it houses the crack police force. It is also a place from where, once you fell in, you might never emerge.

The policeman looked at us with a feline gaze as we, in turn, looked at the man he had placed before us. He was named Mohammed Zakariyya and had been arrested a few days before, at a checkpoint.

"They discovered the weapons we had hidden underneath the seat," Zakariyya told us.[2] His companion tried to drive off, leaving Zakariyya in the hands of the police. The driver didn't get far. The Police Mobile Force officers opened fire, killing him. Abdullahi Kaura and I had seen the red hatchback, full of holes, rear window smashed, in the yard of the Borno police Headquarters.

The police got Zakariyya to tell them where he was going with the weapons. He led them to a large house in the suburbs of Damaturu, capital of the neighbouring state of Yobe. The Joint Task Force of police and military laid siege to the property, and a gunfight broke out that lasted for five hours. The JTF stormed the house and found half-a-dozen wounded gunmen and several women and children. The rest of the men had escaped, leaving their families behind. In the yard of the house there was a patch of overturned soil. When the police dug there, they found a huge cache of arms; high calibre automatic weapons, rocket-propelled grenades and launchers, AK-47s and boxes of ammunition. Two of the remaining survivors died in police custody a day after they were paraded in front of journalists.

Zakariyya had driven on three of these arms smuggling missions, he said. Each time he and his accomplices drove 120km out of Maiduguri to meet a man who ferried weapons downriver from the mountainous Cameroonian borderland. He brought them half a dozen AK-47s and a handful of boxes of ammunition in a canoe each time. They loaded the car then Zakariyya drove it through Maiduguri to Damaturu.

"I was hawking shoes and phone chargers when they came to me," Zakariyya said describing the first time he said he met the men, three months before, at the end of 2010. "They bought some things from me and afterwards they asked me if I could drive and I said yes. Then they told me what they were into."

When they spoke, Zakariyya knew exactly who the men were, and what that meant.

Indeed residents of Maiduguri had known these men's ilk since long before. As Zakariyya said: "They used to preach in the open, so everyone was aware of who they were..."

"They" were a hard-line Islamic sect who had established themselves between 2005 and 2009 at a compound in Maiduguri's Railway district. Dubbed "Western education is forbidden" by their neighbours for the unflinching stance they took on secular education in their public preaching, they had gradually been gathering adherents, bringing more and more people under their influence.

A member who called himself Abu Dujana, his *nom de guerre* taken from one of the companions of the Prophet, described the atmosphere of the sect's Maiduguri headquarters in almost cult-like terms. The pace of life inside was dictated by their charismatic leader Mohammed Yusuf, who set and enforced strict standards of religious practice.

"Yes, I lived there!" Abu Dujana said proudly, speaking to me over the phone in 2011 after the compound had been destroyed and the group temporarily scattered.[3] "In the whole of this country there is no mosque like that, because of the things Mallam Yusuf used to teach. He reminded us about Islam, his teachings were about the practice of the Prophet to such an extent as some of the practices that had been forgotten were revived, such as praying at night and reading only the Qur'an at all times of the day. There wasn't a mosque like this in the whole of the country where you could go and attain as much knowledge."

The compound in Maiduguri was named after Ibn Taymiyyah, the medieval Syrian jurist who declared Jihad was obligatory against insincere Muslim leaders; in his case the Mongols who had swept into Syria in the thirteenth century. Yusuf also had a base in nearby Bauchi state where a large farm had been established. Estimates put the number of sect members in the thousands.

On 20 February 2009 (a month after I was on the trail of vegetable helmets in Maraba), members of the sect were travelling to a funeral in a large group. The convoy was made up of a large number of motorbikes, and the police stopped them. The police were part of a state-wide special Joint Task Force (JTF) in cooperation with the military, called Operation Flush, set up in 2005 to combat political thugs who had run out of control following elections two years before. The dispute between the group and the police about their refusal to wear helmets became heated. A fight broke out and a policeman opened fire. There were many casualties.

This was not the first time that Operation Flush had crossed paths with the sect, and the group's leadership had already concluded the purpose of the Special Task Force was to harass them directly. In the weeks following this encounter on the road to the cemetery, Yusuf made a series of bloodcurdling speeches, circulated through the north on tapes and DVDs and over Bluetooth connections, calling on Muslims to "come to Jihad":

> What we are facing now is a new catastrophe, like the one Allah told us: *And fear a trial which will not strike those who have wronged among you exclusively and know that Allah is severe in penalty*. In Nigeria in the north in particular there were many catastrophes like the organised war against the Muslims by the Christian group in Nigeria, with the help of the infidel government of this country [...] they killed thousands of Muslims, burned their money, kidnapped their daughters and forced them to do bad things. Now they come up with a new system in the Borno Maiduguri Area. The ruler of that area, who is an infidel, unjust and a renegade person, did not rule according to what Allah has sent. He brought massive amounts of infidels who do not love Islam, the Muslims, the Islamic outfits or any of the Islamic symbols such as the turban, the miswak (tooth stick) and pocket sized Islamic guides. They hit our Muslim brothers with whips and sticks. During the previous week they shot our brothers with bullets, they injured 20 brothers while they were heading to the cemetery for a funeral of three people who died because of a car accident, as well as a child that was dead too.[4]

"Those, O Muslims, are our real enemies" Yusuf said, "should we let them do that to Muslims?"

In another speech he said:

> If Muslims stop doing Jihad, become weak, and accept those infidel laws, it would be a *fitna* (chaos) in this earth and huge corruption like what is happening now. These infidels on the other hand, would continue to occupy the land of the Muslims. Because of that Allah ordered Muslims to be prepared. [...] [This preparation] includes also the material preparation such as learning shooting, buying rifles, bombs as well as training the Islamic soldiers to fight the infidels. You should sacrifice your souls, your homes, your cars and your motorcycles for the sake of Allah.[5]

The state government in Bauchi responded to these speeches by ordering the police to raid their farm, capturing hundreds of members and killing several in the process. The leadership of the sect in the Ibn Taymiyyah mosque compound at Railway in Maiduguri prepared for the arrival of the police and military.

When they came, the police laid siege to the sect's headquarters. "They did not engage us fully, but tried to provoke us, driving along the side of the compound in a jeep," Abu Dujana told me. "We waited until we had our chance and then we took it".

The sect broke out of their encirclement and rampaged through the streets of Maiduguri for four days, engaging police and army in running battles. As well as killing police and military officers, they killed scores of civilians caught out in the open, slaughtering them like rams, cutting open their throats and spilling their blood on the ground.

As the JTF reestablished control of the town, Mohammed Yusuf was captured by the military. They interrogated him in front of journalists who filmed it on their camera-phones. The military then handed Yusuf over to the police. Within minutes, Yusuf was dead. Shot—the police said—whilst trying to escape. Nobody believed them. Policemen were said to have emptied their magazines into his corpse as it lay in the yard of the force headquarters. His bullet-ridden body was displayed to journalists, who snapped pictures.

This was the beginning of the violence that has left thousands upon thousands of people dead and at least one and a half million people displaced, scattered from their homes, with no end in sight.

Even before independence, the north's most prominent universities in Kano and Zaria, like universities across Africa, had developed reputations for left-wing radicalism. During the military era of the 1980s and 1990s they were perpetually teetering on the edge of crisis. Long faculty and student strikes were common, as were frequent clashes with the security services in which students were shot dead. Student unions were at the forefront of democracy campaigns, with the full support of their professors. The military rulers also promoted reactionary cult groups on campuses, disrupting the peace and sowing deeper chaos.

The chiefs of the military governments of Ibrahim Babangida, and afterwards General Sani Abacha, faced a problem; where to send their own children for higher education? This problem became more acute following the annulled election in 1993 and the continuation of military rule. By 1995 Nigeria's pariah status had reached its zenith with the execution of the Niger Delta activist Ken Saro-Wiwa. Places for the sons and daughters of elite families in overseas universities were harder to come by, and to pay for.

Instead many of the high-ranking government officials settled on sending their children to Unimaid, the University of Maiduguri, a small university in the heartland of the Kanuri ethnic group, of which Head of State General Abacha was a member.

"We had everyone there," an alumnus of Unimaid during the late 1990s told me, "name a high official and their sons and daughters were here. They used to have competitions to name the King of Campus, the king was the student who could spend the most in a week: cars, parties, alcohol, gambling, girls, nothing was off limits," said the former student, who didn't want to be named.[6] There was a rumour (which persists to this day) that the runway at

Maiduguri airport was lengthened for use by larger planes, to meet demand for direct flights from North East Nigeria to Switzerland and South Africa, where the jet-set visited their banks and hosted parties.

The excesses of this young elite were marked with rituals of display that celebrated their wealth; particularly fashionable was "naira spray", a form of celebration popularised during the oil boom of the 1970s and often seen at weddings and festivals. In order to honour a talented musician, a fine dancer or a pretty girl, a man of means approaches and scatters a rain of currency over the object of their approval. Notes, the fresher the better, will stick to their skin, coat their clothes and form a carpet for their feet. When the wad is finished the recipient can bend down and pick it all up.

"These young men would compete to see how much money they could spray, they would just spray girls with money, dollars or pounds," the former Unimaid student, who is now a middle-ranking civil servant, said. "When I think of the sacrifices my father made for me when I was that age..." He shook his head.

These stories would have been well known by all of the university cohort and beyond. They were not secrets; quite the opposite; they were acts of conspicuous abandon designed to be spoken of. This was the fetishisation of money, the magic of sudden wealth.[7]

To some this was as clear an example of the injustice and outright paganism at the heart of the infidel state as it was possible to get. Some young disaffected students and university drop-outs gravitated toward the youth wing of the Salafist group at a mosque in Maiduguri. This included the younger scions of the wealthy and prominent families, among them the nephew to the governor of the neighbouring Yobe state, the son of the state secretary of Borno and five sons of a prominent and wealthy businessman who made his money through state contracts.[8] They were likely aware of, if not on first name terms with, the "Kings of Campus". They were drawn to the Salafists, who preached that such spiritual corruption was the cause of Borno's ills. Many of them burned their university certificates when they joined.[9]

Such disgust at excess amongst poverty was not exclusive to Unimaid, but in the north east there was an individual who had become adept at spotting and shepherding the young men of the local elite to him, a man who saw the potential in sweeping up these young radicals to add to his following, a man named Mohammed Yusuf.

Yusuf had been travelling around the north east, preaching, making connections and winning a following at least since the mid-1990s. He was affiliated with the Izala salafists and moved in those circles, actively trying to convert Christian communities in southern Borno as early as 1996.[10] Yusuf drew people to him with his charismatic preaching. Abu Dujana said when Yusuf spoke, members felt he was revealing "the truth"; things about their faith that they did not know, or that they had been deceived about. Yusuf's radical ideas about the infidel nature of the state of Nigeria sparked with many people he met.

He promised paradise in the hereafter and a way to get there. He gave fiery orations at mosques and debated other Islamic scholars on local television and radio. He talked about a great lack of justice as defined by the Qur'an and Hadith in Nigeria, and he offered only one way this could be corrected.

Yusuf and his closest associates were from poor backgrounds. According to supporters, Yusuf grew up an *Almajiri*, living on the street begging bowl in hand. But by the early 2000s he had found a place as a leader of the youth wing of a Salafist group in the orbit of Maiduguri's popular Alhaji Muhammadu Ndimi mosque.

Yusuf's credo has been collected in a book, named *This is our doctrine and our method in proselytization* which was published just before the 2009 uprising. It was a response to a conflict between the group and the Izala in Maiduguri. Yusuf had decried Izala as heretics, in thrall to the infidel state. Izala in return had branded Yusuf's sect as *khawarij*, meaning a misguided, extremist, faction of Muslims, the like of which the Prophet Muhammad foresaw would arise after his death. This represented a definite split between the Izala and Yusuf, who at one stage had been associated with the society. Before the violence of 2009 there were sporadic clashes, almost a gang war, between Izala and Yusuf's supporters in Maiduguri.

The title of Yusuf's book deliberately echoes the titles of similar treatises by Sunni preachers, like Sheikh Gumi's *The Right Faith According to the Sharia*, perhaps in order to lend his ideas credence. While the two clerics share a revulsion for secularism, Mohammed Yusuf went further than his predecessor in his strident anti-state rhetoric. In the book he quotes extensively from Saudi clerics who proclaimed in *fatwas* that "legislation is only for Allah". Mohammed Yusuf wrote:

> However, democracy says that the "rule is by the people" hence there are no objections against being ruled by an unbeliever or a hypocrite or an immoral person under the umbrella of the democratic system, and this entails great danger and immense evil for all that it includes. Therefore we hereby affirm and assent that democracy is a tughut [idolatory] that should not be believed in and should be refused.[11]

The simple truth that Yusuf told his followers was this: anyone participating in the democratic system is an unbeliever, and bound only for hell. Further, Muslims who participated in any form of democratic system were apostates and should therefore be killed by faithful Muslims. This is *takfir*, the belief that a group of Muslims can be "false" and therefore deserving of death. Indeed their killing is said by takfiri ideologues, including Ibn Taymiyyah, to be an obligation on the faithful.

The wellspring of corruption, Yusuf concluded, was the education system put in place during and after colonial rule by Christian Britain. In a chapter titled "The foreign western colonial schools: their poisons, harms and dangers to the nation" it is written:

> Many people have fallen in love with these western schools because of their love for *dunya* [worldly affairs] turning a blind eye to Islamic law. Sometimes they call it a necessity, at other times they differentiate between missionary and state schools. This signifies their ignorance of colonial history and the blasphemous schools, because when they began they had no teachers but the missionaries [...] When the colonisers left they also left Muslims with their disbelief, which they induced. Citizens taught these sciences that the colonisers came with, without any difference neither through addition nor omission. This is Christianization in itself.[12]

Yusuf's book was itself not widely circulated while he was alive. The academic Adam Higazi, who obtained a copy from an Imam in Jos, has found Yusuf's ideas were plucked wholesale from the writings of a small, hard-line group of Saudi clerics, some of whom were active when Yusuf was in the kingdom between 2003 and 2004. Much of the content of Mohammed Yusuf's book is simply copied out of pamphlets by these writers. Higazi found that the work is full of errors; Yusuf misidentifies the suras he quotes from. The work also lacks any critical evaluation of the texts he quotes.

Unoriginal and uncritical they may have been, but Yusuf's words were powerful. His main mode of transmission was through orations which he gave in many towns around the north east. He was adaptable in his approach, preaching on market days rather than on Fridays as usually acceptable by Islamic authorities—an adaption of practice that angered the Izala.

His speeches ranged from crazed topic to crazed topic. He ranted about how Hindus in India killed Muslims with impunity. He ranted about Jews and how the Jews and Christians treated Muslims in other countries. He ranted about a particular devilish apparition that haunted him which he called "this Lugard"—as if the British colonial Governor were still there sitting in his Kaduna residence. The British destroyed the state Othman dan Fodiyo created, Yusuf said. They killed Muslims, destroyed their mosques, burned their *shahada* flag and urinated on the Qur'an.[13]

He picked up followers from the urban and rural poor, tradespeople and the "informal sector", street hawkers, cobblers, blacksmiths, knife sharpeners, tailors.

"I was a carpenter before I met Mohammed Yusuf," Abu Dujana told me and Abdullahi Kaura in 2011. "I was happy in my ignorance of the true religion. But now I am so glad that Allah did not take my life before I discovered the truth".

The "truth" that Yusuf imparted was that the only legitimate way to live life was left to the world by Mohammed in the form of the Qur'an and the Hadith, and that deviating from those had caused the ummah, the Muslim community, to become irredeemably corrupt. This stripping back of everything to an avowed stance on first principles of Islam allowed Yusuf to dispense with any and all objections to his credo. It has been noted that in his debates with other scholars, who were also Salafis, they shy away from tackling him on his interpretation of the back-to-basics approach and concentrated on debating the narrower issue of the legitimacy of Western education. These debates, although meant to disarm Yusuf, may have led a section of society to identify with him more strongly.[14]

In the years before the 2009 uprising, Mohammed Yusuf concentrating on growing his community through *da'wah*—proselytization—and conversion. So sucessful was the group that observers were shocked at the speed and efficacy of the conversion process. Habila Pudza, from Chibok in southern Borno, told me that his uncle was converted from Christianity by the group, much to the entire family's surprise.

Anthropologist Gerhard Müller-Kosack said that a village which he had spent most of his career studying changed "virtually overnight". People of the remote settlement in the Mandara mountains, south eastern Borno, near the border with Cameroon, adopted the signs of devout piety, changing their behaviour over a very short period. When he visited for the last time in 2008, what surprised him most were the women: "Suddenly they were there in the full covering. It was the women at the forefront of the change," he said.[15] During their years in the remote village, high up a mountain, Müller-Kosack and his wife had started a school. He had collected donations from friends and colleagues to buy textbooks. The last time he visited he found the school abandoned; "All the books had been burned; the young women, it was they who made a pile of them and burned them in front of the school."

The speed of the spread of this Islamic fervency troubled many. Pudza told me that his community explained that the rapid and irresistible transmission of the message was put down to other, more mysterious, means; a common story was that the group gave out dates which were enchanted, tainted with cursed blood. As soon as someone ate the date, the story went, they were possessed.

Yusuf was able to move between the many levels of Maiduguri's social worlds. As well as finding adherents among the disaffected youth and the urban poor, his message resonated with the wealthy.

Maiduguri has always been an important trading post, an entrepot city-state where dealers in all kinds of produce, legal and illegal, are based. Its proximity with the borders of three other countries makes it an excellent hub for these businessmen to exploit the arbitrage created by differing state interventions in markets for products like fertiliser, kerosene, diesel and petrol. Trade in Maiduguri's thrumming markets is considerable; smoked stockfish, hand-sized soot-blackened river fish curled and skewered five to a stick, chili peppers, beans and grains, edible oils and meat are all profitable. Trade was so lucrative that even the hours of daylight could not confine them. In 2011 Maiduguri's night markets hopped with life. People came out in at night to browse the food markets freely, among tall piles of spicy deep-fried locusts, or roasted red-billed qelea—tiny sparrowlike birds cooked and sold by the weight in wraps of paper, translucent with grease and eaten whole, skeleton and all.

Agricultural commodities have made the trading elite of Maiduguri a lot of money. The traders are mostly Kanuri speakers, the largest ethno-linguistic group in the north east. These are "new men", somewhat independent of the old Borno aristocracy but, as Kanuris, also unconnected to the Hausa-Fulani establishments of Kano and Sokoto. Much as other burgeoning business elites had been drawn to the Izala since its emergence in the 1970s, some of their number gravitated to Yusuf's Salafist group. Their belief was fervent, their need to purify their soul in preparation for entry into paradise was an imperative for these wealthy men.

According to people familiar with these markets, at least two prominent Kanuri traders fought and died with Yusuf in the 2009 Maiduguri uprising.[16] A third fled with his family after the military crackdown and has since lost all his property to the government.

These were men who had been successful in a world that straddled both illegal and legal markets, a liminal place that has been called "the informal sector" but which upon closer inspection appears to be the core of economic life in the Chad Basin.[17]

Another prominent businessman linked to Yusuf was a director of the northern-focused media group The Media Trust, a man named Mustapha Bello Damagum. In 2007 he was arrested along with Mohammed Yusuf by the Nigerian State Security Service and charged under prevention of terrorism laws. As part of a programme to put young men through Qur'anic education they had funded a number of young boys to go to a Qur'anic school in Mauritania. The boys absconded form the school and presented themselves at the US embassy in Nouakshott claiming they were being trained to be in al-Qaeda. The security services accused Yusuf and Damagum of sending a number of boys abroad for "terrorist training". Damagum has always protested his innocence of the charges saying he was performing his religious duty to help poor young men learn their religion. He was later bailed and the charges were never brought to court.

According to former business associates of Damagum's with whom I spoke, he remains undoubtedly a Salafist by nature.

"He will not even talk to you," I was told when I asked for an introduction.[18] "He is not interested in persuading or debate. He will not feel he has to explain himself to the likes of you. He has lost a lot by being in the public eye and is very bitter. Even me, he thinks of me as being involved in that other world, the one of worldly corruption."

It has been said that Mohammed Yusuf 's preaching was non-violent. This is not true, as speeches from the time show. They reveal that he was espousing a violent ideology from early on, as in this lecture from 2006:

> In this da'wah we agreed that we are going to suffer like Bilal who was dragged to the ground, just like Ammar Ibn Yasir was tortured, just like a spear was thrust into Summayyah's vagina, these are trials that are awaiting, these are the hurdles we want to cross. Anyone who dies in the process goes to Paradise.[19]

In 2007 Yusuf's former teacher, Sheikh Ja'afar Mahmud Adam, himself an ardent Salafist, had gone on record to denounce the group and warn that these ideologues were heading for a violent confrontation with the state. In April that year, on the eve of the general elections, Ja'afar was shot dead as he prayed in a mosque in Kano, it is thought by members of Yusuf's sect. With hindsight, this murder was probably the turning point that made violence in 2009 inevitable.

In the lead up to the 2009 uprising, after the indignity he felt over the motorcycle incident, Yusuf told followers:

> "This Jihad, and those Jihadists, will be rewarded by Allah. Their reward will be their victory over their enemies [...] The Jihad for the sake of Allah and protecting

the borders for the sake of Allah have a great reward. Jihad cannot be done without guarding, protecting and martyrdom operations. Islam needs your bodies and your money."[20]

When I spoke to Abu Dujana in February 2011, I asked him if his group were prepared to send people as suicide attackers, something they had not yet done. He replied: "It is God's will that we shall do this soon." Four months later the group made good on this promise.

In June, under cover of darkness, Mohammed Manga, a 35-year-old commercial driver set out from a camp near Maiduguri for the capital Abuja. In his car was an explosive device prepared by the the people who sheltered jihadists on the run, after their uprising was put down in 2009. This is believed to be either al-Qaeda in the Islamic Maghreb who were then in camps in the Sahara, or Al Shabaab in Somalia, a few days journey east by the old overland Hajj route. He drove into the police headquarters, right past the sentries and up to the front door, usually a busy throng of activity. When he detonated the bomb, five people were killed and over a hundred injured.

Manga was not a poor man, a spokesman for the group said, as reported by the journalist Ahmed Salkida. Manga left his widow and five children an inheritance of N4m (c. £16,000), no small amount. To prove his veracity, the spokesman sent the journalist Salkida a picture of Manga. He is waving as he gets into the car, the cheerfulness of his benign smile undiminished by the AK-47 he holds in his left hand.

"He was calm and never showed fear" the group's spokesman told Salkida. He added that everyone was envious of Manga, "wishing it was their chance to act and gain entry into paradise".[21]

They followed up this mission with another a few weeks later, in August 2011, detonating a huge bomb-laden car in the driveway of the United Nations building in Abuja. At least twenty-one people were slain and scores wounded.[22]

In his preaching Mohammed Yusuf made several references to sayings or texts concerning the day of resurrection. He speaks of the joy the fighter for Jihad feels to die in battle only to be resurrected again and again and again to continue the fight. Yusuf told followers just before the insurrection of 2009 that the true Muslim must "purify his heart", he added:

> Doing this would help him to face the serious matters, and the most important things which should be taken care by him. One of those things is establishing the right spirit for Jihad in himself as well as the meanings of the well, the seriousness and the patience in his mind, heart and feelings; especially in this era, the era of infidelity, where Muslims are no longer ruling the Islamic countries, nor Muslims. The Sun of Islam has faded and the unjust people became the rulers.[23]

Yusuf's use of the phrase "era of infidelity" is significant. The group's own internal myth-making, the things they tell each other to bind themselves together are hidden from those looking in from outside. Nevertheless in Yusuf's form of Islamic rebellion, the notion that the world is ending had traction. By the "era of infidelity" he is referring to is a period where the rule of the world is held by *kuffar* (*arne* in Hausa), unbelievers, and the justness of Islam is ignored. Yusuf told his followers that the world has been turned on its head and what is wrong lauded as what is right condemned.

"There is great *fitna*, widespread within the Islamic nations" he says in another speech. Fitna is rebellion against God's law, strife, chaos and misrule. This condition of the world has a particular significance in Islamic eschatology. Widespread fitna is one of the signs of an impending day of judgement, of the arrival of Yajuj and Majuj. The end times are upon us, Yusuf was saying, and the only course is "to wage war until Islam prevails".[24]

There is no known evidence that Yusuf and the group that remained after his death are what Lugard might call "Mahdists", in the way that rebellious groups in the past believed the Mahdi was coming or could even be brought into the world by an emigration of the faithful. This is perhaps because Mahdism was misunderstood by the British colonial government, who labelled any Islamic radical Mahdist. It may also be that the core ideologues of today's group, with their Salafist roots, view Mahdism as a concept derived from *bid'a*, the innovations of the hated Sufi brotherhoods. They may only talk about it among themselves and the outside world has yet to hear about it.

But when I asked Abu Dujana in Maiduguri what they hoped to achieve by their violence, he said: "We are not looking at the practicality of it, we are motivated by fighting those who don't believe in Allah and the day of Judgement. We will fight people until they believe that God is the only God and Mohammed is his last messenger. Jihad should be done until the end."[25]

This sense of an end is an apocalyptic resonance which sounds deep within the ideological core of the group. There are zealots among them who believe their violence will be rewarded by Allah with victory and that the violence itself will being about, not only a personal entry into Paradise for the fallen, but also bring on the end times and the longed-for day of Judgement. In pursuit of this, compromised Muslim rulers are deserving of death; Muslim civilians too. Boko Haram has slaughtered hundreds even as they pray in mosques because of this takfiri ideology.

It is clear that from the very beginning he was preparing his followers for violence. Among the first generation of followers there were many ideologues willing to unleash violence on the state, innocent civilians, the Muslim establishment and anyone they declared to be kuffar unbelievers. They came from all levels of society, they formed a "counter elite", alienated by resentment over what they saw as years of compromise to the worldly rule of the state. Where in the past there had been compromise with Nigeria's federalism, these men still dreamed of a sharia wonderland on earth, and believed it would come to Nigeria through a war of unending bloody slaughter.

The group's previous experience however, had shown that zealotry alone was not enough. Before the 2009 uprising, the Salafists associated with the Ndimi Mosque in Maiduguri had already made one disastrous attempt at creating an Islamic state. In 2003 a man named Muhammad Ali, tired of Yusuf's slow approach to building a movement, led a band of 200 young men and women (including the sons of some of the prominent citizens) out into what they thought was the wilderness to start society anew. They ended up in the borderlands of Yobe state, near the dry river bed between Nigeria and the Republic of Niger, at a place called Kanamma. They were determined to shun the corrupted world and create a new state of Islamic purity.

This group of aggressive, contumacious, iconoclastic city-dwellers soon came into conflict with the people who already lived in the place they tried to settle. Indeed, conflict was what they sought. They dug defensive preparations in a wooded grove near a water source. They raided local police stations and government buildings to get weapons and to provoke a reaction, which they duly received.[26] After a brief siege the military overran and destroyed their camp. The group were mostly wiped out. A few survivors escaped north over the border, where some can still be found in towns on the Niger side of the border. Others slunk back to Maiduguri.

The military crackdown on the sect attracted attention internationally because the group dubbed themselves "the Nigerian Taliban"—a name which appeared in the local media. But at the time the US embassy concluded there were no links to al-Qaeda.[27]

Mohammed Yusuf had not joined this failed attempt at creating a new Islamic state. After it was crushed, feeling the heat of the authorities, he put himself into self-imposed exile to escape accusations he had something to do with the Kanamma uprising. While in Saudi Arabia it is thought he made links with like-minded Salafi preachers and secured their support. But after a year, he was back in Maiduguri.

On his return, in 2005, Yusuf began re-building his community, this time establishing a mosque and compound in the Railway district of Maiduguri, where he bought land with the help of his father-in-law. This location was key to the group's new incarnation. Instead of stumbling out of the city to a rural place to locate his community, Yusuf stayed in the state capital.

By embedding themselves in the town rather than moving out to the wilderness, the community were able to avail themselves of many more avenues for recruitment and funding.

Maiduguri has in recent years seen its population rise dramatically, the academic Mohammed Kabir Isa of Ahmadu Bello University Zaria says. He has studied the factors contributing to the rise of religious conflict in the north east in programmes sponsored by the United Kingdom's DFID and the British Council. Population dynamics, and particularly shifts in response to the changing environment are significant, Isa said. Desertification is a big problem; the desert is encroaching into farmland by as much as a kilometre a year. Lake Chad, intimately connected with many livelihoods from farming to fishing, is drying up, the water receding toward the border with Chad. The north of the state has always been the most populated, he says, and the constriction of land resources there has, over the last decade, sparked an exodus to the city. According to Isa, before the Boko Haram crisis, local government civil servants thought around 30–35 per cent of the population of Borno State was in Maiduguri:

"It was very densely populated [...] with people who live in areas which are not well laid out, no running gutters, no clinics, no police stations...

"When they come to the city in search of livelihood, the bubble bursts, and they realise there's nothing there. That's when they become easy prey for militant organsiations."[28]

By the end of 2008 the group was operating like "a state within a state";[29] they had their own institutions like a shura council that made decisions and a religious police who enforced discipline. They had a rudimentary welfare system, offered jobs working the land they had acquired in Bauchi and they even gave microfinance loans to members to start entrepreneurial endeavours. Many used the money to buy motorcycles and worked as *achaba*. The group also arranged marriages between members, which many of the poorest could not afford in normal life.[30] Rather than stick out as disobedient aliens, as Ali had done at Kanamma, Yusuf and his people could swim with Maiduguri's social currents, and the community grew as it pulled in the needy.

The Ibn Taymiyyah mosque had been allowed to continue to function because of a deal that Yusuf, the vociferous anti-state iconoclast, had struck with the government. The deal between the state deputy governor and Yusuf had been brokered in Saudi Arabia by leading Salafi Sheikh Ja'afar Mahmud Adam. Yusuf promised that he had nothing to do with the group in Kanamma and would never again preach violent Jihad. But in the years following he ignored this pledge and was be picked up by the security services several times, only to be swiftly released. This led some observers to conclude that he had high level backing from the Governor of Borno, Ali Modu Sherif.[31]

Both Sherif and Yusuf believed that they both might benefit from their association. What Yusuf wanted from Sherif was guarantees of a stronger sharia, a better commitment to a hard line on God's divine law; what Sherif wanted was to win re-election.

Sherif courted Yusuf, providing a lucrative position in the state religious affairs ministry to one of the group's most zealous members, a man named Buji Foi. It is thought that through this, the group accessed state patronage directly. For Modu Sherif, in the quest to "remain relevant" it would have been unwise to reject, discard or fight openly such a potent force as Mohammed Yusuf and his group. At least until he could be completely sure that it could not be bent to his own will.[32]

Ahmed Salkida, who was the first to report on the sect and was close to Yusuf, said that right up until the final days before the rising, even with the vitriol Yusuf spat at Modu Sherif, calling him an "infidel" and calling for his death, Yusuf still believed that a deal could be done with the state and Modu Sherif would come around to their uncompromising point of view. But by that stage Modu Sherif had been backed into a corner. Questions still hang over the speed with which Yusuf was dispatched by the police, and who exactly Yusuf's silencing served. Foi was also murdered by the police mopping up after the 2009 uprising. They stood him in the road and he held his hands to his face and prayed before they mowed him down in a hail of gunfire. A film of his execution remains on YouTube.[33] Also murdered was Mohammed Yusuf's father-in-law Babbafugu Mohammed. Horrified at what was happening during the sect's rampage he had reportedly gone to the security services with an offer to act as a go between to stop the violence. He was never seen again.

After Yusuf's death, the loyalty of his lieutenants to his vision sustained the group in hiding. Under a new leader, Yusuf's second-in-command Abubakar Shekau, their first priority was revenge. The police were the first targets, picked off at their checkpoints in hit and run attacks for their weapons. Higher-ranking police officers were assassinated in their homes, as were local politicians and traditional rulers.

After the uprising, the authorities had seized property belonging to the members of the group. It had been parcelled out to traditional leaders as reward for pointing out members in the days after the 2009 insurrection, when hundreds of men accused of being sympathisers of the sect were extra-judicially executed.

The group were coming back to murder people they branded "enemies", robbing them of what they called "spoils of war", booty that belonged to the jihadi as sanctioned by the Qur'an.

This looting quickly turned to other targets, only tenuously involved in the 2009 conflict, or not involved at all. In 2011 Maiduguri experienced an upsurge in armed robberies of some specific, strategically useful targets. Waiting for an aeroplane from Abuja to Maiduguri in 2011 Abdullahi Kaura and I were told by a man that his friend, a pharmacist, had been robbed and murdered in his shop just days before. As well as cash, his entire stock of medicines was also taken. Our informant said his friend was not the first pharmacist to be robbed in that manner.

Abu Dujana made it clear how comfortable he was with twisting his avowed principles to the expedient circumstances:

"All we know is that Islam caused us to wage Jihad," he said, "if you kill a person anything that has belonged to him has become *ghanima* [the spoils of war], and is halal for you. Anyone whose property we have taken must have been helping the government we are fighting."

Between 2011 and 2014 it seemed that Boko Haram went from the tattered remnants of a radical group to a fully fettered terrorist outfit within a short period.

They struck at will across the north east and beyond, unleashing a bombing campaign that hit Maiduguri, Jos, Kano, Kaduna and the capital Abuja. They launched devastating co-ordinated bomb and gun attacks on the security services in Kano. They attacked churches, universities and schools, bus stations and markets, killing thousands of people.

In 2013 the government declared a state of emergency across the north east. In Maiduguri, the military and police enforced a tight curfew allowing civilians outside for only a few hours. Many people, especially those from so-called "settler" communities—mostly Christians, migrants from other parts of the country who were never considered indigenes no matter how long they had lived in the north east, left the city. A film by a BBC reporter working undercover showed devastated streets, burned out cars and empty or looted businesses.[34] Even with the military presence, Boko Haram had the run of the city, and de facto control of most of Maiduguri.

The expansion of Boko Haram, the growth in the numbers of people necessary to carry out such widespread and varied attacks, is now thought by observers to point to an encompassing of virtually all violence under the "Boko Haram" umbrella. Violence that was not necessarily connected to the core of the group, its shura council of Emirs, was assumed by observers lacking any true way of verification, to be part of a Boko Haram campaign.[35]

"This is a time when someone can just walk into a village, shout 'Allahu Ackbar!' fire a gun in the air, and everyone runs away… it's impossible to say who is 'real' and who is not, the concept ceases to be meaningful," Mohammed Kyari, Vice Chancellor of Modibbo Abba Technology University and a long-time observer of Boko Haram told me.

Simultaneously, Boko Haram is thought to have opened its doors to other pre-existing criminal networks, the armed robbers, like the 'Yan Kalare or the Sara Suta, to operate under its auspices. In preceding years, the Nigerian retail banking sector had seen great reform. Fewer people travelled with large amounts of money between cities, or stored it in their homes, as they had done before. Now money was held in protected banks and ATM machines, this made it harder for armed robbery syndicates. But when Boko Haram emerged, suddenly it seemed that banks were being robbed all over the north east.

It is thought the main group of political thugs in Borno, known by the name Ecomog (but unconnected to the peacekeeping operation) were absorbed into Boko Haram. Previously these men, who were used by Sherif to strong-arm elections and chase away opponents' rallies, had not been known for their Islamist dogma as much as their cultish beliefs; in spirits that could make fighters bulletproof or invulnerable to harm. The attraction of being able to loot and rob with impunity under the banner of Jihad, and as people fled Boko Haram's ferocious reputation, was obvious.

In 2014, with the help of local militias known as the Civilian Joint Task Force, Boko Haram members were driven from their hideouts in Maiduguri in what was the first major reversal since their return in 2010. These vigilante groups joined forces with the military to scour communities where it was suspected Boko Haram sympathisers were hiding the group. Many were brutally killed by the vigilantes. It seemed that the vigilantes were at times even directing the military at points, the lines of command blurring.[36]

As Boko Haram fled the city for the second time, stories began leaking out about the places they had been hiding. People in Maiduguri said they found evidence of strange rituals, shrines and more; body parts, corpses and jerry cans and bottles filled with blood, some of them labelled "virgin".[37] In the time since, other stories of cultist behaviour have emerged; survivors who fled incarceration in some Boko Haram camps say that they were subjected to cannibalistic rituals. Their captors were full-blooded cultists, they say, who used juju and charms to make themselves invulnerable, to walk through the bush "like ghosts".[38]

As Boko Haram used the Qur'anic injunctions surrounding the spoils of war to entice armed robbers into their fold, they also expand their conflict by exploiting pre-existing chauvinistic hatred within communities across the north.

The group's first large scale bomb attacks had been in Jos, the religiously divided city and location of a number of "inter-communal crises" where Muslim and Christians have killed one another in successive riots. Boko Haram had hoped to wreak revenge against the Christian Berom community, who held the reins of state power at the time and whose people had been filmed eating the barbecued flesh of Muslims following a bloody clash between the communities in 2011.[39]

The first bombings of churches occurred in the Bukuru area of Jos South, the heartland of the Berom whose man, Jonah Jang, held the position of Governor. The first reports were very cautiously worded by Nigerian newspapers all too aware of the conflagration that could be caused by reprisal attacks. Boko Haram wanted to insert themselves into that conflict and spark a war between Muslim and Christian. This was a tactic they expanded across the north east.

After they had been pushed out of Maiduguri, an event Shekau would later refer to in a video as the group's "Hijra",[40] they became more like roving bandits, raiding villages across the north east taking what they wanted and sowing chaos in their wake. They raided the fringes of Lake Chad and around the Mandara Mountains, and the Sambisa forest, areas of rough and difficult terrain, whose paths are now laced with booby traps.

Where Boko Haram raided and who they subjected to their violence closely resembles the patterns of raiding in the disputed territories of the nineteenth and early twentieth century.[41] Violence was done to people who had been the victims of raids on pagan communities in the past. Where the latter had been subjected to long histories of slave raiding they were more likely to have resisted Islam. These communities in turn were more likely to have taken up Christianity when it came to north east Nigeria during the colonial era, but in some places this did not begin until the 1970s. In many of these communities adoption of Christianity was a form of resistance to hegemonic Islam. Now Boko Haram's violence was directed against the figureheads of communities that had long histories of disputes with Muslim communities.

The motives underlying these conflicts were land, lineage, inheritance, control of the resources of patrimony. Land usage and ownership is complicated, as for generations a family might farm an area, investing their energy into the land, without actually owning it. They may derive their rights from tradition, word of mouth handed down from one generation to the next. Conflict over such ad hoc agreements is common. The festering resentment was further enabled by an absence of trust in institutions like courts or local government to mediate such disputes. Ethnic politics gives communities some protection, with the larger community usually able to exert their will over others.

Boko Haram's victims were often Christians, especially in southern Borno, where churches were bombed and congregations slaughtered, pastors and local traditional rulers assassinated.[42]

To the east of the Mandara Mountains is a fertile lowland plain which supports several villages and towns before you reach the twisting river that forms the border with Cameroon. It is host to a large Christian population who control large amounts of land, albeit in a part of Nigeria where state power is mostly just a rumour.

In late 2013 Boko Haram came down from the mountains and over-ran these towns, chasing all the Christians away. Survivors in internally displaced people's camps in Adamawa told academic Adam Higazi that the Muslim population aided Boko Haram in rooting out the Christians, killing the young men and burning down their families' property. As the Christians fled, survivors told Higazi, their Muslim neighbours cheered.[43]

Boko Haram built a great following in the Mandara Mountains themselves. The anthropologist Gerhard Müller-Kosack, who has spent a long time studying the montagnard people of the region, thinks that the swiftness of Boko Haram's takeover owes a great deal to the social conditions engendered by the region's history.

In the aftermath of the First World War, he contends, when the British took over this area from the Germans, the colonial authorities picked some of the mountain people and elevated them to be local leaders. These emirs were handpicked by the colonial power, as Lugard had done after his campaign against the Sokoto Caliphate. This new elite were, to some degree, romanticised by the British as hardy mountain people, much as the British thought about the Fulani as being a more "noble race" of African. The newly empowered elite came down from the mountains and based itself in Gwoza where its leaders, replete with the trappings of power given them by the colonialists, sat in courts over the inhabitants on the plains. But mountain life lent itself to a large number of smaller communities, many and diverse identities. The people who had been empowered did not represent all of the montagnards.

One of the largest of these groups were the Dgwheɗe. "They have a long history of conflict with the Gwoza elite," says Müller-Kosack. The Dgwheɗe were independent and had a strong sense of their own identity and had continued to refuse to come down from the mountains, he said. This resistance was seized on by the Gwoza elite as "uncivilised behaviour" which coloured their attitude toward the mountain people since. "They were looked down on by the others" said Müller-Kosack. "They were stigmatised by the emirs in Gwoza as idiots who didn't want to come down the hill." They were marginalised and came off the worse in the conflicts over who had what rights to land and the disbursement of government patronage.

In the early 2000s the mountains were hit by a new wave of religious fervour, with Izala at the crest. "I noticed that, particularly among the young people, because they had been stigmatised as idiots, this new religiosity gave them a new identity, it served them quite well. They became purists," Müller-Kosack said. "There was a great degree of opportunism about it."

The young people were particularly exposed to this as they had been the ones who left their mountain communities and gone to Maiduguri to search for work. After generations of not wanting to be Muslims, the situation was totally reversed. "Suddenly within a year or two everything changed," according to Müller-Kosack "You would see it at funerals, and particularly the women, all the young women would be wearing their Islamic dress, and there were only a few grandmothers who wore the leaves around their waists."

Islam presented a powerful new identity that a group could use. Perhaps their generation would be different, would hold new power, over their enemies, the entitled Gwoza elites. "There was a very opportunistic motive for this, to shed this stigmatisation, to create a sense of belonging, to shed this mountain backwardness," said Müller-Kosack.

In the words of Yusuf's teachings, they found an Islam that said the traditional heads of the religion were unbelievers, worthy of death. These Dgwheɗe members of Boko Haram were said to be among the most fanatical fighters during the Maiduguri insurrection of 2009, reportedly running headlong into police fusillades, holding only knives and machetes.[44]

In 2009 when Müller-Kosack visited the village he had lived in and studied, he discovered that things had drastically changed. Before he had been very popular, thought of as the village's own white man. But when he returned he discovered his house had been burned down. One of his friends came to him and told him that his son had been killed in the 2009 Maiduguri uprising.

He doesn't believe that Yusuf sparked this up-swell in religious fervour, but that he somehow harnessed a zeitgeist. And after the crackdown in 2009 his remaining followers were aided by the ones among them who had come down from the mountains.

"Boko Haram came to the hills to hide in the caves," Müller-Kosack said, "the ones who joined Yusuf in Maiduguri led them there and they hid in the caves, much as their forefathers had done when they were hiding from slave raiders right up until the 1920s".

The Dgwheɗe were by no means the only community to join Yusuf. As the group grew, their ability to draw more people to them increased, with the broadening range of ethnic and kinship ties. Once some people joined, they got their friends and relations in too. A persuasive force drawing others in was the promise of a new identity this new sect granted, and potentially the ability to settle long-held scores and grievances.

In other places Boko Haram simply recruited people to fight for them for money. In 2014 young, jobless men in Diffa, across the border in Niger, told the BBC's Thomas Fessy that they had been paid over $3,000 per mission to fight for Boko Haram in Nigeria.[45] Boko Haram insurgents, slain as they ambushed a military unit, were said to have been found with a thousand dollars in crisp notes on their bodies.[46]

"Whenever they go anywhere they break into a bank," said Atta Barkindo, a PhD researcher at SOAS, University of London.[47] He travelled through Adamawa in 2015, as the military pressed Boko Haram back. "They move with money in huge Ghana-must-go bags of cash, wherever, and with that kind of money they are able to pay [...] And that's why no matter how many members of Boko Haram are killed it always seems as if their number never dwindles."

Where intentions aligned with other people willing to doing anything for money, some confusing situations came to light. When a bomb went off at the headquarters of the Church of Christ in Nations evangelical congregation in Bauchi, close to the city of Jos in February 2012, it was thought to be the work of Boko Haram. However the escaping bombers were caught and revealed to be—by some reports—members of a rival faction of Christians involved in a financial feud with members of the bombed church.[48] It is now thought Boko Haram provided the explosives and paid them to carry out the operation.

The opportunistic search for further funds is also probably behind Boko Haram's shift in attitude toward kidnapping. In 2012 it became clear that a split had emerged in the group. It was revealed that two Western hostages had been held by a splinter group calling itself *Jama'atu Ansarul Musulmina fi Baladis Sudan* (otherwise known as Ansaru).[49] They released a manifesto saying they were rejecting Boko Haram's takfiri ideology of targeting Muslims, and instead would attack international interests in northern Nigeria, as well as the Federal Government. Negotiations for the two men's lives broke down, and Chris McManus and Franco Lamolinara were executed in the toilet of a house in Sokoto after a desperate last-ditch attempt to rescue them failed.[50]

At the time, a Boko Haram spokesman told the BBC Hausa Service that their organisation had nothing to do with the kidnapping, that they would not kidnap, that it was not their way. A year on however, things had changed. A French family visiting a Cameroonian national park near the border with Nigeria were taken on their way back to Douala when their 4x4 got stuck in mud. A few weeks later Boko Haram put out a video message saying they held the family. A ransom of about 3.5m Euros was paid and they were eventually released.[51] Other Westerners have been kidnapped: a French engineer and a French priest survived their ordeal. A group of seven engineers in a compound in Bauchi, however, were executed when the operation to seize them went wrong. The kidnapping spread. Boko Haram are also said to have taken the wife of the deputy prime minister of Cameroon's northern region and ten Chinese workers from a building project.[52]

Abubakar Shekau has become famous as the leering, ranting face of Boko Haram, or as they dubbed themselves after their return in 2010: *Jama'atu Ahlus wa Sunnah Lida'wati wal Jihad*, 'The People Dedicated to the Teachings of the Prophet and Jihad'. Shekau issued twitchy challenges to US President Barack Obama, Israeli Prime Minister Benjamin Netanyahu, French President François Hollande, Queen Elizabeth and the deceased former Tory Prime Minister, Margaret Thatcher.

In his many videos released to Western media he can be seen aping the communications of other jihadi groups, first al-Qaeda then Islamic State. Following the 2009 scattering of the Ibn Taymiyyah compound it is thought some of the group sheltered in al-Qaeda in the Islamic Maghreb training camps in Mali, or fled along the old Hajj route to Somalia where they met up with Al Shabaab. The bombing of the UN building in Abuja in 2011 was an overture to al-Qaeda's injunction to attack "the far enemy". The explosive device was one of a limited number provided by their hosts while they were on the run, according to a spokesman.[53] However, the bombing of the UN building remains the only attack on an international institution in Boko Haram's history. The dearth of other high profile foreign targets, despite many being available in Nigeria, has been read by some as evidence that the attack was possibly part of a deal with their al-Qaeda affiliated hosts during their time on the run. Once it was paid off, Boko Haram returned again to their local priorities, namely creating an Islamic state in Nigeria.[54]

"Shekau! Eat the heart of the infidels, since infidels want to disobey Allah," the grimacing man shouted in a video released in 2014.[55] In many ways he embodies the very picture of the inflexible zealot. But under his leadership, opportunism has been as important as fervour.

The north east of Nigeria is a region where the state, specifically the security a state is supposed to provide in its most basic form, was already weak and ineffective. Boko Haram have put those already weak institutions into an almost complete reverse. The consequence of this is that violence was unchecked and is now more visible, and that a new tidal wave of violence was just unmanageable. The heart of the state had already been eaten hollow. Just how thin the influence of the rule of law actually was in north east Nigeria had been painstakingly revealed to all. Many seized on this opportunity with gusto.

In the office at 'the Crack', the home of the Special Armed Robery Squad in Maiduguri, Zakariyya was finishing his account.

As a boy, Zakariyya was brought up by his grandmother. His father was not around while he was growing up and for a great part of his youth nor was his mother. This could have been because after his father divorced his mother, she married another man who wanted nothing to do with the boy. It could also have been for another reason: in Hausa the word for an independent woman, divorced with no husband, is the same word as it is for "prostitute".

After some time, Zakariyya said, his mother returned. She came back with some money, but when that ran out, he said, the family didn't have enough for Zakariyya to continue to attend school (this is likely because she had other, younger, children to care for). He had to leave school unfinished to go out hawking. Selling shoes and phone accessories he was able to take home between 2,000 or 3,000 naira a week (c £10). At twenty-two years old, Zakariyya says he is married to two wives, and has two children.

"They promised me 200,000 naira," he said "but on the first trip they only paid me N70,000 and on the second trip they gave me only N40,000."

"I was never in favour of their ideology", he said. "They threatened me, they said now that I knew what they were and who they were it is either that I do what they wanted or they will kill me. You cannot know their secret and just go. Once you know you have to be part of them or they would just get rid of you. I was afraid for my life."

When he was caught by the police, he told them what they wanted to know straight away.

"And now the security forces have arrested me I have pledged to assist them. Even as it is now I'm in trouble, if they get me I'm a dead man."

Zakariyya's voice was very faint. At that moment he looked very small.

Boko Haram's reaving existence across Borno, Adamawa and Yobe went largely unchecked by the military. They became bolder and bolder and began attacking towns in large fighting groups, travelling in convoys of stolen Toyota Hiluxes. They would routinely warn towns in advance of their coming, in an attempt at meeting Qur'anic injunctions on Jihad which stipulate the holy warrior should inform their enemies of their arrival, the time of battle and even their strength. This was in order to ensure that if victory was theirs, the jihadis would know that their victory was down to Allah's will. Everything is predestined, and a man cannot change his fate.

Their tactic was to arrive in a town and announce themselves at the mosque. After they rounded up all the people there, they would demand the young men of the village would either join them or die. In February 2014, fifty-nine young boys were lined up outside their school dormitory and murdered, their bodies dumped on a fire.[56] Also that year, two video clips surfaced. The first shows a truck parked on a bridge. In the truck are perhaps a dozen young men of about Zakariyya's age. They pull the men from the lorry, throwing them to the ground. The young men's elbows are bound behind their backs. They take the first young man and put his head between the side rails of the bridge. A man puts the barrel of an assault rifle against the back of his head and pulls the trigger. The first lets go of the boy's arm and the lifeless body falls off the bridge into the river below. They do it again and again and again until the truck is empty.[57]

In a second clip, thought to have been filmed somewhere in the vicinity of Bama in Borno in November 2014, the camera advances through a group of armed men toward a single story building. In the background, single shots can be heard ringing out. When the camera reaches the building the viewer can see that the door is barred, like a prison would be. The picture grows dark as the camera lens transitions from the bright sunshine to the dark interior. Then out of the gloom the coloured shapes of men lying down on the ground appear. Several gunmen walk among them, repeatedly and nonchalantly firing into the bodies that cover the floor. They keep firing and firing for close to 10 minutes. A young man in yellow, wearing a white hat turns to the camera, points at it and says of the killing "Wherever we go, we shall kill, slaughter and scatter. That is our job. Because of the covenant we have with Allah we cannot live with unbelievers on the same land." He says, "Abubakar Shekau, our leader, we are the bullets in your gun."[58] I am reliably informed the young man in yellow, who appears to be about seventeen or eighteen, is Mohammed Yusuf's eldest son.

These two clips were not circulated to Western journalists by the group as they were not meant for foreigners. These were among clips that were circulated by Boko Haram aimed at a local audience. These clips spread virally, not via the Internet but from Bluetooth enabled phone to Bluetooth enabled phone. Their wide spread showed what power they had, the purpose being to terrify and subdue, and also to reinforce the belief that because it was happening, it was Allah's will. A Qur'anic injunction states: "And the soul will not die but with the permission of Allah; the term is fixed; and whomsoever desires the reward of this world, I shall give him of it, and whomsoever desires the reward of the hereafter I shall give him of it; and I will reward the grateful."[59] The message in the clips was an extreme interpretation of that sura; here were God's instruments, doing his work, and no man could prevent it.

In another video made of the March 2014 attack on the Giwa barracks in Maiduguri, Boko Haram fighters can be seen advancing on the military base, in the suburbs of a state capital under emergency rule.[60] The fighters, many of whom are little more than boys, make almost no attempt to seek cover during their advance. When they broke in, which some have claimed they did with the help of collaborators in the military, they freed 800 people from the cells of the building converted into a prison in the grounds of the military barracks. Here there were undoubtedly people who were also not in Boko Haram before they had been picked up by the military joint task force—they would have ranged from the poor, people from outside of town, people without anyone to speak for them, or the victims of others trying to settle scores, people who had been fingered by CJTF members for reasons all of their own. They now faced a choice, they couldn't stay in the prison, as to do so would mean they would surely die there. If they left and struck out on their own they faced the almost certainty of being recaptured. Or they could leave with the group who had just breached the wall of the prison.

The terrible fate that met those who did not go with the militants was discovered by Amnesty International: their research indicates 645 people, the ones who did not flee with Boko Haram, were rounded up and executed, their bodies dumped in a mass grave.[61]

Many young men must have joined Boko Haram because they were unable to sway the circumstances of their fate. For many like Zakariyya it must have seemed to be simply their destiny to join Boko Haram, or to die.

Atta Barkindo argues that as Boko Haram press-ganged more people into joining, so these new members broadened the group's scope for further recruitment. "Some joined to protect themselves and their families," he said, "some joined because they got personal letters from Boko Haram. The new members come from these villages, and they know who is from what village and they have friends, they would say 'we know this person is courageous lets go and get him' they will even send you a personal letter saying if you do not come we will target your mother, your dad."

"I saw soldiers manning roadblocks in Mubi, Kanuri men who showed me personal letters from Boko Haram demanding they leave the army and join them or their family would be killed."

There were others who could not prevent themselves being sucked into the clutches of Boko Haram. In the police office known as 'the Crack' Zakariyya had finished speaking. From the chair behind him, the policeman now raised his voice.

"We have someone else here, would you like to see them?"

The door opened again and a grey shape slipped into the room. It was a young woman, cloaked in a charcoal grey jilbab that covered her entire body. On her back was slung a sleeping baby, holding her hand was a wide-eyed toddler.

Her name was Yakakka. She was married to one of the men who had escaped the firefight at the house in Damaturu.

She set her children down, resting her sleeping baby in her lap. The head of the youngest child lolled over her leg, it looked like someone had just turned the baby off. The toddler looked around, bewildered and scared, two wet fingers in its mouth.

"When I met my husband, he was working as an *achaba*," she said.[62] "I liked him, so we got married." They lived for a time in a house in Maiduguri until they were evicted by the landlord because they could not pay their rent, she said.

"We went to live in Damaturu, in the house with many other people." The family were all together in one room of the large house. Although she says she was aware of who Mohammed Yusuf's group was before 2009, she denied knowing that the place she was living was a commune run by the group and that her husband was a member. Even if she was aware, and was lying out of justifiable terror that what she said would leave her at the mercy of her captors, there would have been little she could have done about it.

"We heard the gunshots outside. My husband told me to stay in the room he went out. That was the last I saw of him," Yakakka said. She was arrested as she tried to flee the house, along with some of the other wives. In the cells at 'the Crack', she was being kept separately, in her own room with her children, she said. She was being fed, but was obviously traumatised and terrified. "This is me here now. Look at me," she said.

"We are holding her here and won't release her until her husband surrenders himself," the policeman said.

Holding to ransom the wives of Boko Haram members became a covert policy option of the government and by 2014 the Joint Task Force had reportedly seized scores of women, among the hundreds of male Boko Haram cadres already held in jail. It was said that one of Abubakar Shekau's wives was among these captives. In several videos he demanded the release of their Boko Haram detainees and their womenfolk.[63]

For much of the time that Boko Haram ravaged the north east, they separated women from the men and in at least one reported case shooed the women away after lecturing them on proper Islamic practice. Later, at some point in 2013, this changed. The young male adherents of Boko Haram, who already looked to the group to provide the meaning of their spiritual war, their cash and livelihood and as a way of extorting vengeance for previous grievances, also wanted access to something else they could not get; namely women.

This had a cruel practicality to it. The fighting groups were living on the move, and needed camp followers; people to do the backbreaking slave-work, to carry, wash and to sweep. They would also continue their policy from the days of the Ibn Taymiyyah mosque of arranging marriages for their members. But this time they took the women as chattel from communities they had "defeated".

In April 2014 a group of Boko Haram fighters descended on the town of Chibok in southern Borno state. With many stories swirling around trying to explain what happened that night, one account says they intended to engage the military based in the town, with the hope of looting their armoured cars and weapons. It has also been reported that the main target was a brick-making machine and other building equipment.[64] In any event the military pulled out before Boko Haram arrived. It is not known exactly how they knew the attack was coming, and whether the insurgents had warned them it was about to happen.

On their arrival, rather than confronting the security forces the Boko Haram column found instead dormitories full of young girls who had been staying in the town in order to take their exams the next day. The fighters decided to take two hundred or so girls with them and waited for five hours while they stole enough trucks to take them into captivity.

Twelve of the girls escaped as they were being taken from the village. Human Rights Watch interviewed one of the escapees. She told them they did not at first realise who the men were:

> Two men told us we should not worry, we should not run. They said they had come to save us from what is happening inside the town, that they are policemen. We did not know that they were from Boko Haram. The rest of the men came and started shouting 'Allahu Akbar' and at that moment we realized, they were Boko Haram. We were told to be quiet. One of them told us that the horrible things we heard happening elsewhere, like burning houses, killing people, killing students, kidnapping people, would happen to us now. We all started crying and he told us to shut up.[65]

The resulting global outcry about this particular act, as opposed to any other act of brutal murder they had previously carried out, took the leadership of Boko Haram somewhat by surprise, observers have said. They capitalised on it, rushing out a video that showed Shekau standing in front of an armoured car: "I am the one who abducted your girls," he gloated, "you think you know about human rights but you know nothing." The girls who had become Muslims would be "married" off to his commanders he said. The others would be "sold in the marketplace… I will marry a girl at 12, I will marry a girl of 9," Shekau leered.[66]

Just a few days later, the shortest gap between video releases, another was posted. This showed the girls being held in a forest glade, chanting the *shahada*, the creed of the faith. Shekau, filmed in another location in front of a green background, in an exultant tone said: "These girls, these girls you occupy yourselves with… we have indeed liberated them. These girls have become Muslims."[67]

There was worse to come. In June 2014 female suicide bombers began to attack targets across the country, including what is believed to be the group's only attack on Lagos, a failed suicide bombing of a gas shipping terminal. The use of women, it was initially suspected, was done for practical reasons; women attracted less attention than male fighters and could get past vigilante roadblocks to their targets without being searched.

By October 2015, ninety female suicide bombers had killed a reported 500 people and injured over 700 in just over sixteen months. They were deployed in groups of two or more to maximise the number of casualties in an attack by staggering the explosions in an attempt to kill people responding to help the victims of the first detonation.[68]

A 13-year-old girl, one of three strapped with a suicide vest and sent to attack a textile market in Kano in December 2014, told police that her father had put her forward for the operation.[69] Women and girls were being coerced to do this. The stream of female suicide bombers contained a potent propaganda message: that Boko Haram is prepared to destroy the things the West holds most valuable.

But there might be something else at work. It is clear part of what attracts men to the sect is exertion of control over women. But as with so much of what happens inside Boko Haram, women's role in the sect has yet to be fully understood.

Stories have emerged from people working for NGOs in the north east that all-female groups exist among Boko Haram, not only acting as wives and camp followers but as fighters, spies and firebrand recruiters.[70] for example, in July 2014 three women were arrested in Adamawa, part of a clandestine recruitment cell according to Nigerian security services. [71]

In the minds of Western observers it appears obvious young girls, too young to give meaningful consent to anything, are being coerced into destroying themselves. But it is becoming apparent that while many women join Boko Haram because they are coerced by male family members, women also join for reasons that are no different from men.

In this world where the concepts of coercion and consent to do not hold any currency, adopting a radical identity can become a paradoxical form of empowerment, says Chitra Nagarajan, who coordinates civil society groups in the north east with a British aid funded programme.

The stories of what happened in the village Gerhard Müller-Kosack studied have stayed with him. "It was the girls who burned the books in the village, not the boys. It was the girls who were the most noticeably radical. It's very puzzling."

Atta Barkindo is working with the Nigerian government's programme to de-radicalise the men and women that they have captured. He says there are generally three different types of people in Boko Haram: people who have fallen into it through fate, swept up into it and could not escape. Then there are those who joined for opportunistic reasons, or to exploit the chaos that Boko Haram represented, or for a salary paid in hard currency. Finally there are the ideologues, the people who really believe in Mohammed Yusuf's teaching, the coming end of days, the promise of resurrection and paradise for the jihadi who is "pure of heart".

"The people who joined for money, many of them are ready to give up," Barkindo says, "They want to come back into the world, they are sorry, there is hope they can be rehabilitated." The ones who were swept up or coerced are trickier cases. In March 2015 the Nigerian military began a concerted push to chase Boko Haram out of the territory they had held ahead of the general elections. As they advanced, Boko Haram simply melted away leaving many of their "wives" and camp followers, their female slaves, in forest glades where they were found by the advancing troops.

One such group of young women were settled in a camp for internally displaced people in Adamawa. Shortly after though, the women were moved again, this time to a secure camp in a military barracks. They could not be allowed to stay with the other displaced people because, it was said, they were calling their captors, telling them where they were and asking them to come and get them.[72]

Like the child soldiers in the civil wars of Liberia and Sierra Leone, or the Lord's Resistance Army in Central African Republic and Uganda, so thoroughly had they accepted their new lives in the group that their old ones had been almost completely erased. The possibility of finding them again is uncertain.[73] From a comfortable seat in a developed country, with pluralistic politics and a functioning education system, it may be hard to comprehend this. The degree to which people who have little agency accept fate can seem mystifying to those of us who feel we have so much choice in our lives.

As for the ideologues in Boko Haram, Barkindo thinks their world may be beyond reach. "They will never talk to you," he said. "When they are brought in front of you they don't even look at you. They have nothing but contempt." In detention they are kept separately form the people judged to be of the other types, because combining them is too dangerous.

"They have this belief, what I understand is that they believe the world is sort of like a motorpark. They are the passengers, they are the ones who are going somewhere, to paradise. The rest of us are just hawking peanuts."

Outside 'the Crack' Abdullahi Kaura and I were shaken by our encounter with Zakariyya, Yakakka and the police.

"What will happen to them?" I asked.

"The woman, it seems they have some value for her." Kaura said. "I wonder if there is someone official we can talk to, someone who can step in..." his voice trailed off as he looked back at the entrance to the police station, "but I don't think..."

"They're going to kill that boy aren't they?" I said.

Kaura nodded.

9

KILL ZONES

The sentry at the gate of Giwa Barracks was a large man, so large in fact that his bullet-proof vest rode high over his bulging gut. The breadth of his belly and chest strained the clips running down the middle of the vest holding it to his body. The camouflaged fabric was stretched and bent out of shape around his bulge. His helmet too was ill-fitting, the strap held so tight around his chin that it pulled the rim of the helmet down over his forehead and squeezed his cheeks. The only thing that did look serious about him was the assault rifle.

Aminu, our driver, rolled his Mercedes slowly through the chicane of barrels blackened by night-time kerosene fires. The sentry bent and looked inside. Seeing me in the back seat, he said: "*Oyibo,*[1] well done."

Kaura leaned over the gear stick to the driver's window and in the voice he reserves for protocol, equal parts politesse and firm order, said: "We are from the BBC. We want to speak with the Commanding Officer."

"Is oga inside?" the sentry asked his colleague.

"They are coming back just now," came the answer.

"Wait inside," the sentry said, waving us through with a giant hand. We drove down a straight road, lined on both sides with dry-looking trees. Ahead there were a few bungalows which looked like classrooms. It seemed to be mostly open space, with about a hundred yards of dusty-dry grass between the 15-foot-high perimeter wall and the buildings. To the right was a large blue roofed building that looked like a church. The area was dotted with trees which gave the appearance of a university campus rather than a military installation. We parked and got out of the car to kick our heels waiting for the CO.

"Did that look like a bulletproof vest to you?" I asked.

Kaura's brow furrowed.

"All the soldiers I've seen, I'm not sure those things they're wearing are bulletproof vests."

"Why do you think that?"

It had been bothering me since we arrived in Maiduguri. Although it was a while since I had seen a bulletproof vest—on a hostile environments training course, where journalists learn first aid—I remembered the feel of the heavy waistcoats; the inflexible Kevlar, the big pockets at front and back holding the ceramic plates that provide most of the protection. The plates are heavy and the jacket stiff, it hardly warps or stretches, and they don't have clips up the front.

"Looks like a lifejacket," I said, "you know... stop you drowning?"

All the soldiers of the Joint Task Force I'd seen manning checkpoints in Maiduguri looked as if they had arrived there by yacht. The jackets were an inch and a half thick, but the material under the camouflage fabric looked soft and squidgy. They looked light, not at all like the bulletproof vests I had seen before. "You've been on HEFAT training," I asked Kaura, "does it look like the bulletproof vest you tried on?"

"Why would they give them lifejackets?"

"I dunno, why don't the military give soldiers good equipment?" I asked back.

"I've seen them wearing the same in the Delta," said Kaura.

"Exactly, I can see why they give them lifejackets in the Delta, in and out of boats all day, soldier's more likely to drown than get shot. But here?" I waved my hands at the dust and dry grass that stretched for hundreds of miles in every direction.

"Maybe they're both?"

"Maybe that's it... Or maybe that's what they tell them..."

Kaura started shaking his head. I'd gone too far, forgetting that too-overt cynicism from outsiders can provoke a defensive response, even in those who could produce great theses on the subject of what is wrong with Nigeria.

At the gate an armoured car pulled into the barracks, followed by a convoy of cars and another armoured vehicle.

"How are we going to find out?" I said, "Ask the sentry if I can poke him to see if his jacket is made out of sponge?"

"No, I wouldn't advise it," said Kaura.

The convoy was upon us. In the lead armoured vehicle was a soldier with a large machine gun sticking out of the top hatch. I nodded at him, pointing

Kaura's attention with my brow to the thick vest the soldier was wearing. Kaura rolled his eyes at me and laughed.

Car doors were opened for the officers and they strode toward the bungalows. The convoy was dismissed and drove into another part of the barracks we couldn't see, the armoured car farting diesel smoke as it went.

One of the officers stopped and beckoned to us to come. He turned out to be the CO's aide de camp. We followed him into his office, where he welcomed us, and sat down at a wide desk. Behind him unintelligible circles and triangles were drawn on a whiteboard.

Regrettably, the ADC informed us, we had just missed a press conference where we could have asked our questions. The CO had just flown to Abuja for a very important meeting and would not be back until next week. He politely, but very resolutely, refused to answer any questions in his CO's stead. As soon as it was clear we weren't getting anything here my mind began to wander: how much sponge would it take to keep two bulletproof ceramic plates and a heavy soldier buoyant?

We drove out of the gate of Giwa Barracks, ruing the wasted trip. I gave the sentries a wave. They didn't wave back.

"Definitely a lifejacket," I said, but Kaura shook his head.

That was the entirety of my glimpse inside Giwa Barracks in 2011, before we knew what was going on there.

* * *

"Permit me to end this discussion on a personal note..."

Muhammadu Buhari, former military head of state, retired general, serial election candidate, was speaking to an audience at the foreign policy think-tank Chatham House in London, just weeks before the 2015 elections were to take place.

Buhari, not a naturally effortless public speaker, was meticulous and slow about it. When he speaks English his Hausa accent is rich and strong; "p"s and "f"s can slip into each other, "b"s become "v"s and vice versa. He read from the page, enunciating every word, only glancing up from the paper briefly in between paragraphs like a schoolmaster taking a register. The speech was a rather dry affair. He used a long list of figures and quoted from reports on the state of "freedom" in Africa to draw a picture of a continent that, he said, had been washed by a wave of democratisation. But as he continued, his metaphor becoming somewhat Cnutian; this wave had not "consolidated", it was at risk of slipping away without delivering the dividends the population expected.[2]

The speech had elicited a guffaw from someone at the back of the audience. This was when Buhari promised to ensure government agencies only had one set of accounts. The laughter was either because what Buhari said seemed frank acknowledgement that in the past crooked double accounting was routine, or that the laughing man thought he would believe it when he saw it. But as the retired general drew to a close, an expectant silence grew in the audience of Nigerians and Nigeria watchers.

"I have heard and read references to me as a former dictator in many respected British newspapers. Let me say, without sounding defensive, that dictatorship goes with military rule... Though some might be less dictatorial than others."

"I take responsibility for what went on under my watch. I cannot change the past, but I can change the present and the future." In the front row, his new opposition party allies broke out the applause.

"So before you is a former military ruler, now a converted democrat, who-" there was laughter now, like the applause it too came from the front row. Was it laughter of relief? "-is ready to operate under democratic norms and subject himself to the rigours of election processes for the fourth time."

Buhari smiled—an acknowledgement of the front row's approval? He had executed a neat rhetorical pirouette, taken something used against him and flipped it back onto his side. This is a savoured skill in Nigeria, where everyone from the street seller to the politician must verbally construct the world in which their power will have meaning.

"You may ask why is he doing this?" Buhari said, "It is a question I ask myself all the time too. And here is my humble answer; because the work of making Nigeria great is not yet done."

The martial pedigree of Muhammadu Buhari's family goes back to precolonial times. He was born into the family of a district head in Daura, Katsina state, in Nigeria's north-west. His mother's father and grandfather had been military leaders or *Dogarai* (head of the palace guard) in the court of Emir of Daura. Another great grandfather was a commander under the warlord Rabe, until Rabe tried to kill him. Buhari's ancestor escaped death in Bornu and led a group of men west, raiding as they went, until they settled in Daura.[3]

This family history may have had an effect on his choice of career, but perhaps of greater influence was an address the Emir of Kano gave his school class while Buhari was a teenager. In the years approaching Independence, the northern elite had realised that perhaps they had not only neglected education but also their participation in the military.[4] Following a coup in Iraq in 1958, the emir told Buhari's class if soldiers could topple a dynasty descended from the Prophet, then the sons of Nigeria's prominent Muslims had better join the army.[5]

The advice was prophetic; in 1962 Buhari was one of two boys from that class to be accepted into officer training. Just four years later, in January 1966, soldiers ended the first republic in a coup. At this point Buhari was a junior officer and wasn't particularly influential in those events, or the counter-coup that took place in July of that same year. But in the years that followed, during Nigeria's civil war between 1967 and 1970, Buhari rose to being an infantry brigade commander. In 1975 General Yakubu Gowon, the military head of state in the period after the unsuccessful secession attempt, was removed in a coup and Buhari's friend General Murtala Mohammed installed as head of state. At this point, Buhari became part of the military government, serving in Maiduguri as governor for the North East region.

Less than a year after, however, Mohammed was assassinated by a group of officers from Nigeria's "middle belt". Their coup failed and in the following weeks the loyal officer cadre was re-consolidated at the heart of the military government. Buhari was moved back to Lagos from the North East and appointed Federal Commissioner for Petroleum and Energy. Over the next three years, under the military leadership of General Olusegun Obasanjo, he reorganised the ministry and the national oil corporation to create the Nigerian National Petroleum Corporation (the institution which manages the state's share of the oil business today). He was the NNPC's first chairman until the return of civilian rule in 1979.

In 1983 the Second Republic, mired in the rampant corruption of the administration of Shehu Shagari, was toppled anew by the military. Buhari was the General Officer Commanding of the 1st Mechanised Brigade stationed in Jos, Plateau state, when the plotters struck. They decided Buhari, as the most suitable senior officer, should be installed as head of state.

In power, Buhari and his Chief of Staff Major General Babatunde Idiagbon enacted the "War Against Indiscipline", punishing civil servants who turned up to their offices late, or who were not "on seat" at all. Corrupt officials were jailed. He used military decrees to clamp down on the press and public. In the street military officers with hide whips administered corporal punishment for the slightest infraction, usually sets of painful bounds from a squatting position known as "frogjumps".

Another oft-remembered aspect of Buhari's crackdown on law and order were a series of public executions. Convicted drug traffickers, murderers and armed robbers were marched up to telegraph poles driven into the sand of Bar Beach in Lagos, and shot by firing squad. The executions were broadcast on national television. One undated film clip shot by the Associated Press shows soldiers leading convicts from between the dunes. Some are still wearing crisp wide-lapelled floral shirts and flares, the smart clothes of up-and-coming men-about-town. Some are crying and praying, others stern and sullen, smoking a last cigarette. An excited and eager crowd rush up to a barrier manned by soldiers who whip them back. They push forward nonetheless, calling out to the men as they were bound with strong rope to the poles, the rope digging into their torsos. The firing squad take several volleys to kill the men, their faces become twisted masks of pain, bodies hanging against the tight cords. The bodies are put unceremoniously into rudely made wooden coffins.[6]

Perhaps the most audacious occurrence during Buhari's administration was the Dikko Affair. A former Second Republic minister named Umaru Dikko had reportedly stolen millions of dollars and fled to London. Buhari wanted him back in Nigeria to face charges, but the British government refused to extradite him. Instead, the Nigerian security services engaged a Mossad-trained hit team to kidnap Dikko. The Israelis seized him from the street outside his Bayswater home. The plan was to drug Dikko, put him in a crate and fly him back to Lagos. He would be kept alive by an Israeli doctor, shipped in the crate alongside him, monitoring his vital signs. When the alarm was raised, UK Customs officials noticed the irregular arrival of a Nigerian Airways plane at Stansted airport, and very suspicious of two large crates waiting to be loaded onto the flight. They discovered the sleeping Dikko and the doctor in one of the crates and two more Israelis in the other.[7] Buhari claimed the government did not sanction the operation, but because the Nigerians who couriered the crates were diplomats from the High Commission and they had tried to claim the crates were "diplomatic bags", the incident caused the United Kingdom and other countries to break off diplomatic contact with Nigeria for several years.

After his release from house arrest following the 1985 Babangida coup, Buhari was kept out of the way of the military government that followed. He was later given a role as the head of the Petroleum Trust Fund, a parastatal organisation that directed tranches of money cut from oil revenues to infrastructure projects like roads and boreholes. Despite accusations he favoured projects in the north, and persistent accusations of money missing from the fund, none of this mud has stuck to Gen. Buhari himself.

Quite the contrary, in the years following the 1999 return to democracy, during Nigeria's Fourth Republic, Buhari's reputation has undergone something of a renaissance. There is no denying the incredibly high regard that he is now held by the northern Nigerian street. Young people who were possibly not even born when Buhari was military leader flock to see him in vast numbers. His personal reputation for probity and honesty has gained him a wildly enthusiastic following. At public rallies they shout "*Sai Buhari, sai Gaskia!*"— Buhari and the truth!

Most often remarked on is the humble manner in which this former head of state lives. Both Nigerians and foreign visitors, diplomats and ministers, all comment on the modesty of his house in Kaduna. While it is by no means a hovel, it is spartan in comparison to the palatial mansions that have become the norm among former politicians.

"When I visited him, he opened the door to me himself, he has no phalanx of servants, just a single office assistant," former US Ambassador John Campbell told me. "He still uses the same car he had in the 1970s," Campbell added, "in my experience of Nigerian politicians, it's unique."[8]

People in the north speak of him in almost saintly terms. In 2011 one of the largest crowds I have ever seen turned up at the old Racecourse in Kano to catch a glimpse of Buhari in the distance as he campaigned in the election. At the edge of the crowd of thin young men, standing on their tip-toes, hustling to press forward, it was not really possible to see the candidate. I didn't dare venture into the heart of the multitude. Crowds like that can be dangerous places. I was afraid if anything went wrong I (and potentially hundreds of other people) would be crushed to death in a stampede.

In contrast the reputation of the People's Democratic Party in the north, with some exceptions, was that of narrow self-interest with a history of not delivering on its promises. Opposition parties have held the governorships of several northern states. Nationally, however, the People's Democratic Party held too tight a grip on the "machinery on ground" for any opposition parties to find purchase. Despite his popularity Buhari did not win elections in 2003, 2007 and 2011.

The high regard for Buhari is by no means universal. Like all politicians in Nigeria, he is a divisive figure: feared, hated and mocked by people from other regions of the country. In the early days of the Fourth Republic Buhari told *NewsWatch* magazine that he "would die for the cause of sharia".[9] This was widely interpreted by other parts of the country where Muslims did not hold some form of state power to mean he was committed to the cause of replacing secular law with sharia across Nigeria. This statement dogs him to this day among Christians, those in the north and the south.[10] In every election he has contested, the Lagos-based newspapers have printed adverts paid for by "concerned citizens" groups referring to Buhari's authoritarian roots and warning that people never really change.

Some have sought to puncture his image as an honest man, pointing out that his second wife Aisha (Buhari has been married twice but—unlike other prominent northern Nigerian big men, they were not co-wives in a polygamous family) has been photographed wearing a Patek Phillippe watch. If genuine, the watch costs upwards of £30,000.[11] Of course this is small beans compared to the hundreds of millions of dollars looted by Sani Abacha, the military head of state between 1993 and 1998, now being returned to Nigeria by Swiss banks,[12] but it is a crack in the firmly held image of Buhari as a modest and simple man.

But there are other ways in which Buhari resembles the rest of the Nigerian elite. He has family connections by marriage, and therefore by some small degree of societal obligation, to other northern figures who don't share his glowing reputation. He travels to London to see a doctor instead of risking the Nigerian health system. Some of his children were educated at expensive private schools favoured by wealthy Nigerians who don't wish to send their children to overcrowded, low-achieving Nigerian institutions. His children from his second marriage went to British universities where they completed their degrees without having to endure indefinite faculty strikes, poor teaching and minimal educational resources.

But Buhari's family life has not been completely isolated from Nigeria's woes: in 2012, Zulai, his eldest daughter from his first marriage, died from complications from sickle cell anaemia after she gave birth to a baby in a Kaduna hospital.

While his image as an incorruptible politician has impressed outsiders and rallied northerners, it has not always elicited positive responses from other members of the Nigerian political class. His dogged pursuit of high elected office, at times when all his putative allies in opposition deserted him, has made him something of a laughing stock among the political elite in the past. Before 2015, people wondered aloud "when will this man give it a rest?" and "what does Buhari do in between elections?" What foreigners saw as an adherence to principles, Nigerians see as political naivety. People who are involved in politics, even those from the same region where he draws his core support, say that his obtuse refusal to play the game of politics by Nigerian rules indicates Buhari is in some way deficient or slow witted.

In fact, he possesses a quick and very dry wit which he uses self-deprecatingly. But this does not detract from his reputation as a stern man. His dress is most often sombre and his face seemingly in a semi-permanent frown; his downward-turned mouth is fringed by a small moustache which is meticulously barbed into a shape that went out of fashion, in Europe at least, sometime during the mid-1940s.

He is recognisably a military man. In the auditorium of Chatham House, Buhari told the audience; "Boko Haram have put Nigeria on the international terrorism map." The military had been "poorly equipped and improperly incentivised" to deal with the problem, he said. This would cease under his stewardship, he added, saying; "I know the army".

Can what Buhari does be any worse than what has gone before?

In the early days of the insurgency, even before the north east was placed under a state of emergency, long go-slows snaked from the many police checkpoints that carved up Maiduguri. Driving through town in March 2011 Abdullahi Kaura and I were regularly trapped in queues so long the sandbags of the police checkpoints were not actually visible for most of the wait.

This was not just an inconvenience. Once we heard the sound of sirens rushing toward us and a blue police pickup truck screamed past. Its flatbed was thick with green-bereted mobile policemen, bristling with weapons. Later, we heard the police had shot up a car, killing two young men. It was said the car had, unwisely, tried to execute a U-turn before they got to the chicane. Wherever Kaura and I went in the city it was the same story; Boko Haram were bad, but to the mind of the ordinary people of Maiduguri—at that point at least—the police were the immediate, daily, and deadly, threat.[13]

The police's appalling relationship with the people meant that at a stage when the group were still relatively weak operationally, citizens would not come to them willingly with information. They feared, in an entirely justified way, that they would be arrested, detained, tortured and extorted by the officers of the state.

The roadblock checkpoint has remained the chief method of population control and crime prevention used by the police, their most visible point of contact with the inhabitants of a region under threat from insurgents. These have routinely been used to extort money from commercial drivers and harass the population in general all through the Boko Haram insurgency. Kaura and I observed that even in the inky black night of a neighbourhood with no street lights, at a time when vulnerable police outposts were being raided and police killed for their weapons by hit-and-run gunmen, police officers still worked to a default system: shining torches in drivers' faces, squeezing money from the local population plying the road. After all, their superiors would still be expecting their regular cut, the price of being given a lucrative position to milk. Many of the officers would also have to regularly kick the proceeds back to the men who loaned them the fee to join the police in the first place.

As Boko Haram became more deadly, bombing markets and bus stations, slaughtering thousands of Nigerians, Muslims and Christians alike, people's faith in the Joint Task Force of the military and police did not improve.

Some of the things that the government did in the name of security actually aided Boko Haram. When I spoke to Abu Dujana in Maiduguri in 2011 the fighters did not practise any sort of counter-surveillance discipline over their telephone usage. I was able to speak to Dujana by phone in several calls over two days. In the months after, Boko Haram put forward a spokesman by the name of Abu Qaqa to represent them. He would regularly call the Nigerian journalist Ahmad Salkida in Abuja. Salkida would put his phone on speaker so assembled journalists could hear him and ask questions.[14]

In 2012 there were indications that the Nigerian security services were beginning to use this to their advantage during a period of pushing back against the sect. Several Boko Haram figures were arrested, showing there were possibly pockets of competent counter-insurgency agents inside the security services, with networks of informants and use of communications intelligence.[15] One of the men captured was thought to be responsible for bombing a Catholic church in a town close to Abuja at Christmas the year before, where forty-six worshippers had been killed.[16] Another was arrested as he met a Senator from Borno in his house.[17] The last contact Abdullahi Kaura had with Abu Dujana was around this time. Dujana told Kaura that the group were aware that the military had begun tracking them down using their mobile phones. As a consequence Boko Haram started attacking cell phone masts, blowing them up.

But a few months later, when the government declared a period of state of emergency across three states in May 2013, it was also directed that all cell phone networks should be cut off. This was ostensibly because Boko Haram were using mobile phones to detonate bombs. However cutting off communications did not slow Boko Haram down. In fact it simply accelerated a tactic which they themselves had started. They had developed parallel communication networks for their cell structures and were still able to carry out bombings and deadly attacks during this time. Some have also said that this action contributed to making Boko Haram into a different, more devastating, kind of operation.[18]

Before cutting the phones off, officers in the security services were issued with communication devices that did not use GSM mobile networks in the hope that the military would not be hampered. But the cut-off alienated the population from the army and deepened the economic decline of the area. In some cases traders and businessmen in Yobe had to travel as far as Kano just to make phone calls. Those in Maiduguri and Adamawa were stuck. In Adamawa and Yobe the phone connection was restored in July 2013, a couple of months after it was disconnected, but in Borno it persisted for several months, well into September.[19]

When Boko Haram gunmen strode into the Yobe town of Benisheik in September 2014, the town was in the midst of its weekly market, the crowds there were swelled by those who had travelled from Borno to make telephone calls. At least 160 people were killed.[20]

When the phone lines did return, it was supposed to be following a nation-wide SIM card registration drive, after which all telephone numbers would be able to be linked to an ID document and an address. However, this was not an easy thing to do successfully. While I was waiting in line at a mobile phone business in Bauchi in 2013 to register a SIM card, a young security guard suggested I buy a "pre-registered" SIM from him on the sly. I waited around to see how his hustle worked. Whenever he saw a gap, the young man jumped in and registered a SIM card to sell on. The company technician doing the registration did not object and stubbornly refused to meet anyone else's eye while it was happening. While I was waiting for my details to be entered, I saw the guard slide over the form with the registration address: it was Bauchi's Shadawanka barracks.

Not all military officers had specialist alternative military communication networks. The military also uses mobile phones and cutting off the GSM network made keeping in touch with non-military personnel very difficult. This communication with non-military civilian informants was to become more and more important.

In 2012 and 2013 Boko Haram were able to seemingly strike at will. They proved to be very versatile, launching endless bombing attacks on churches, gun attacks on mosques and motorparks, breaking into prisons to free their members and hammering the police and other security forces in coordinated attacks. They bombed the capital, targeting the newspaper *This Day*. Their attacks formed mini campaigns against these different targets, they would pursue one type of target or method in several places across the north east and then turn on a sixpence to pursue another direction. By 2013–2014 the group of insurgents who had at first flitted through the darkness were vying with the security services for control of Maiduguri. Despite a dusk-to-dawn curfew, they had the run of the Borno state capital. The official security forces were seemingly unable to respond other than by deploying ever rudimentary and brutal tactics.

Faced with official institutions who were unwilling or unable to respond effectively, communities turned to unofficial ones to fill the gap.

Like many parts of the Boko Haram story, the origins of the disparate vigilante groups that became known as the "Civilian Joint Task Force" is contested. By some accounts they were spontaneous groups that sprang up to defend individual communities, but others claim that many were first started by former Boko Haram members who wanted to leave the group and could only do so by taking up arms against them.[21]

"In the old days we used to run away from gunshots. Now we have become so fed up with Boko Haram we run towards them," a young vigilante member in Maiduguri told the writer Alex Preston, who visited the city for *GQ* magazine in 2013. Following Maiduguri's example Civilian JTF groups were popping up in other affected towns and taking the fight to the insurgents. The CJTF had the ability to breach the gap between the military and the insurgents in one important respect:

"The soldiers do not know Boko Haram," CJTF commander Abubakar Mohammed told Preston, "my boys know the locals, know if someone strange moves in, if there is something suspicious."[22]

This grassroots resistance to Boko Haram was praised as a panacea, and the vigilantes were heralded as heroes and an indispensable part of the fightback against Boko Haram. They took the JTF to the sect's hideouts and dislodged cells of fighters from the city. But that was not the end of the interaction between Civilian JTF and the military. As time went on just who was in charge of who became confused.

As Boko Haram shifted their tactics once again, from occupying Maiduguri to inhabiting forest and mountain hideouts, emerging to attack military posts and loot villages, the importance of the CJTF vigilantes increased. In many places they were absorbed into the military as a sort of adjunct unit who could sniff out the sleeper members of the sect, the ones giving fighters intelligence ahead of their attacks. Mobile phone footage of their operations, shot by vigilantes themselves and unearthed by journalists working for a television documentary team, showed that the CJTF at times seemed to be directing the army units. They were in control of the operations to "screen" people and root out

Boko Haram suspects. After a Boko Haram attack the vigilantes would prevent people leaving the neighbourhood. They were looking for unspecified marks on the body—said to resemble the burn pattern of a hidden weapon, hot from firing and pressed to the torso, or bruises in the shoulder from the recoil of an assault rifle. But there was no definitive way of spotting a sect member.

The documentary makers tracked down people who had fled the areas before the vigilantes had done their worst. One man watched the mobile phone footage and glimpsed a missing friend being lined up by vigilantes and who, he said, was not part of Boko Haram. Footage has also emerged of vigilantes participating in mass executions, hacking at the necks of suspects with long knives, egged on by men in military fatigues.[23]

Official security tactics were hardly refined. Even without the intelligence from the vigilante the JTF would swoop in and force everyone to lie down. The people they discerned to be members of the group were arrested and taken away.

One man who had been arrested in this fashion told Amnesty International: "Some people were trying to arrange their kaftans, the soldiers shot and killed some of them on the spot."

The man, named by Amnesty as Ahmed, was taken to a place the JTF called "Guantanamo", a prison facility in Damaturu, Yobe. They were kept in terrible conditions: cramped, unsanitary and without food and water. "Many of my colleagues did not make it," he said. The police "will tie your hands behind your back with the elbows touching and then one of them with walk on your tied hands with their boots. Your hands will remain tied and then they'll pour salt water on your wounds."[24] This was being done in police and military bases all over the north east, including Maiduguri's Giwa Barracks. Here more brutal torture was meted out on people—some of whom were almost certainly completely innocent.

Elsewhere, the military swept through villages and towns, killing everyone they found, burning houses, cars and motorbikes, utterly destroying places they believed to be centres of Boko Haram—without attempting to discern between combatant and civilian. The town of Baga was one such place, according to human rights organisations.

On 15 April 2013 Boko Haram gunmen reportedly attacked a military patrol as it was passing the town. By the end of the next day, Human Rights Watch says, over 2,000 homes were burned to the ground and 200 people were killed.[25]

The military issued characteristically strenuous denials that they engaged in such scorched earth policies, saying there were not that number of buildings in the town to start with. Human Rights Watch and Amnesty produced "before and after" satellite images to show the burned houses and witness statements to say that the perpetrators had been the military.

In response the military accused Boko Haram of being responsible for the massacre, the burning, the carnage. (The sect's fighters have certainly on other occasions used military uniforms as cover to approach towns, and indescriminately destroyed whole populated areas, including Baga, again a year later, in 2015.)

But reports by Human Rights Watch and Amnesty International claim with some confidence that in 2013 hundreds of people were buried in dozens of mass graves around the town, something that the sect have not been known to do. In other attacks they simply left the dead where they lay, or threw them in wells. However there have been several occasions where the military have been alleged to bury bodies en masse.

Amnesty International and Human Rights Watch say what happened at Baga could constitute a war crime. It is part of a pattern of military activity that in 2015 prompted Amnesty to release the names of nine commanders, including the top military service chiefs installed by President Jonathan, and recommended the case go to the International Criminal Court.

Overkill was not the military's only problem.

In June 2014 Sahara Reporters, the Nigerian citizen journalism website run from New York, posted a film they had been sent by a soldier said to be serving with Delta company of Operation Taskforce Mike, stationed in Gwoza Local Government Area.[26] The film shows a group of soldiers trying to bail water away from a flimsy hut that was unfortunately erected in a dip in the ground. The dip probably wasn't perceptible before the rain came, unless you knew especially what to look for. Two soldiers, complaining loudly, scoop water out from the six inch deep puddle that their hut sits in. A number of other men stand around filming them on their camera phones. They laugh and joke and poke fun at the soldiers' futile efforts to remove the water from the hut.

"The damage caused by the rain is much," the man holding the camera says. Someone comes and asks him something and the cameraman asks in return; "The OC?" (officer Commanding) The soldier who asked the question, wearing a rain mac with his hood up, shrugs. The OC doesn't seem to be around. Then the soldier in the mac asks the cameraman to snap a picture of him standing next to the soldiers bailing their hut out. After that, the cameraman walks around their base, showing the gun emplacements they dug, now unmanned and full of water.

The camp is on the plain below the Mandara Mountains and was part of the military's defences of Gwoza town. Boko Haram fighters were at that moment to the west, establishing bases in the Sambisa, a huge area of rugged forest, riven with impassable dry gulches and rocks, from where they could launch attacks after being pushed out of Maiduguri in 2013.

Toward the end of the clip, the soldier goes over to a large baobab tree. The mud on the plain is thick and blue-black. As he walks, the soldier's boots make a shucking sound. Dangling from the branches are plastic bottles. "This is the place where we hang our phones to make calls" he says, "keep them inside until there is network". It isn't entirely clear if this is their only form of communication with the outside world, but none of the other soldiers in the clip seem to have any other communication equipment.

Sahara Reporters said the footage was taken in May. In July that year Boko Haram fighters emerged from their camps in the Sambisa forest, smashed through the military's defences and took Gwoza, overrunning the garrison. Boko Haram released a video afterwards in which Shekau gloats over their victory.[27] At the end you can see the soldiers fleeing the military base, into the hills behind it. Even running for their lives they look slow. Defeated, they lumber up a hill. One scrambles to get a better position and he suddenly collapses out of sight, picked off by one of the baying fighters now shooting from the soldiers' own barracks.

The video shows thin young men in rough and dirty kaftans, loose turbans tied on their shaved heads, looting the armoury and carrying out all kinds of weapons. They whoop cheer and cry "Allahu ackbar!"—God is great—joy flashing in their eyes as they hold aloft heavy weaponry and boxes and boxes of ammunition, ammunition that was never used in the fight against the ragged, dirty teenagers who now possessed it.

The attack was so successful it prompted Shekau, convinced of Allah's provenance perhaps, to declare that Gwoza was at the heart of a new Islamic state, although there has been some dispute about the details of this pronouncement. There has been some suggestions that Shekau meant to associate himself with the Caliphate emerging at almost the same time in Iraq and Syria, the Islamic State of Iraq and al Sham (ISIS). The more likely option is that Shekau wanted to announce the existence of their own Islamic State in Nigeria. There is some scholarly debate about the words Shekau used, and their proper meaning; was it *khalifah*—'caliphate'—or *dawlah* meaning 'state'?[28]

Shekau's pronoucements are not reliable political statements. He is bombastic, prone to bouts of verbal bloody flux. Boasting and envy are as likely to be among his motives as political science.

Whatever the truth of Shekau's declaration, it was an unequivocal crushing defeat for the Nigerian military.

"Many of the Nigerian military officers I have met are individually very good," James Hall, a retired Colonel in the British Army and former Defence Attache to the British High Commission in Nigeria told me.[29] "They are committed, bright, patriotic and motivated." But after years of working in Nigeria Hall came to realise that across the military as a whole, any individual ability was covered by a blanket of institutionalised incompetence. "The biggest problem they face is that they lack the 'systems of systems' to manage the military effectively," Hall said.

The military, leery of embedding journalists into its ranks, has only allowed access to its workings on a small number of occasions. One of the resulting films, by Vice News video journalist and former Navy SEAL Kaj Larsen encapsulated the problems of the capacity and capability in the Nigerian military.[30] The film was broadly positive about the military and upbeat about their capabilities. It featured a spirited interview with a Nigerian Special Forces soldier, who was clearly well motivated, disciplined, enthusiastic and with a clear idea about what his job was and how best to achieve it. Nevertheless the film also showed less salubrious behaviour: infantry on the front line of Boko Haram-held territory getting blind drunk the night before a major offensive, crowding the camera, slurring they were going to "fuck Boko Haram in the ass". The next day the whole division lined up to march into Boko Haram-held territory in single file, to reduce the likelihood of tripping a mine. This was a very real risk; indeed the military's bomb disposal team discovered one such device buried in the sand of a pot hole. This discovery, however, came only after the whole division had marched over it. Eventually, the soldiers were unsuccessful in overtaking the town they were trying to retake it from Boko Haram and had to walk back to where they had come from while the air support flew in.

Years of promoting officers on the basis of their loyalty, not to the trade of soldiering, but to a reward scheme and parallel economy of patronage has taken its toll. For years men have been joining the military with the help of rich patrons who pay the fees demanded. They do so in order to avail themselves of the financial opportunities open to them. As the journalist Patrick Cockburn said of the collapse of the Iraqi army at Mosul in the face of the Islamic State in August 2014, despite the billions of dollars spent on it by the Americans; "the military collapsed because it is staffed by investors, not soldiers."[31]

This involvement of the military in corruption comes from the top down. With the government budgeting huge amounts of money for defence and security, $5.8bn in 2014 alone, there was ample incentive for the top brass not to be effective.[32]

A researcher with in-depth knowledge of the situation told me a story about the budget for the military: "Cash was flown up from Abuja to Maiduguri airport, direct from the Central Bank, still in its plastic wrapper, where it was unloaded and taken in an armed convoy to a government house. Later that day the same convoy returned with the money again, loaded it back onto the plane which then took it back to Abuja. This was not done secretly; everyone who worked at the airport saw it."[33] The inference is that the money had been shared out and was being returned to Abuja "converted to the use" of someone else, other than the purpose it was meant for.

Corruption, poor organisation and training can explain much of the military's low capacity, but there was another factor; the government's analysis of the situation favoured avoiding problems and passing off responsibility.

Questions surrounded the effectiveness and authority of former President Jonathan's leadership since even before the death of his predecessor President Umaru Musa Yar'Adua, who succumbed to a chronic illness after a long period in hospital in Saudi Arabia. Yar'Adua was barely conscious for months, and returned unable to live without life support machines. This leadlerlessness left Nigeria in a legal and constitutional crisis.[34]

After a spell as acting president Jonathan acceded to the presidency after Yar'Adua's death in May 2010. By then Nigeria's government had been in a state of confusion for some time. The ruling party was riven by power tussles precipitated by Yar'Adua's inaction. Where the previous president, Olusegun Obasanjo, had been a canny operator who seemingly knew how to play all the factions of government off against each other, under Yar'Adua and Jonathan all that seemed to disappear. Aso Rock, as the presidency is known, had become enshrouded by the fog of secrecy and storms of backbiting.

Whatever is said about his time in office, it cannot be denied that Goodluck Jonathan's rise to power was a remarkable democratic anomaly. Despite having been the deputy governor, then governor of a major oil producing state, followed by vice president, and then acting president, before 2011 he had never actually won an election in his whole political career.

When he took over as president, there was a problem, namely the delicate matter of "power rotation" and zoning, the power-sharing formula that formed a sort of gentleman's agreement at the heart of the People's Democratic Party government. Between 1999 and 2007 Olusegun Obasanjo, a Christian from the south-west had been president. In 2007, according to the agreement, it had been the north's "turn" and Umaru Yar'Adua, the former governor of Katsina and brother of Obasanjo's best friend Shehu Musa Yar'Adua, was supposed to serve for two terms. When Jonathan, from Nigeria's "south-south" region, took over in 2010 and was then elected in 2011, he effectively tore this agreement up.

This added another potent force to the secrecy, betrayal and power-struggles; ethnic and regional chauvinism. Buhari, nursing wounds after being defeated again in 2011 in what he thought were unfair, fraudulent, circumstances, made remarks to the effect that there would be "chaos" in the year to come. This came after he was slow to condemn election violence blamed on opposition thugs that raged for almost two weeks and left hundreds dead. This was reported as without the power-sharing deal, the north would be made ungovernable. These impolitic remarks, like the ones he made about sharia in 2001, would come back to haunt him.[35]

Following his election in 2011, Jonathan and his aides saw Boko Haram as a "northern problem" and did not treat it seriously. It is thought that Jonathan believed that it was a trap being laid for him by northern elites, and he resisted being pinned down on the issue. In 2012, during the earliest days of the insurgency, Nigeria's ambassador in Washington signalled his government was resisting the designation by the US State Department of Boko Haram as a Foreign Terrorist Organisation.[36] This designation would have brought more financial scrutiny on cash flows in and out of the country. At the time, Ambassador to the US Adebowale Adefuye said Nigeria did not want to 'cause any more woes to its citizens travelling through foreign airports'. This was something of a dog whistle phrase, which would have been noticed by people who might be moving illegal cash into or out of the country, who were most likely not Boko Haram at all. Eventually Boko Haram did receive FTO status, but not until many more had died.

As if to highlight the inconsistencies in his approach, at the same time, in 2012, Jonathan accused northern leaders of sponsoring the "ghosts" who now haunted the north. In another speech he implored the US and UK to come to the country's aid to fight what he said was 'al-Qaeda in Nigeria'.

Confusion and inaction became the hallmark of policy. During the furore over the kidnapping of schoolgirls form Chibok, Jonathan refused at first to believe it had happened at all. He also refused to give any order to act for weeks. In the face of protests by the Chibok families and civil society groups, Jonathan's wife, First Lady Patience Jonathan, ordered the detention of two activists, accusing them of trying to shame the presidency.[37]

In January 2014, perhaps sensing that *something* should be done, Jonathan sacked all the top military service chiefs and installed new ones. But the replacements he chose only served to feed the atmosphere of mistrust and regional chauvinism; all of them were from the south-south or the east of Nigeria. In order to place the people he wanted, Jonathan reportedly had to forcibly retire at least 100 senior officers in line for promotion ahead of the ones he picked.

This, then, was the atmosphere in government as Boko Haram was growing. The upshot was that there seemed to be no political will to fight Boko Haram, not from President Jonathan, who thought it could cost him the election in 2015, nor from the service chiefs who, as soon as they eliminated Boko Haram would lose the money they were being paid.

Even though vast budgets had been, on paper, given to the military to fight Boko Haram, in September 2014 President Jonathan asked the National Assembly permission to borrow another billion dollars in order for the military to purchase arms; by now the presidency was becoming desperate, spurred by a gradual realisation that there seemed to be nothing his government could do.[38] Instead of the administration assessing their own inability to act, analysing the reasons why and reforming, they blamed outside forces.

In November that year, Ambassador Adefuye used a speech to the Council on Foreign Relations to blame the United States for Nigeria's inability to deal with Boko Haram. Speaking to a group of very angry diplomats and Nigeria-watchers, Ambassador Adefuye said: "We find it difficult to understand how and why in spite of the U.S. presence in Nigeria with their sophisticated military technology Boko Haram should be expanding and becoming more deadly." The audience reportedly shifted in their seats uncomfortably as Ambassador Adefuye said that Washington's refusal to sell weapons to the country hindered their ability to deal with the situation.[39]

US arms sales to foreign powers are controlled by the Leahy Act which prevents American companies providing combat material to countries whose militaries have poor human rights records. The British government had long banned the sales of deadly weapons to Nigeria, allowing only exports of non-lethal equipment to the military and police. This ban was not an idle, unused sanction. In 2012 a UK-based weapons dealer was arrested and charged over a shipment of Chinese AK-47 rifles he brokered for Nigeria in 2007.

But as James Hall told me, getting kit is the least of the military's problems. The culture of the systems surrounding the management of the army does not allow for materiel they do procure to be used effectively.

A good illustration of this, he said, is the Nigerian drone problem: "In 2011 the Nigerian government bought eight Israeli drones. Three years later they were still in the warehouse in Ibadan in their crates, because the people who procured them did not buy the special software or the training programmes to use them," Hall said.

The military are like "magpies", he said, obsessed with shiny things, but unsure of what to do with them when they got them. "They think there's a big red button that they will push and sort out the problem, but it's not like that," he said, "most of them just don't get it, and the ones who do have to deal with their colleagues before they can make any reforms."[40]

The suspicion in which the British and American government held Jonathan's administration cannot be understated. I was reliably informed that when mapping out how the UK Foreign Office would respond to any situation that unfolded after the 2015 elections in Nigeria, the "worst case scenario" was named "Jonathan 2", referring to a second term for the former vice president.[41] The British government's desire to cooperate with the Jonathan administration in terms of military training evaporated, Hall said, when military personnel based in the Niger Delta returned to Nigeria from an overseas training programme on boat-handling skills, provided at great cost by the UK military. On their return, the soldiers were instantly transferred to the north east, rendering their new skills useless. This was the final straw, which put a strain on the long term relationship between the two countries forces.

Speaking to me in 2014 Hall said: "What it would require is to start at the bottom with a long term officer-training programme, where you take a cadre of junior officers train them and follow them as they progress through the military, over twenty years. At the moment there isn't the appetite for that."

The military incapacity wasn't just a matter of incompetence, he said. "It is true that countries who have experienced military coups hobble their military to prevent these things happening again."

"The Nigerian military has traditionally favoured heavy weaponry, mechanised divisions, armoured divisions. These were the types of battles that were fought in the civil war. But counter-insurgency is different, you need to be on the move very quickly." The Nigerian military, with its unresponsive chain of command and accent on heavy weaponry is not set up for that, Hall says. Quick-moving and adept fighters would perhaps not appeal to political leaders who knew how such forces could be used by ambitious factions of the military to take power.

There were many stories about how military insiders were unhappy about the way the war was being prosecuted. In 2014 I heard from several retired army officers, and other people with connections to the army, who said that serving soldiers they knew reported that their commanding officers were regularly rotated without warning and replaced with unfamiliar new commanders. They also heard how soldiers on patrol in the north east were only given 20 rounds of ammunition, insufficient to fight even if they did engage.

This precaution would fit with efforts to restrict the ability of junior officers to rebel against their seniors and had a dramatic effect on the fight against Boko Haram. Given the way that the insurgents often travelled in large numbers, it would be a brave captain who ordered his troops to engage the enemy. The retired officers I spoke to said they were receiving reports from friends that troops would be pulled back from engaging the enemy at the last minute.

This was not particularly surprising to Hall, who said; "In those circumstances I can see and understand why they wouldn't want to engage the enemy!" Much better—from a longevity perspective—to melt away.

In September 2014 and in May 2015 scores of Nigerian troops were convicted in secret courts of mutiny, and many were sentenced to death. The exact reasons for their refusal to follow orders have not been officially released.[42]

The inaction of the military was so striking that, in July 2014, the insurgents discarded the usual tactics of guerrilla warfare and began claiming territory. They set out from their camps in the Sambisa forest and swept into the town of Damboa, in Borno, but instead of leaving as they had done in other attacks, they stayed. From there they expanded, and town after town fell. So unopposed were they that at one stage they controlled over 70 per cent of Borno state. They blew up bridges, leaving just one of the roads into Maiduguri still open. For weeks people lived in panic, thinking Boko Haram would march in at any minute. They pushed west along the border with Niger and south through Gwoza toward Yola in Adamawa state, turning west toward Chibok. As Boko Haram claimed more and more territory, pushing along the border regions of both Cameroon and Niger they probed deeper into Cameroon, fighting gendarmes, kidnapping the wife of a local politician and robbing banks. Nigeria's neighbours began to get really concerned. In late 2014 Cameroonian troops began pushing Boko Haram out of villages on their border. The Cameroonians pressed further into Nigeria, turning up 80km inside the border at Konduga in September where their government claimed, erroneously as it turned out, that its troops had killed Abubakar Shekau.[43][44]

Of particular concern to Chad was the road that stretches down through Cameroon to the port of Douala, particularly along the stretch from Maroua to Garoua, where it runs closest to the border with Nigeria. This is a major trade route where imported goods can enter the landlocked country, hence in January 2015 the government of Chad sent troops to Cameroon in order to secure the border with Nigeria.

Also in January 2015 there was a massacre by Boko Haram fighters at Baga, which by now had been battered several times by both the military and the insurgents. Many people fled into Chad, onto islands in the lake. No-one knew exactly what had happened as there was little way of getting information out of the area from people who had fled for their lives in terror. Two weeks later Abubakar Shekau claimed the attack in a video, where he also threatened the leaders of Chad, Niger and Cameroon.

Following the kidnap of the Chibok girls in 2014 the leaders of Nigeria Chad, Cameroon and Niger had agreed, at a summit in Paris, to form a multinational force to fight Boko Haram. But there had been little trust between the group of nations.

After the Baga attack, Chadian troops also crossed the border with the Nigerien army following suit. One of the towns they entered, pushing Boko Haram out, was Damasak, just across the dry river border from the Nigerien town of Diffa. Joe Penney, a photojournalist from the Reuters news agency flew in to Damasak shortly after the Chadian and Nigerian armies entered.

"There really wasn't a fight for Damasak, when the Chadians came Boko Haram just pulled back," Penney told me.[45]"By the time the Chadians arrived, everything was destroyed or looted, gone." When Boko Haram pulled out of town, ahead of the advancing soldiers they sent a number of unarmed young boys toward the Chadian line. "This boy told us that morning their *mallam* woke them and said 'Today you will meet your creator' and sent them to walk toward the advancing troops," presumably as a rudimentary distraction to aid the fighters' escape. Some of the young boys were killed before the advancing soldiers realised they were unarmed.

When he arrived, Penney said, women had gathered around the command post and were being given food and other aid by the troops from the Multi-National Task Force, but when Penney was there there were no Nigerian troops in Damasak. The women told Penney that as the Boko Haram fighters left, they took with them all the young women they could, as many as five hundred. After he reported this, the Nigerian army immediately issued a press release saying this was a fabrication, but Penney stands by his story.

"It's what the Nigerian military do. They denied it the next day, when in reality the nearest Nigerian military position was 80km away. How could they verify?"

The incursion into Damasak was just one of the cross border movements that occurred in early 2015. When they marched into towns that had been taken over on the fringes of Lake Chad, they dragged down Boko Haram's black and white *shahada* banner and replaced it with the Chadian flag.

"My concern" says Penney "is that they have gradually circled all of these little islands in Lake Chad, where actually thousands and thousands of people live, and after the rains they will go in and just wipe everyone they find out. Kill them all."

It is a tactic that has been used elsewhere in this conflict. The 2015 election was due to be held in February but it was postponed for six weeks. This, the government said, was to allow the military to improve the security situation in the north east to allow elections to be held. Many asked why it had taken the military so long to do this; why they left it so late before the elections. But the government did not respond clearly, maintaining that Washington's refusal to sell it weapons was to blame for the persistence of the problem. It was then that the Jonathan administration decided to contract a private military company to help the army in its mission.

Specialized Tasks Training Equipment and Protection (STTEP), run by veterans of the apartheid-era South African military who were also former partners in the infamous private military company Executive Outcomes, were contracted by Nigeria in late 2014. This happened at around the same time as the seizure of $9million by the South African authorities from a private jet belonging to key Jonathan ally and head of the Christian Association of Nigeria, Ayo Oritsjeafor, as it landed in Johannesburg.

In an interview with a magazine website aimed at the special forces community, STTEP's chairman Eeben Barlow said the special "strike force" the company assembled, from its own mercenaries and the best the Nigerian military had to offer, had a massive effect against Boko Haram in driving it out of the territory they held.[46] Part of the winning tactics was their use of helicopters. The company had to bring in its own, as the Nigerian military's air support was unreliable. (One of Nigeria's last functioning jets, one of the remaining Alpha fighters bought by the Second Republic, crashed in September 2014 while on a test flight out of Yola. The pilot was thought to have died in the crash, which was put down to an accident. A week later however, he featured in a Boko Haram video, where he was brutally beheaded with a farm axe).[47] On another occasion early on in the deployment of the mercenaries a helicopter crashed, killing three members of the team on board.[48]

The success of the lightly armed strike force was dependent on being able to constantly pursue Boko Haram. To achieve this they used the helicopters to ferry in supplies and fresh troops to keep pressing on. They used trackers, men adept at following people through the bush by following the insurgent's spoor. The strike force was able then to "frog jump", Barlow said, into position ahead of the enemy. Then, using intelligence provided by the mercenaries, the military designated an area as a "kill zone", where every contact assumed to be a hostile enemy is wiped out. With help from STTEP the military drove Boko Haram from Gwoza in March and pushed them back to their cave complexes and deep forest bases, where the rest of the military has continued to keep them on the back foot, albeit slowed by booby traps and heavy terrain.

In March 2015 Muhammadu Buhari and the newly unified opposition All Progressive Congress party won the Nigerian election, defeating Goodluck Jonathan convincingly. While every election since 1999 had been contested in the courts amid allegations of vote rigging and violence, this time, in a move without precedent in Nigeria, outgoing President Jonathan called Buhari to concede defeat. There would be no lengthy court battle and, for the first time in Nigeria's history, power switched from the ruling party to the party in opposition. The story of the election in the north was one of a ruling party whose political big men could no longer deliver their areas for the presidential election. Advancement in voter technology made the traditional rigging practices more difficult while Christian minorities, alienated from the PDP by its inaction over Boko Haram, voted for Buhari in droves.

The People's Democratic Party had been captured by Jonathan's cronies, and the All Progressives Congress, a coalition of politicians driven out of the PDP after clashes with Jonathan, and his wife, took advantage of this. The APC prevailed in an election thought too close to call, which surprised most outside the country. But in hindsight, there were many Nigerians who had been observing a gradual shift of momentum away from the PDP toward the APC over the previous two years.

It is possible that the rapid change in the army's fortunes that occurred in the six weeks after the announcement of the election postponement was connected to the growing prospect of Buhari winning. If Jonathan was sunk, a top military man might be given to think, a more aggressive attitude could save their job. In this, however, they were wrong. Buhari sacked all the service chiefs in July 2015, replacing them with new appointments, two of whom are from Borno state. The new Chief of Army Staff's first action was to hold a press conference in which he got down and did push ups with his men, in an attempt to distance himself from the previous regime's commanding officers, who were all very large and unfit.[49] "Definitely not a pot-bellied glutton", one poster on the Nigerian social media forum Nairaland wrote.

Since taking over, Buhari has been feted by both the governments of the United States and the United Kingdom. They see the 2015 elections as giving his administration a much better mandate than Jonathan had to lead the country, and seem much more comfortable dealing with Buhari than they were with the previous government. Buhari has been invited to both London and Washington for audiences with the President and Prime Minister, something which Jonathan was explicitly denied.

"With Buhari's election, the concerns raised in respect to Leahy [the Leahy act preventing arms sales] will likely go away," former US Ambassador John Campbell told me in June 2015. Shortly before Buhari was inaugurated and travelled to London, the British government announced a "refreshed" twenty-year military training partnership with Nigeria, of exactly the duration James Hall said was inconceivable under Jonathan just a year before.[50]

During the election Buhari made much of his knowledge of the military and his prowess in fighting an earlier radical insurgency that convulsed the north east—the 'Yan Tatsine, the followers of the "One Who Curses", Marwa Maitatsine.

Although not as internationally remembered as the War Against Indiscipline, the executions and the frogjumping civil servants, or as diplomatically disrupting as the Dikko affair, Buhari's time in office was marked by two 'Yan Tatsine riots that occurred in Yola in 1984 and in Gombe the following year. The history of that engagement, however, may not reveal such an uncontested military victory after all.

After the 1980 massacre in Kano in which Marwa Maitatsine was killed, and the further flare-ups of 1982 in Borno and Kaduna, the surviving 'Yan Tatsine went underground. They regrouped in Jimeta, a ward in the city of Yola which is now the state capital of Adamawa (at the time this state was called Gongola). Surviving members, some of whom had been arrested, interrogated, imprisoned and then released after the Kano revolt, took up residency in a number of slums and squatter camps. Buhari's military government received regular intelligence updates from the police, mostly reports about how they prayed at every hour of the day and night.[51]

In February 1984, after a number of minor scuffles between members of the sect and police monitoring the group, it was decided that the sect's activity needed to be curtailed and the members arrested. When they approached the Vinikilang slum, members of the group ambushed a police unit and seized their weapons. They started a riot, burning down homes in the neighbourhood, setting the people running in panic. They took women captive and holed up in a place called Dobeli, repelling all attempts to dislodge them from their stronghold, armed with a few guns stolen from the police, swords, machetes, knives and bows and arrows.

On the third day of the rampage, Buhari came to the city himself. Among the sect members, it was believed there were still innocent civilians trapped by the conflict. Over the next two days the police tried to rout the group, turning off all water and electricity into the area and calling on the rioters to let bystanders go. After yet another police assault was repulsed, the commanding officer asked that the army instead move in.The entire area was declared a "prohibited zone" for civilians, in effect giving the military a free hand to "liquidate" anyone they found inside.[52] The military shelled the area with heavy artillery until it had been flattened.

As the army moved in, the surviving members of the sect fled, burning everything in their path. Hundreds lay dead. An estimated 30,000 people, half the population of Jimeta, were homeless.[53]

After a day of combing through the wrecked slum, defusing unexploded booby traps, control was handed back to the police. To mark the end of the operation the military were given permission to march over the ruined area holding their regimental colours aloft.

But it was still not over. A few dozen members had escaped, diving into the river Benue to swim for their lives. Under the leadership of a man named Musa Makanaki (Musa the Mechanic) they re-grouped in the Pantami ward of Gombe town in Bauchi state. In April 1985, a year after the Jimeta clashes, after monitoring the sect for some time the police and state government decided to arrest some of its members, who were jailed without charge. Makanaki issued an ultimatum: the police should either charge their members, or release them. If they did not, the sect would burn Gombe to the ground.

That evening, the military governor of Bauchi declared on television that the "fanatics would be arrested by all means". Forewarned of the arrest plans, the sect laid an ambush and the next day the police, sent to arrest them, blundered into it. Police casualties were high, and the army was again deployed to bring the situation under control. Although several members were reported to have escaped the clutches of the military, over 100 were killed, and hundreds imprisoned.[54]

Those in prison faced a terrible fate. After the riot in Jimeta, 800 had been arrested. Between April and May of 1984 the government teased out from those they had arrested who were actually sect members, eventually releasing 265 people. The rest, including those arrested at Pantami, were locked in unventilated cells without water or food and simply left to die in jail. Prison records showed that most of the 'Yan Tatsine died of heart failure, starvation, thirst or disease.

According to Sabo Bako of Ahmadu Bello University Zaria, who interviewed surviving sect members in the early 1990s for a PhD thesis, in the cells they were reduced to cannibalism.[55] By 1988 the remaining members were released, some of them deported to Chad and Niger from where they had come.

"I have tried to win the confidence of those who are scared of me..." retired General Buhari told the audience at Chatham House. A nervous laughter rippled through the hall, "... because of my antecedence," he concluded with a knowing smile. Buhari had been asked about corruption, and about all the investigations that might be possible, dating all the way back to Independence.

He had met with many important Nigerians he said, from all over the country, "and whenever I meet them, I make sure to tell them that I shall draw a line... If we go back all the way to the 1960s, we may end up not achieving anything."[56]

Buhari had been speaking for about an hour when he was asked was his attitude to the future of sharia law in Nigeria. It was the last question in a batch of four, and after he answered the first three, he retook his seat.

In a clamour, the audience called: "Sharia! Sharia!" Buhari looked puzzled as he was reminded he hadn't answered the final question. He quipped: "Ah! You see I love sharia so much it slipped my mind. Sharia law is limited to the level of the customary court" the presidential candidate said, "the federal court comes above it, and if anyone wants to change it, let them change the constitution first!"

It was a politician's answer. Buhari has achieved a deal of political refinement in the past few years. The question among many watching Nigeria is how deep will this change go? What really is the All Progressive Congress capacity for positive reform? The general perception among most diplomats, analysts and journalists I have spoken to is that even if Buhari is the right man to lead Nigeria during this crisis, he is only one man.

He does have his allies, this time. After elections in 2003, 2007 and 2011 the rump of the opposition left him high and dry, pursuing doomed court challenges to the elections alone. They opted instead to come to terms with the PDP government. But now the opposition group sat in the front row at his public appearances, clapping and laughing. I don't think I was alone in wondering where exactly Buhari's line would be drawn, and which of the many people who had allied themselves with him would find themselves on the right side of it?

As everyone left the Chatham House auditorium, it had begun to rain outside. In order to avoid competing crowds of pro and anti government protesters in St James' Square, everyone was directed out of a side door. None of the departing audience, however, wanted to step into the street and get wet. This created an immovable block and a backlog of people in a go-slow through the Georgian building. Inside, the former Lagos Governor, Ahmed Bola Tinubu, one of Buhari's new allies and a key person in delivering the election in the south west, called his driver to the side entrance to pick him up. As the car came around it blocked the way of a London black cab and a truck delivering building supplies and narrowly missed a cycle courier. Within seconds they were all yelling at each other, pointing fingers in each other's faces. The protesters, hearing that the audience were leaving the venue by a side door, ran around to jam the street, all dressed in matching sloganed T-shirts over their normal clothes, waving placards, uulating, singing and dancing and blowing horns. I stood back, watching the scene unfold.

10

STRANGE CARTOGRAPHY

"Look, really there's something you have to understand..."

Kaura and I were driving to Kaduna under a grey September sky. We had started out in the early morning when the green verges were still lush and wet and before the cool breeze was replaced by muggy, dead air. From time to time we would drive through showers that slapped the windscreen with fat drops of water.

For most of the journey we discussed the current crisis, and the general state of Nigeria more broadly. Our discussions seemed to return always to the same point. It was one I have discussed many times with many people, always over different specifics, but it usually comes down to a version of the same core argument: what, in Nigerian affairs, can be attributed to Nigeria's culture of careless management, low institutional capacity or even outright chaotic idiocy, and what can be attributed to the calculating actions of conniving cabals?

Kaura is from Nasarawa, a very rural, heavily forested state to the south-east of the capital. I was telling him about a pair of Zimbabwean farmers I bumped into when I first arrived in Nigeria, at Lagos airport. The men, father and son, had left Zimbabwe after their farm was seized by Robert Mugabe's Zanu-PF government. The pair were following some friends who had already moved to Nasarawa at the personal invitation of the governor. They and their families were starting over, full of hope and enthusiasm for their new venture: four grid points on a map, land leased to them by the state government. The land would have to be prepared from scratch, turned from forest into productive commercial farmland.

"The land is so fertile, it's amazing," Dion, the younger man had said. "There's potential for several crops out of a single season. I've never seen anything like it. Managed right, Nigeria could be an agricultural powerhouse."

A year later I bumped into Dion again. Things were not going well. They were struggling to get finance from Nigerian banks. "Nobody understands seasonal lending for agriculture," he said, exasperation creeping into his voice, despite his best efforts. "It's a standard practice all over the world, but here, because no one has done it for years, they just said it couldn't be done. They didn't have a clue, we had to take the bank manager to the state legislature to show him the law that made it possible. We had to get the gazette of legislation out and point to the law on the page."

I heard that, around six months after I met him for the second time, Dion and his father called it quits and left Nigeria, disillusioned. Other Zimbabwean farmers remain, but finance has been a struggle for them. I thought their trouble was an example of how incompetence and poor capacity in one area, in this case banking, held back progress in another important developmental sector: commercial farming.

But Kaura wasn't having it. "No no no. I'm sure if you were to look into that case more closely," he said, "you would find someone was holding them back, someone didn't want them to succeed. I'm certain that they must have had links to politics?"

I remembered then a story that the men told me. When they first arrived the Governor of Nasarawa threw a party at government house for them. He invited the governors of neighbouring states and, when welcoming the Zimbabweans, he turned to the other governors and said: "See, here are my white farmers... Now where are your white farmers?"

Kaura smiled, lifted his hand from the steering wheel and opened his ringed fingers to reveal his palm. "You see?"

"But don't you think that's just a bit speculative, I mean, it's at best a rumour, isn't it?" I said.

"Listen, what you have to understand is most times, when you really look... in Nigeria, rumours, they have a way of turning out to be true."

This may seem like a strange thing to say, but in a surprising and important way, he is absolutely right.

* * *

In April 2014 Stephen Davis, a 63-year-old retired Church of England clergyman, travelled to Nigeria. He was about to embark on a secret and incredibly dangerous mission.

Davis wanted to use connections he had among Islamic radicals to try to open a dialogue with the kidnappers of the Chibok girls in order to bring about a positive resolution to the situation.

This was not the first time he had done something like this.[1] In 2004 he and a local activist helped engineer a truce in a war raging between several gangs and the military in the creeks of the Niger Delta. These gangs of "boys" were a product of Nigeria's violent elections. They were given weapons by politicians in the run up to the 2003 polls and promised money in return for providing the muscle their masters needed to bully the election process. But when the elections were over, the boys were dropped, cut off. These crude militias of unemployed youths retreated deep in the creeks, the waterways that wind like a labyrinth through the brackish mangrove swamp. In their camps they could do what they wanted, they drank, took drugs, raided local villages for young women, fantasised about what they would do if they had money, bragged and swaggered. They also recreated ancestor cults, picked up from the talk of their parents and grandparents (who in most cases had abandoned these beliefs in favour of Evangelical Christianity).

From these camps they skirmished with the military and police Joint Task Force and ran extortion rackets against multinational oil companies, kidnapping foreign workers and blowing up pipelines, spilling crude over the land and into the water. They also acted as muscle for another criminal concern; oil bunkerers—thieves who robbed unquantifiable amounts of crude from pipelines in return for guns, cocaine, and cash from rogue oil traders. All this was the source of a dramatic disruption in the flow of oil from the well heads to the export terminals. Millions of barrels a day were shut-in, Nigeria's funding was choked off.[2]

This was not an easy thing to untangle. The oil thieves had connections to the politicians and godfathers who had armed the boys in the first place. There were also connections to the military the boys were regularly fighting. This is the complicated web of criminality that is woven into the state, with criminal syndicates deeply embedded in Nigerian political society.

The peace Davis negotiated in 2004, with the Niger Delta People's Volunteer Force, led by a man named Dokubo Asari, did not hold. Once Asari's boys were out of the way, other groups got in on the act. The promised pay off for Asari's boys and a programme of job training never materialised and the brokered deal dissolved. But Davis had developed a clear picture of how this system worked, and understood it very well. He could read the lay of the land, even the bits that were occluded by a fog of theatrical deception, bits which might otherwise be impenetrable to him as a white outsider. These parts were filled in by informants, amenable local activists who had their own picture of how things worked.

In order to find a more permanent peace, he concluded, there had to be a political will on behalf of the politicians to provide job training and opportunities for the boys they had picked up and then dropped. The political "godfathers" who bore responsibility for the gangs' creation should be reined in with stern action to curtail their activities.

It wasn't until 2010 that concerted pressure was put on the militants to disarm. An uneasy cessation to the conflict in the Delta was negotiated by the government of President Yar'Adua firstly, and then Goodluck Jonathan. They threw money at an amnesty programme, gave key militants plum positions in government agencies and called upon local politicians to cooperate, many of whom were connected to Jonathan by ethnicity or political obligation. The peace will, in all likelihood, be temporary. Most likely it will last only as long as the money does.

During the 2004 peace process Davis had established himself as a negotiator. He won friends in Obasanjo's presidency, but he also made enemies. Davis told me he had to leave Nigeria following the peace deal with Asari after a contact in the military told him he "could no longer protect him" from the bunkering syndicates on whose toes he had apparently trodden.

In 2008 though, Davis was back in Nigeria. That was when I met him, after he helped me arrange an interview with the brother of an imprisoned leader of a Delta militant group. However Davis either did not let on, or I did not cotton on to, the fact he had other business in Nigeria at the time. According to interviews he gave in 2014, he was there at the request of President Umaru Yar'Adua, travelling around the north, talking to radical Islamic groups, trying to establish forums for interfaith dialogue.

Among the many sects he encountered were, he said, the group who would rise up in Maiduguri in 2009.[3]

I spoke to him again in 2009, this time from London. Davis told me he had been diagnosed with stomach cancer. He was responding well to treatment, he said, adding he was taking each day as a blessing. I got the impression during our conversation that the prognosis was bleak. A few weeks later he wrote an email to journalists he had communicated with over the years. He owned up to managing a website which hosted many useful documents about the shady world of oil theft, gun running and Delta gangs, under the pseudonym "Stephanie Omunna". He asked us to download the documents we needed, as the website would shortly be taken down. The email had an air of finality about it, as if it was from a man who wanted to tie up loose ends.

But Davis did not succumb to his illness. When he heard about the Chibok kidnappings, he was back at his home in Western Australia. He had been in remission from a serious illness, one which in most cases is terminal, for almost five years. The news of the kidnapping had a dramatic effect on him.

"I have three daughters," he would tell a Nigerian journalist later, "I just cannot stand the thought of what those girls are passing through. I have spoken to an escapee who described how she was being raped for forty days by militants. I can't stand it. It is heart-breaking."[4] It is hard not to conclude that after Davis was confronted with the possibility of his life's imminent ending, he wanted to use his remaining time to achieve something.

Davis reactivated contacts he made travelling the north. He hoped they could get him where no other white Westerner had gone voluntarily, into the company of Boko Haram's leadership. He put himself in the hands of his interlocutors, and went to the north east to seek out people with a reputation for terrible violence, with no back up or method of escape if things went wrong.

He emerged again, three months later, with a remarkable story.

Around northern towns and cities most afternoons—particularly Fridays after prayer—you can find men sitting in the shade of a tree, chewing kola nut and ruminating. As they talk, young street hawkers might be attending to their hands and feet with their manicure kits. If it's a Friday, perhaps a quiet, purse-lipped, barber might be scraping their heads with a razor.

On the ground nearby there is likely to be a tarpaulin spread out with newspapers laid in rows, their mastheads and page one headlines visible, the most enticing splash of them all on top. For a fraction of the cover price, newspaper vendors allow people to read one and replace it. In addition to newspapers, radio is an important medium. The BBC, Voice of America and Deutsche-Welle all have Hausa language services that reach millions of people on medium-wave. Local FM stations like Kano's Freedom Radio are also listened to avidly, so much so that the stereotypical image of a Hausa man is be-kaftanned, wearing a round, peak-less kube cap at a rakish angle, cycling slowly along the road, pressing a transistor radio to his ear.[5] People sit around poring over the articles, declaiming them aloud, others interjecting with praise or mockery for the dramatis personae; usually the big men of the political elite—or otherwise football, sometimes both simultaneously, always vociferously.

The news pages and feature sections of newspapers are dominated by interviews with politicians and political players. Most stories have what look like fairly unpromising headlines. If they are illustrated with photographs, they are usually dull photos of large, elegantly-dressed men shaking hands with other large, elegantly-dressed men. The articles themselves are arcane, written in a syntax full of journalese which I always found difficult to follow. For two years at the *Daily Trust* it was my job to edit much of this copy. Often I found if I tried to unpick it, to find out what was actually being said, the news angle crumbled away to dust. It was not uncommon for the subjects of these interviews to say one thing and then a few paragraphs later they might directly contradict themselves. Often in these moments I would find myself seeking out the senior political reporter, to ask in ever more desperate tones: "But what is this story ABOUT Hameed? He's said one thing here and then the other here... I don't understand." On these occasions Hameed looked at me pityingly. "They are politicians, they talk from both sides of their mouths," was all he said. Attempts to get reporters to pin the subjects of these stories down during interviews were resisted. The sheer volume of comment from people who seemed to be minor figures on the issues of the day was difficult to understand. Their interjections always seemed to muddy the waters as much as to clarify them.

One day I noticed an article in which a big political player countered an assertion made the previous day by another politician. In doing so he asserted that something else entirely was true, but he provided no supporting evidence to prove it; he simply contradicted the previous statement. I asked a colleague; "How does he know that? Why should we believe what he says if he can't substantiate it?"

My colleague said simply: "He may know because he is part of that group of people who would know".

It was a long time before I realised that the importance of many of these stories was not necessarily what was being said, but that the person featured in the article had spoken. What the reader was being told was, this person—the constituency and ethnic identity they represent—has a role in the debate at hand. In the parlance of Nigerian politics they were "relevant".

The newspapers were confusing for the outsider because, unlike in much of the European or American press, most of what was printed could be classified as a "who story"—where the primary aspect is the fact that the object of the story spoke, the actual content of the speech or press release is secondary. Ignoring celebrity "news" and sports, the list of people who merit a "who" story in American or British public affairs is quite short.

This is not so in Nigeria, where the cast of people meriting a "who" story is as broad as the political elite itself. For the political player, appearing to have an inside track is the route to advancement, even if it is off track. In the logic of "settlement" the purpose of these accusations is to make the accuser someone who has to be settled too.

Consequently there is a high level of corruption in the media. Journalists are poorly paid by their employers, who are aware that they are providing their employees acess to a marketplace where they can hustle among political players, who are more than willing to pay for their services. Journalists interviewing prominent people are often relegated to the role of stenographer. Often the journalist has indeed been paid to write the story by the article's subject. The lines between who the journalist is actually working for—the media outlet, which might not actually pay, or the members of the political elite, who do, are blurred. The media are focused not so much on breaking scoops, as operating as a trade paper, showing who is up and who is down in the market of Nigerian politics.

Journalists themselves are often the children of small-time traders, teachers, or low-ranking military officers; the children of parents outside the petro-political elite, who scrimped and saved to put their child through education—often only able to send one of their children to university, the child upon whose shoulders all their hopes rest. Journalism is an opportunity to convert this investment into access to the patrimony being circulated above their parent's heads. Often the journalists' mission is not to shine a light on the powerful, but become their spokesperson. Many aim to hitch their tender to a bigger yacht in the hope of catching a rising political tide.

This is all very well understood by the Nigerian readership. And yet, perhaps contrary to what might be expected; that such corruption would lead to people to abandon these corrupt media streams—people cogitate over the one sided, dense and confusing articles. They are read with great care, absorbed at length.

People in Nigeria know that politics is done behind closed doors in secret deals brokered at midnight meetings in swish Abuja neighbourhoods between a cabal of leaders. Newspaper readers scour interviews with the leaders of ethnic cultural groups, former generals or senior members of the senate, trying to divine what was going on behind the veil of politics. While few of these people accuse each other outright of corruption and criminality explicitly, innuendo and attack spin are common. The goal is to advance the negotiating power of a particular group the politician represents, in what has been called "ethnic entrepreneurialism",[6] the ultimate purpose of which is to corner the market in patrimony. The prize is maintaining or increasing their position and maximising their share of the proceeds of patrimonial politics. The best players of the game will be able quickly to exploit shifting alliances and master the use of imperfect information. The observers too become experts at reading the gaps.

These days discussions about the intent and origin of the political elite do not just happen under a dogonyaro tree. Most people are involved in at least one, and possibly several informal discussion circles. These groups, especially among the political elite, have a long history. They were pivotal for the independence generation, the discussion group being the place where young activists obtained an education and circulated anti-colonial ideas. They persisted among people through the periods of military rule. Indeed, it was the attempt to lift these sorts of institutions out of their ethnically polarised nature that contributed to the failure of the 1992–3 transition to democracy under IBB. Although the process was aborted by Babangida, and the bringing together of the social associations that were to be the foundation of the political parties was a failure, it at least recognised how important the informal association is in Nigeria.

As well as these forms of association, people now participate in on-line message groups, chat forums, email reply chains and proto-social media websites like Nairaland.com and Gamji.org (these are popular websites where anyone can write op-ed articles or rejoinders to others), and of course now Facebook and Whatsapp (Twitter is not as popular for these discussions in northern Nigeria as its character limit does not suit the kind of discussion style of long-form articles and rejoinders, nor the idiom of Hausa language culture, which avoids getting to the point directly).

In the absence of reliable institutions of record that are trusted across the barriers of politicised ethnicity and identity politics, these forums are where people "meet" to construct their Nigeria, establish in rhetorical terms what is going on and defend their version with fierce argument. What people find persuasive in these settings can be influenced as much by their personal background, their identities, as by verifiable fact.

My reservations about the stories that people tell themselves about Nigeria always came down to one question, which seems to be hardly ever asked or answered: "How do you know that?" How one knows something in Nigeria is as much to do with who you are, as what it is.

Despite this reflexive unreliability, it does seem that political decisions, especially in the issues surrounding the sharing of government patronage and influence, require such wide compliance from other interest groups that many people could have a handle on the inside track. While the perception is that this is all done at the level of the leadership "inner circle", it must also be acknowledged that there are many inner circles in Nigeria, at the national level, the state level, the level of the various ethnic groups. There are few inner circles that are completely watertight when it comes to information. Everyone in the cabal has their own interest, and sometimes that is better served by talking.

Nigeria is not a society of political secrets. It is incredibly difficult to keep one, it seems. The main players don't do anything alone, they are always accompanied by aides, servants and factotums ready to spill the beans to a political rival who will call in the media when it's time to rubbish their opponents. Unlike the "whatever you say, say nothing" attitude of secretive politics elsewhere in the world. Nigeria's political discourse could be more accurately said to be a mass of narratives; often it's impossible to distinguish what is true from what is false.

And once something becomes known, printed in the media and declaimed in public, a funny thing happens. By some method of strange cartography it is assimilated into charts mapping an intricate and fascinating landscape, with its switchback trails and hidden caves, striated with ha-has.

There are no institutions which have the ultimate ability to determine which of these features are real and which are invented. Instead most people deal with this in a very counter-innovative and interesting way. As the story is repeated in the echo chambers of public discourse, crossing from media to discussion group to spokesman and from there back into the media, garnering more strength at every stage, until eventually so many people believe it that it becomes—functionally and for all intents and purposes—true.

Perhaps unsurprisingly, the explanation stories, narratives that explain what Boko Haram is, are legion. Some of them are absurd; most of them are plausible. Some of the stories have changed over the past five years, but many of them are contradictory, or at the very least problematic.

Most analysis starts with Boko Haram as a local insurgency with local aims, but others say that Boko Haram is the frontier of a new internationalist jihadi movement. Even that is not simple; some people see Boko Haram as connected to al-Qaeda. Others point out Boko Haram has made *bay'ah*—a pledge of loyalty—to al-Qaeda's other arch-enemy, Islamic State.

When they returned to north east Nigeria in 2010 Boko Haram was about vengeance, avenging the name and following the revolutionary ideas of Mohammed Yusuf. But others say, contradictorily, that Boko Haram is a group of thugs used by the political elite to maintain the status quo.

Boko Haram have said themselves they want to destroy the corrupt Muslims of the north east and strengthen Islamic law there. But some assert

Boko Haram want to Islamise the whole of Nigeria. Others say they are the tools of the northern elite who have tried to push for stronger implementation of sharia, and failed to do so before; or in other words Boko Haram are far from being outsiders; rather, they're hot-wired to the heart of northern Nigerian politics.

Simultaneously, however, there are people who say Boko Haram are a rag tag bunch of illiterates with no links to anyone; a rag tag bunch of illiterates on an impossible quest to destroy the secular state. To other observers Boko Haram is the creation of the military, sponsored by a high ranking officer—a Christian from the South East to boot.

Boko Haram is, allegedly, a plot by the United States to destroy Nigeria. Or Boko Haram's activities and its members are sponsored by the northern political elite. Boko Haram is part of a southern Christian government's attempt to wrest power from the north. To others, Boko Haram is part of a caliphate that seeks to remove every border between Nigeria and Baghdad, unifying it under the singular law of Islam. Alternatively again, Boko Haram is a hyper-local drive for greater power by, ethnically Kanuri nationalists.

Can all of these things be true at the same time?

There are deeper twists in the story. It has been said that Boko Haram's focus on the conflict in Plateau state shows they want to get involved in the near-twenty-year long simmering conflict there. Abubakar Shekau himself said so when he angrily condemned Christians in Jos for killing and eating Muslims in 2011. But there are credible stories that Boko Haram has Christian members. Can these people who profess to hate the Christians on the Jos Plateau also be cooperating with Christians, right up to and including paying them to bomb Christian churches for them?

The stories about Shekau are also contradictory. Abubakar Shekau is a mastermind, involved in every decision; Abubakar Shekau is like the father of a household, in charge but only consulted on certain things and who allows the running of the organisation to be delegated to his emirs; Abubakar Shekau is a clueless, mentally ill drug addict, isolated and hidden away from the rest of the sect. Abubakar Shekau is actually three men. Abubakar Shekau is dead.

Their appreciation of history is also grounds for disagreement among analysts. Boko Haram are obsessed with the legacy of Shehu Othman dan Fodiyo, and speak of him often. And yet some analysts insist that Boko Haram is a modern expression of the ancient and noble Bornu Emirate, historically the sworn enemies of Sokoto. (If that were true, why would they not talk about the Safayyids and their legendary Champion El-Kanemi?)

Boko Haram are a threat to neighbouring Chad. Or Boko Haram are a creation of Chadian oil barons, with the acquiescence of the president, with eyes on as yet untapped reserves on the western side of Lake Chad.

Boko Haram are illiterates from the lowest parts of society; Boko Haram control the lucrative smuggled petrol, chili and smoked fish trades. Boko Haram are a rag-tag militia; Boko Haram have better weapons than the Nigerian military.

Boko Haram are floating on a sea of weapons that flow south from Libya on the falling tide of Gaddafi's ouster. Boko Haram are boosted by weapons and explosives from Niger Delta hoodlums.

Boko Haram hate Western education to the extent they attack schools and slaughter and enslave school children. Boko Haram use the products of Western education; weapons and ultra-modern communication tools like the internet.

Boko Haram are funded by Saudi Arabia; Boko Haram are funded by European companies paying ransoms.

Boko Haram enslave women. Boko Haram have units of fighting women. Boko Haram dupe and brainwash young women into carrying suicide bombs. Young women are at the forefront of the group's radicalisation, leading it, not following.

Boko Haram are located in remote camps far away from towns and cities. Boko Haram can appear at a moment's notice in strength.

Boko Haram are hard-line Salafist Muslims. Boko Haram are cultists who indulge in blood ritual and charms.

Boko Haram would stop if their goals were met. Boko Haram will never ever stop.

Distinguishing between these narratives can be impossible, especially as many proponents will simply say that they have a direct line to the source and are the only ones who know anything for real. The others, they invariably say, are simply clueless.

The narrative is so confused that it is impossible to untangle with any certainty. What is more understandable is a meta-narrative of the tellers. The truth is that all of these contradictory stories cannot be properly understood until it is realised that the importance is not in what is being said.

The narratives seeking to explain Boko Haram, describe who they are and what they want, are broadly divisible into genres. Which genre you are inclined to prefer is often dependent on your identity. There are the stories told by southern Christians and the stories proposed by northern Muslims. Further to this there are the tales told by northern Christians and other minority groups in the north. There are also narratives that originate from outside Nigeria, and are told by analysts from outside, looking in.

Some of the stories were wild and outlandish. The version that said Boko Haram were an attempt by the US to destroy Nigeria was based on reports in the Nigerian media of Washington think-tanks who forecast that the country could break up in 2015 or 2030, combined with a well circulated story that someone from the US Embassy in Abuja visited Mohammed Yusuf while he was detained before 2009.

As Raufu Mustapha of Oxford University has written, some of these stories can be set aside easily, but others are more difficult to dismiss. He has studied these narratives extensively, and says they fall into three different types: those that focus on the religious, the political and the military elements. All of the stories, Mustapha says, lack fundamental evidence to confirm them, but are very persuasive to observers nonetheless. They are big on speculation, short on evidence.[7]

Most of these stories refer to Boko Haram as a player in Nigeria's electoral politics, with specific reference to the hotly contested election of 2015. Supporters of the government of Goodluck Jonathan asserted Boko Haram were funded and supported by northern big men as an attempt to destabilise Nigeria and oust Jonathan from power. Close confidants of the president, like Edwin Clarke, an elder of the Ijaw people—the ethnic group in the Niger Delta from whom Jonathan hails—used the media to issue calls to his counterparts in the north to "rein in their boys". Pastor Ayo Oritsjeafor spoke of the threat of Boko Haram as being primarily one based in the desire of northern elites to "Islamise" the whole of Nigeria. Another Jonathan ally, the Niger Delta militant Dokubo Asari, said that if the northern elite used Boko Haram to scotch Jonathan's re-election, the Ijaw would "set the country on fire".

Other people pointed to Buhari's supposed remark, widely circulated as true, and yet not quite accurate, that the People's Democratic Party fixing the 2011 election to allow President Jonathan to continue as president despite it being "the north's turn", and tearing up the power rotation agreement, would make the country "ungovernable". Boko Haram was the embodiment of this threat, they believed.

Jonathan himself had at certain points endorsed this view. Journalists who were granted an interview with him after the Chibok kidnappings told me the president believed engaging with Boko Haram would be to step into his enemies' trap. Instead of which, they decided to shun the insurgents.

Among northern Nigerians, people tended to veer in the other direction, to see Boko Haram as part of a government plot to keep Jonathan's clique in power. Proponents of these theories pointed to the weakness of the Nigerian military, and the repeated instances of how they would retreat rather than confront the sect, allowing Boko Haram an effective free rein. Time and time again I heard that this was uncharacteristic for a military lauded all over the world for its peace-keeping efforts overseas.

As an example of the kind of evidence people relied on for this interpretation, in Zaria I spoke to Professor A.S. Mohammed, of Ahmadu Bello University, who told me he had been in contact with serving soldiers, young men he had sponsored to join the military, who had told him Boko Haram were being aided by Nigeria's own forces. Mohammed had heard this from several people, who told him it was that it was common knowledge around the barracks that soldiers had seen other Nigerian military personnel fighting on Boko Haram's side during firefights with them in the bush.

When I said I had reservations about this, Mohammed replied: "I too had the same reservations at the start, but when you hear the same thing, or similar stories time and time again from different people, you start to believe it."[9]

Allegations concerning military personnel on the other side of firefights were similar to a report that featured on the Voice of America Hausa service some weeks before, in which an unnamed soldier told the news outlet that he had seen a soldier he knew well, a man who had trained him in how to fire his weapon, moving through the bush.

Another common feature of these stories is the "mysterious helicopter". In 2014 a group of elders in the Borno political elite, retired civil servants and military officers mostly, calling themselves the "Borno Yobe People's Forum" held a press conference where they asked the government to respond to reports they had received about unexplained military helicopter sorties from military bases.[10]

The report does not say how the military retirees obained this information, but it is likely to be from similar kinds of sources as A.S. Mohammed's: serving soldiers who they have sponsored from their area as a form of patronage.

Of course it is possible that there are military officers who are colluding with Boko Haram.[11] Just as there were members of the Liberian peacekeeping force who were selling Nigerian military weapons and equipment to both sets of rebels, any opportunity for self-enrichment cannot be ruled out.[12] But the narrative put forward that there is high level involvement, connected to the People's Democratic Party, seemed to be outlandish. If they were getting their information from people in the service, then the quality of that intelligence might be conditional on how much that person knows.

These stories are founded on the assumption that the state is otherwise capable of dealing with something like this, as it has done in the past. As the spokesman for the Borno Yobe People's Forum, former Chief of Air Staff, Air Vice Marshall Al-Amin Dagash said: "How did a little band of rag-tag misguided youths metamorphose into a well-kitted, well-armed killing machine moving freely in convoy of vehicles and supported by helicopters?"

This refusal to believe that the institutions of Nigeria's security could be laid low by a band of "rag-tag" misguided youths seems to be at the centre of this idea that the situation is being orchestrated by some organ of a powerful "deep state".

On the other hand, accounts by outside analysts seemed to concern themselves with the degree to which Boko Haram were aligned with other groups of international jihadis.

Here two overarching narratives have been deployed. The first is that Boko Haram used its international connections in pursuit of its own local goals. The other posits that northern Nigeria is the frontier of international Jihad, and that Boko Haram were, up until 2014, being influenced by al-Qaeda, via the Ansaru splinter group of Yusuf's sect.

The first version, that Boko Haram are a local group with local aims, plays down the direct threat they pose to Western capitals and sees a limited role for international actors. The second suggests that the governments of Western nations should see Boko Haram in terms of how it poses a threat to them. The importance of the connections with al-Qaeda seemed to evaporate in the summer of 2014 when the forces of the Islamic State launched themselves onto the world stage, overwhelming the Iraqi military in a manner that resembled how Boko Haram had turned the tables on the Nigerian military in the country's northeast.

Goodluck Jonathan has also advocated versions of the story that emphasised the role of foreign forces. He drew attention to the group's overseas connections and asserted they were the representatives of al-Qaeda in Nigeria, in the aftermath of the botched rescue of two Western hostages. He appealed for money from the international community to help Nigeria fight the enemy of the West. Military spokesmen have also emphasised the foreign nature of Boko Haram, telling any journalist with a pen that the fighters they were encountering were foreign. Exactly how foreign was debatable; the countries commonly listed were Chad, Niger and Cameroon, just over the border.

All the different genres of narrative concerning Boko Haram speak to different experiences of a broad and complex phenomenon. Simultaneously, these experiences are happening in a place where there are no institutions of record that anyone in a highly fractious society can fully trust.

The questions that these accounts seek to address are about where Boko Haram sit in the spectrum of Nigerian political culture, using the tropes of previous political conflicts. Among the questions are: who are their sponsors or godfathers? Into which part of the Nigerian patrimonial network do they fit?

But existing analyses of Boko Haram do not provide satisfactory answers to many of the key questions. There is no reason why they should, as that is not their purpose. Accounts of Boko Haram are mostly self-serving. They do not rely on evidence and use interpretations to direct policy, and seek to further the interests of the group within a theatre of politics concerned only with keeping a grip on the sources of patronage.

Given the partisan nature of most of the accounts, it is perhaps unsurprising that they often contradict one another. If one assesses them they all seem to have weaknesses—one might even call them "plot holes". To get to the bottom of this, an analyst might be forgiven for suggesting it would be helpful for an independent observer, someone without an iron in the fire of Nigerian politics, to contact the group and really find out what it is all about.

When Stephen Davis re-emerged from his mission, he gave several revealing interviews to reporters. He had come face to face with Boko Haram commanders, he said, and furthermore he had come within a whisker of retrieving some of the kidnapped Chibok girls.

Using the connections he had made among Islamic radicals, he facilitated a meeting with Boko Haram commanders in a remote village, at considerable risk to his own life. He told journalists: "When confronted by groups with an AK-47 in my face they'd say 'You are American we have to kill you. When you say no I'm not American they think you are British and say 'you will still die', but when I say I'm Australian, they say 'that's alright'. I have no idea why but it's certainly been helpful."[13]

They informed him that Boko Haram was not all together in one place, rather it was split over half a dozen or so camps across Borno state. In addition to that, there were other camps outside Nigerian territory, in Chad, Niger and Cameroon. The Chibok Girls had been taken beyond Nigeria's borders, they said.

The people he spoke to were not implacably opposed to dialogue, he reported. They had political demands that could be met. Specifically, they wanted compensation for widows of slain fighters and—contrary to the groups perceived anti-education stance—they wanted training and job opportunities, education to better their lives and prospects.

Davis tried to persuade them to release a small number of people as a goodwill gesture, to open up a dialogue. After much persuasion they agreed to arrange a limited release, initially of eighteen girls from among the two hundred who had been taken from Chibok. The girls were sick and in need of medical treatment, he said.[14]

The arrangement he brokered was that Boko Haram would bring the girls over the border back into Nigeria to be dropped off in a village. From that moment there was a mad dash to get everything ready: "The president gave me a military jet, got me up there (to the border region), and a military convoy with ambulances. In the local hospital they set up a trauma unit to bring the girls back to. The deal was that Boko Haram would bring them over the border from Cameroon to a village, they would leave the girls there and then call us and tell us where they were... That would give us an hour for us to get to the village and an hour for Boko Haram to get away."[15]

It was a breakthrough, a chance to bring some girls back. Davis resolutely believed it was also a first move towards a solution to the wider situation: "This was the first step to a peace deal," he said.

"We got the call on the appointed morning, and there were far more girls than we thought, twenty vehicles with upwards of sixty girls. So we set out with an ambulance convoy and it was a four and a half hour trip in the end because the roads were so bad."

The pick-up location was a farm at the edge of a very remote village in Borno. They had difficulty finding it and when they finally arrived they found no girls waiting for them.

"It was just dark as we got close to there, we were led a bit of a merry chase around the way, when we reached the remote village and a remote farm outside of it we had missed them by about fifteen minutes," Davis said.

The explanation he was given hinged on a truly amazing sequence of events. Because the police had announced there was to be a reward for the return of the girls, another group of people had tried to kidnap them from the rendezvous point. The Boko Haram commander who Davis had been dealing with later told him that they had been keeping an eye on the place where the drop had been scheduled, but someone other than Davis's convoy showed up first to take the girls.

"What of the girls?" Davis recounted, "the girls were back with Boko Haram. What of the people who took them before we arrived at the village;

well the commanders said they had 'taken care' of those people. They didn't give many details but I'm sure it wasn't a pleasant outcome."

With the girls back out of reach and Davis's efforts being frustrated seemingly by unseen hands, it was a disappointing outcome for everyone.

But Davis learned something about Boko Haram that could be useful in understanding them further. He said that it was this very frustration of his efforts that indicated there was a powerful hand behind the group.

As part of the same interview Davis named two individuals who, he said, were funding Boko Haram and as part of that process, directing the group toward targets. He named a former northern governor, and a high ranking military officer.

"Some of the most prominent and influential politicians in Nigeria are the sources of funding for Boko Haram, and indeed as a sponsor you can participate by nominating targets" he told Arise TV in August 2014. The key part of this analysis was that this political funding had been continuous all through the group's life and had a material effect on the group's decision-making.

It was a familiar situation to Davis: "We've had this in the Niger Delta," he said.

These politicians were seeking positions in opposition to the government of Goodluck Jonathan at the 2015 elections. Funding Boko Haram was part of their strategy, Davis said. President Jonathan thereby faced a dilemma: he could not go after these men because to arrest them would be construed by outside observers as being anti-democratic, and countries like the the United States and Britain might cry foul over the polls.

The only way to progress, he said, would be to take out the sponsors. "Those guys (the Boko Haram commanders) they have told me clearly that they will not do any deal because the sponsors will direct the other guys to kill the ones willing to enter into a peace deal," he said.

At the same time, Davis seemed to go some way toward voicing support for President Jonathan and the government, clearing the President from involvement in the clash of political thugs; "people don't really understand how much this president has done to try and stop this," he said.

This was a fairly clear vision of what Boko Haram was. According to Davis, Boko Haram was not only the creation of Nigerian political players, particularly those in opposition to the PDP government of President Jonathan, it was also their continuing project. These shadowy figures not only provided seed funding for the group as election thugs, Davis said, but continued to support them even after 2009, when Boko Haram had been targeting local leaders and even family members of the man he accused of continuing to sponsor them.

Davis didn't really go into the specifics of how the military commander he accused of sponsoring Boko Haram interacted with the group, but he said that the military were benefiting from the conflict, and by naming the highest commander—who had just been sacked by the president some time before in a change of the service chiefs, suggested that the collaboration stretched right to the top.

At a point in the future, Davis said, the control of the politicians would be overtaken by the connections with international jihadi groups and Boko Haram would become a self-sustaining phenomenon. Once this happened, Davis said, the group would be impossible to destroy within twenty years. But at the time of the interview, in August 2015, this had not yet occurred. Something could yet be done to avert it.

Almost as soon as Davis had spoken, however, the fog of confusion seemed to descend again. Other people began to attack his version of events.

The former *Daily Trust* journalist Ahmed Salkida who had been in contact with Mohammed Yusuf frequently before his death and reported on the early days of the sect, had flown in to Nigeria from political exile in the United Arab Emirates at about the same time as Davis to try to negotiate the Chibok Girls' release himself. Salkida (who says he maintains communication with the group's leadership) took to Twitter to denounce Davis and say he had not been anywhere near the real group. "The #BH ideology like #IS wil neva entertain Muslims tht don't share their blief (let alone a Christian clergy) to negotiate on their behalf" he tweeted.[16]

Another journalist claimed Davis had likely never left Abuja and was like John le Carré's "Tailor of Panama," who suited his stories to match his paymaster's designs and advance himself.[17]

In December 2014, the Department of State Security arrested the people Davis had been in contact with in the north east. They said Davis and his associates had been part of an elaborate hoax. Davis's interlocutors had pretended to be Boko Haram at the behest of a senior politician who had an interest in sinking the person Davis accused.

A group of seven men were "paraded" before the press by the DSS, accused of conspiring to "spread falsehood and undermine efforts of the government to end terrorism." The DSS spokeswoman Marylin Orgar called Davis a "self-styled negotiator" and said that he had no link with the Presidency. The people who were assembled in front of journalists then confessed they had constructed, along with Davis, the accusations in order to extort blackmail and discredit the people Davis named.[18]

This form of show confession is common in Nigeria, and cannot be relied upon in any internationally recognised legal sense. Few Nigerians would have taken them seriously. It is only indicative of how the waters are muddied, and how unreliable the official institutions of state are in finding fact.

Davis himself responded that the DSS were working on behalf of the man he named. The developments were even more peculiar because if Davis is correct, it appears the intelligence institutions of the state in this case are working to undermine an account of Boko Haram that, on the whole, put the then president in the clear. Very little appeared to make sense.

There is no reason why it should. Even though Davis had, at face value, been in contact with apparently powerful members of the organisation, had gone to the heart of the remote region and seen a certain amount for himself, it was still not enough to eliminate ambiguity.

Far from making everything clear, what Davis brought back from his dash into the bush was more confusion. His revelations simply merged into the conspiracy narratives. At best all his information seemed to do was create a new genre. In this version, as elucidated best by the Nigerian blogger and freelance activist Peregrino Brimah, there were two distinct Boko Harams. The original Boko Haram, the "Yusufiyya sect", a group with well defined aims and, until 2009, peaceful methods, had been wiped out in 2010 by a second Boko Haram. This second posited group were referred to as "Political Boko Haram", or "Boko Haram 2". According to Brimah—who quotes only Stephen Davis and Wikileaks cables about the uprising in 2009 as sources—this new group consisted of men armed directly by the military for the purpose of doing the bidding of the cabal at the heart of the PDP. This conclusion, incidentally, was completely at odds with the narrative Davis himself presented.

No one can hold the full picture of what is going on. Davis, even though he believed he was speaking to the genuine group and was in the right place, could not account for the reason things did not go as planned. Into that gap he projected what he knew about the way clandestine relationships between militants and political actors worked in another area of the country, and transferred that understanding to this locale. As the Nigerian security blogger Fulan Nasrullah has written, analysts transfer their understanding of other situations onto Boko Haram, and this has resulted in a picture that is "way off" from the ground reality.[19]

The experiences of Boko Haram are so varied that it has led to general confusion over what they actually are. The reason it is so hard to know anything about Boko Haram, and indeed Nigeria, for certain is that it operates under conditions of a continual crisis of epistemology, where it is impossible to verify any fact, and all accounts are filtered through the political objectives of the players involved.

What accounts for the wide variety in "Boko Harams" which people experience? Boko Haram is—at its heart—still an unknown quantity. We don't know how they operate, how the centre of the organisation maintains its grip on its fringes, how they coordinate or what stories they tell each other to keep them doing what they do. We have no idea what their internal myth-making consists of. Even when someone goes into the north east to meet them, they cannot return bearing an uncontested truth. Nigeria is a place where personal power operates in a space that is entirely unregulated by a trusted institution of record, or the uncontested rule of law. Instead, the forces that have the most influence are ambition, identity and politics. Every individual's action is an exertion of power with imperfect information, any gaps are filled in with their own version of the story. This is as true for the members of Boko Haram as it is for everyone else.

When it is so difficult to distinguish fact from fiction, all rumours might as well be true.

11

OFF WITH THE RAT'S HEAD

In the summer of 2015, following the murder of thirty-eight tourists in Tunisia by a gunman inspired by the Islamic State, Lord Ashdown of Norton-sub-Hamdon, better known as the former Liberal Democrat Member of Parliament Paddy Ashdown, addressed the House of Lords. Ashdown, an international statesman and former Special Forces soldier, said history could be roughly divided into two kinds of period:

> In one of them, the gimbals on which power is mounted are steady, stable and unchanged—these are predictable times, times when we can look ahead with confidence and know what will happen. They are not necessarily peaceful times but they are at least unbewildering times. Then there are the second phases, which are the times of change, when power shifts—these are turbulent times, puzzling times and, all too often, bloody times.[1]

The world today, having been under the first set of conditions for the period of living memory, he said, is now moving into the second period, with bloody, unpredictable consequences.

He later told the BBC: "The world of the future is going to look a lot less like the world of the last fifty years, an American dominated world, and much more like the world of the nineteenth century."[2]

In early 2015 the Nigerian military began pushing Boko Haram out of the territory they held. They retook Gwoza in March, driving the insurgents back into the Mandara Mountains and towards the border regions around Lake Chad.[3] At his inauguration in August 2015 President Buhari charged the military to eliminate Boko Haram by Christmas.[4] In November Nigerian newspapers reported the military spokesman saying preparations were being made for the "final push" to clear the group from the Sambisa forest.[5]

It was just after this tide turned against Boko Haram in March that Abubakar Shekau made a formal pledge of loyalty to Islamic State in an audio message released on the internet.[6] This pledge of loyalty, known as *bay'ah*, was acknowledged and accepted a few days later by a spokesman from the Islamic State's media arm, Al-Furqan.[7] The group began releasing much slicker video productions, showing military operations and executions, under the brand of ISWAP, Islamic State West Africa Province.

This appeared to clear up many of the ambiguities left hanging by Shekau's August 2014 announcement of the establishment of an Islamic State in Nigeria. It would seem that the window that Stephen Davis referred to, the gap between Boko Haram being a local movement influenced by politics in Nigeria and a group firmly under the wing of an international jihadi movement, had closed.

But questions still remain. The timing was interesting. Had Shekau finally, unambiguously, pledged the group's loyalty only when they were under pressure? Why didn't IS recognise their fellow travellers in Nigeria before now? What does the connection mean in practical terms?

Boko Haram have in the past turned to international partners for help when they were in trouble. They sheltered in jihadi training camps following the uprising in 2009 and made overtures to al-Qaeda, even going so far as to write letters to Osama bin Laden.[8] Security sources in 2014 told journalists bin Laden wrote to the Somali jihadists Al-Shabaab, giving them advice, but there is no publicaly known evidence that the al-Qaeda leader ever sent an epistle to Boko Haram. Their association with al-Qaeda only resulted in one attack on an international target—against the United Nations building in Abuja. While this was terrible, it was but a minor encounter compared to the unmeasurable slaughter they unleashed on Nigerians.

Despite the 2015 military reversal, the group has not lost its ability to sow mayhem. It has simply withdrawn from the open field and returned to its clandestine tactics, hiding in mountain caves, or in chaotic city slums, using suicide bombers to attack soft targets like mosques, markets and motor parks. In November a suicide bomber struck a market in Yola killing at least thirty-two people. The attack came just days after President Buhari visited the city.[9] Yola itself is further south than the territory Boko Haram previously controlled in 2014. The next day a bomb went off in Kano, further indicating their reach. Hundreds have been killed in this way since the command was given to "eliminate" Boko Haram, contributing to their rating by the Institute for Economics and Peace as the world's most deadly terrorist organisation, surpassing the Islamic State themselves.[10] It is far from certain that northern Nigeria can be automatically counted as being a subsidiary outpost of ISIS, rather than a distinct phenomenon of its own.

It is doubtful that whatever the renewed vigour the military can muster will be enough to completely root out Boko Haram. When Abubakar Shekau said they were coming to "eat the heart" of the infidel state, what was it he thought he would find? The ability of the state in Nigeria to provide its basic functions, to provide a forum for pluralistic politics, to guarantee its people security, to provide its citizens with the educational tools they need for modern employment, have already been eaten by the people charged with providing them.

All of the problems that beset the Nigerian state that allow Boko Haram to thrive, described in the preceding pages, still persist.

This, it could be said, is the "new normal". In a way this is the real connection between Nigeria and the Islamic State; northern Nigeria, like parts of Iraq and Syria, is a geographical space where the idea, the commonly agreed rules of the modern nation state, formed in the post-War period by the European colonial powers of the nineteenth and twentieth centuries, no longer apply. The creation of this zone represents the boundary between the two historical periods identified by Lord Ashdown.

But more than this, the fight against Boko Haram is not just a fight between jihadi militants and the military. It is a conflict over Nigeria's very identity. At question is this: is Nigeria a secular state, governed by what we recognise as the agreed principles of the rule of law, or has Boko Haram exposed it as something else?

If the Middle East would be more recognisable to a nineteenth-century statesman, as Lord Ashdown says, I feel Nigeria would be more recognisable to a boy, brutally whipped from his home, a victim of slavery, transformed by Victorian manners who maintained a mystery deep within him. Dorogu would have readily understood Nigeria's present inner torment. Certainly more easily than those who have grown up in a world where the gimbals of power were more firmly held.

Tellers of Hausa folk stories use a phrase to signify their tale is at an end. They say *kunkurus kan kusu*, which means "off with the rat's head."[11] Like the old British folklore tale ending "a mouse did run, and now my story's done," the idiom serves as a rousing call to the audience, to remind them of the difference between the story world and the real. It means that a thing is done and finished with.

Although this book may be at an end, I am afraid the rat is still running.

ACKNOWLEDGEMENTS

This book was researched and written between spring 2013 and autumn 2015, but it draws on my ten years involvement in Nigeria.

Since I arrived at the *Daily Trust* newspaper in Abuja in the spring of 2006 I have had many teachers, patient people who took the time to explain things, and forgave me when I didn't understand. The true roll call is far too long to be fully acknowledged, but I am indebted to my colleagues (in no particular order) Abdullahi Idriss, Abdulazeez Abdullahi, Habib Pindiga, Ahmed Shekarau, Abdulkarim Baba Aminu, Abdullahi Korau Zango, Dafe Ujorha, Abdullahi Tasiu, Hameed Bello, Emmanuel Bello, Zainab Kperogi, Aliyu Abubakar, Idris Ahmed, Hassan Abdul, Nasidi Yahaya, Soliu Hamzat, Tashikalmah Hallah, Hassan Karofi, Yushau Adamu, Shehu Abubakar, Ben Auta, Ruby Rabiu, Anas Galadima, Abdul-Rahman Abubakar, Mahmud Jega, Ismaila Lere, Mohammed Haruna, Safiya Dantiye, Zainab Suleiman, Sam Egwu, Attahiru Musa, Lawal Ibrahim, Afolabi Sotunde, Haruna Ibrahim and everyone else who worked at the dusty house in Lusaka Street, in the days before they occupied a glittering glass tower. I was employed to train young journalists, but they taught me more than I could ever teach them.

I am also indebted to Senan Murray and Russell Smith, without whom I would not have got a job reporting from Abuja for the BBC. Working with Joseph Winter and Lucy Fleming on the Africa Desk of the World News Website was one of the most rewarding experience of my life, their hard work and commitment is the core of the BBC's online reporting of Africa. I have incredibly good memories of working with the BBC Hausa Service office in Abuja, and would like to thank them all for their support and help during that period, including Ahmed Idris, Bashir Sa'ad Abdullahi, Ibrahim Dosara, Mansur Liman, Umar Suleiman Akko, Jimeh Saleh, Chris Ewokor, Fidelis

Mbah, Adeola Osinuga and Mary Iroanya. I'd also like to thank Joe Boyle and Jude Sheerin, Martin Plaut, Mary Harper and everyone else at the BBC World Service who advised and helped me while I was reporting.

I have met some amazing journalists and researchers in Nigeria over the past ten years. I am very privileged to have worked with or shared stories with them over a beer or two. So here's to you: Alex Last, Christian Purefoy, Ed Harris, Sarah Simpson, Katy Pownall, Randy Fabi, Will Connors, Elizabeth Dickinson, Alex Gillies, Chris Albin-Lackey, Eric Gutschuss, Nick Tattersall, Jon Gambrell, Matt Green, Tom Burgis, Joe Brock and Gillian Parker. I also would like to thank Paul McHenry and Jonathan Phillips for putting me up when I was homeless in Abuja in 2011 while pursing the research that would go into this book.

Also indispensable was the support of my fellow Naija-philes and great friends in Britain, in Oxford and London and elsewhere, without whom I would have been totally lost: Olly Owen, Adam Higazi, Hannah Höechner, Zainab Usman, Alex Thurston, Marc-Antoine Pérouse de Montclos, Murray Last, Aaron Zelin, Antony Goldman, Jeremy Weate, Chris Newsom, Thessa Bagu, Bashir Bagu, Elizabeth Pearson, Atta Barkindo, Bala Liman, Elizabeth Donnelly, Noel McGeeney, Leo Traynor, Henry Mang, John Smith, Ryan Cummings, Jacob Zenn and Andrew Noakes. Thanks to those of you who read chapters or early drafts of the book and gave feedback; your help and kind comments were much appreciated. Thanks also go beyond the family of Nigeria-obsessives: to Sam Blair who shared his experience of the creative battle with me when it was most needed.

I would like to acknowledge and thank the people who gave me their time to be interviewed for this book, Hadiza Usman, Yahaya Shinko, M.K. Isa, A.S. Mohammed, Abdullahi Ladan, Ahmed Gumi, Balarabe Musa, Katrina Korb, Abdulmajid Sa'ad, Gerhard Müller-Kosack, Habila Pudza, James Hall, John Campbell, Yakubu the vigilante and Capt. Umar Abubakar. Thanks are also due to others in Nigeria and elsewhere who helped me during the research, including Ahmad Salkida, the first person to report on Boko Haram, Chitra Nagarajan, who works with civil society groups in the northeast, Saratu Abiola of the Testimonial Archive Project, and Simon Thompson and Lilian Breakall, who work on education with the programme funded by the UK's Department for International Development. Thanks are also due to Mannir Dan Ali, the executive editor of *Media Trust*. I am especially thankful for the help and assistance of Mohammed Kyari and his colleagues at the Moddibo Adama University of Technology, Adamawa.

I would also like to thank all the other journalists who have done amazing work covering the Boko Haram story, great reporters like Aminu Abubakar, Hamza Idris, Isaac Abrak, Tomi Oladipo, Phil Hazlewood, Michelle Faul, Sunday Alamba, Drew Hinshaw, Will Ross, Mike Smith, Monica Mark, Tim Cocks, Alexis Okeowo, Chika Oduah, Jina Moore, Joe Penney, and Glenna Gordon.

Much of the research for this book was conducted with the help of Abdullahi Kaura Abubakar, now the BBC's roving reporter in northern Nigeria. We went to Maiduguri together in 2011 and collaborated again in 2014. He has been a strong presence during my time in Nigeria and I appreciate his experience, calm, effective manner and his friendship.

It must not go without saying that I am very thankful to Michael Dwyer and everyone at Hurst. Michael's belief in this book and in my ability to complete it were an inspiration.

I can't end without acknowledging four other people, without whom this book would not exist. First of all, thanks to my parents Helen and John, who have always encouraged me in every way. The final two people I would like to thank are Kabiru Yusuf, CEO of Media Trust, the publisher of the *Daily Trust* newspaper, who changed my life when he brought me to his amazing country. I also want to thank Isa Sanusi. Without his friendship, wise council, encouragement and deep and abiding humour, I would certainly not have stayed for long.

Na gode.

NOTES

PREFACE: THE STRANGE TALE OF JOHN HENRY DOROGU

1. Kirk-Greene, Anthony, and Paul Newman (eds), *West African Travels and Adventures*, New Haven: Yale University Press, 1971.
2. Ibid.
3. Barth, Heinrich, *Barth's Travels in North and Central Africa; Vol. 1: Tripoli The Sahara and Bornu; & Vol 2. Timbuktu, Sokoto, the Niger, West and Central Soudan*, London: Ward, Lock and Co., 1890, v2, p. 101.
4. Kirk-Greene and Newman (eds), *West African Travels and Adventures*, p. 11.
5. Ibid., p. 93.
6. Whitehead, Clive, *Colonial Educators: The British Indian and Colonial Education Service 1858–1983*, London: I. B. Tauris, 2003, p. 33.
7. Ibid.
8. 'Boko Haram; What's in a name?' SahelBlog, Thurston, Alex, https://sahelblog.wordpress.com/2013/01/07/boko-haram-whats-in-a-name/
9. Kirk-Greene and Newman (eds), *West African Travels and Adventures*, p. 14.
10. Ibid., p. 15.
11. 'Shekau proclaims Islamic Caliphate', *Daily Trust* http://www.dailytrust.com.ng/daily/top-stories/32604-shekau-proclaims-islamic-caliphate accessed 08.10.2015

1. IF YOU CAN'T BEAT THEM, SHUN THEM

1. Sarki, Sarkin in the posessive, or "snake killer", is the title granted the ancient kings of Hausaland. It comes form a legend where a prince of Baghdad slew a serpent that guarded a well in Daura, the oldest Hausa kingdom, and married Daura's queen. The kings of the Hausa city states are from this bloodline. The title exists today as a form of patronage available to emirs.
2. The term used by the first West African Muslims for what the Arabs called Sheikh.

3. Bello, Muḥammad, and E. J. Arnett, *The Rise of the Sokoto Fulani*, Kano: Kano Emirate Printing, 1922, p. 50.
4. Ibid.
5. Last, Murray, *The Sokoto Caliphate*, London: Longmans, 1967, p. 23–4.
6. Hiskett, Mervyn, *The Sword of Truth: The Life and Times of the Shehu Usuman dan Fodio*, London: Oxford University Press, 1973, p. 47.
7. Bello and Arnett, *The Rise of the Sokoto Fulani*, p. 49.
8. Ibid., p. 117, and Hiskett, *The Sword of truth* pp. 47 and 73.
9. Bello and Arnett, *The Rise of the Sokoto Fulani*, p. 50.
10. Ibid.
11. Last, *The Sokoto Caliphate*, p. 23.
12. Hiskett, *The Sword of Truth*, p. 18.
13. Ibid.
14. Ibid., p. 37.
15. Trimmingham, John S., *Islam in West Africa*, Oxford: Clarendon Press, 1959, p. 81.
16. Ibid.
17. In his account of his father's life Mohammed Bello refers to a learned woman, who claimed to communicate with Sufi saints.
18. Bello and Arnett, *The Rise of the Sokoto Fulani*, p. 25.
19. Tremearne, Arthur, *The Ban on the Bori*, London: Heath, Cranton and Ouseley, 1914.
20. Ibid., and Bello and Arnett, *The Rise of the Sokoto Fulani*.
21. Tremearne, *The Ban on the Bori*.
22. Ibid.
23. Ibid.
24. Ibid., p. 136.
25. Ibid., p. 133.
26. Hearing this, Tremearne, who was also an officer in the British Army, prosaically suggested a nocturnal species of bird that he knew of. But his informant was not having it; "Any of the old men can tell the difference," he said "and they also know by the sound if the owner of the soul is dead or just sleeping."
27. Ibid.
28. Ibid.
29. Ibid., p. 176.
30. Hogben, S.J., and Anthony Kirk-Greene, *Emirates of Northern Nigeria*, London: Oxford University Press, 1966.
31. Hiskett, *The Sword of Truth*.
32. Bello and Arnett, *The Rise of the Sokoto Fulani*, p. 18.
33. Trimmingham, *Islam in West Africa*.
34. Johnston, Hugh, *The Fulani Empire of Sokoto*, London: Oxford University Press, 1967.

35. Last, *The Sokoto Caliphate*, London: Longmans, 1967, p. 10.
36. Bello and Arnett, *The Rise of the Sokoto Fulani*, p. 11.
37. Hiskett, *The Sword of Truth*, p. 36.
38. Trimmingham, *Islam in West Africa*, p. 92.
39. Hiskett, *The Sword of Truth*.
40. Higazi, Adam, 'Mobilisation into and against Boko Haram in North-East Nigeria', in Cahen, Michael, Marie Emmanuelle Pommerolle and Kadya Tall (eds) *Collective Mobilisations in Africa: Contestation, Resistance, Revolt*, Leiden: Brill
41. Hiskett, *The Sword of Truth*.
42. Ibid.
43. Interview with Ahmed Gumi, September 2014.
44. Cruise O'Brien, Donal and Christian Coulon, *Charisma and Brotherhood in African Islam*, Oxford: Clarendon Press, 1988.
45. Trimmingham, *Islam in West Africa*, p. 81.
46. Hiskett, *The Sword of Truth*, p. 36.
47. Bello and Arnett, *The Rise of the Sokoto Fulani*, pp. 24, 26.
48. Ibid., p. 37.
49. Hiskett, *The Sword of Truth*.
50. Last, *The Sokoto Caliphate*, pp. 4, 10.
51. Bello and Arnett, *The Rise of the Sokoto Fulani*, p. 20.
52. Hiskett, *The Sword of Truth*.
53. Ibid., p. 66.
54. Last, Murray, 'From Dissent to Dissidence: The Genesis and Development of Reformist Islamic Groups in Northern Nigeria' in Mustapha, Abdul R. (ed.), *Sects and Social Disorder: Muslim Identities and Conflict in Northern Nigeria*, Woodbridge: James Currey, 2014.
55. Last, *The Sokoto Caliphate*, p. 4
56. Hiskett, *The Sword of Truth*, p. 58.
57. de Saint Croix, F.W., and Garba Kawu Daudu, Kano: Bayero University, Centre for the Study of Nigerian Languages, 1999, p. 18.
58. Hogben and Kirk-Greene, *Emirates of Northern Nigeria*.
59. Riesman, Paul, *Freedom in Fulani Social Life*, Chicago: University of Chicago Press, 1998, p. 29.
60. Ibid.
61. Ibid., p. 231.
62. Ibid., p. 117.
63. Ibid., p. 129.
64. This is not the same for women. As Risman says, in Pullo society women are believed not to require the special liberating relationship between man and cow, because they are inherently closer to nature through their ability to bear children. Reisman, p. 257.

65. This is not to say that these are innate, racial characteristics of the Fulani. Pastoralist nomads are often thought of as being a "people apart". Traveller after traveller has written in a romantic mode about them, early anthropologists were tempted to see links between the Fulani and the "noble dynasties" of ancient Egypt. This was probably mainly down to a characteristic Fulani look; tall, straight nose, lighter skin. European travellers commented on the "purity" of their race and bloodline, these myths and legends and ideas of racial purity were no doubt encouraged by the Fulani's own myths about themselves and their chivalric existence. But the narratives of Fulani culture do reinforce a number of these as ideal behaviours for a Fulani. Individual Fulani are, of course, able to live up to them with varying degrees of success or failure.
66. Bello and Arnett, *The Rise of the Sokoto Fulani*, pp. 17–18.
67. Johnston, *The Fulani Empire of Sokoto*, p. 24.
68. Hiskett, *The Sword of Truth*, p. 19
69. Ibid.
70. Johnston, *The Fulani Empire of Sokoto*, p. 28.
71. Last, *The Sokoto Caliphate*, p. 7.
72. Johnston, *The Fulani Empire of Sokoto*.
73. Hiskett, *The Sword of Truth*, p. 75.
74. Smith, Michael, *Government in Zazzau, 1800–1950*, London: Oxford University Press, 1960.
75. It is believed that if someone had displeased him he would summon them to his court, with a friendly proposal. When they arrived as commanded he bid them stand before him. Unknown to the summoned, Yunfa had dug a pit under the mat that covered the floor and filled it with spears.
76. Hiskett, *The Sword of Truth*, p. 72.
77. Ibid.
78. Hodgkin, Thomas, *Nigerian Perspectives: An Historical Anthology*, London: Oxford University Press, 1975, p. 248.
79. Bello and Arnett, *The Rise of the Sokoto Fulani*, p. 95.
80. Ibid.
81. Last, *The Sokoto Caliphate*, p. 228.
82. Ibid., p. 232.
83. Hiskett, *The Sword of Truth*, p. 106.
84. Last, The Sokoto Caliphate, p. 231.

2. DISPUTED TERRITORY

1. Sattin, Anthony, *The Gates of Africa; Death, Discovery and the Search for Timbuktu*, London: Harper Collins, 2004.
2. Kirk-Greene, Anthony (ed.), *Barth's Travels in Nigeria*, London: Oxford University Press, 1962.

3. Barth, *Barth's Travels in North and Central Africa; Vol 1 Tripoli The Sahara and Bornu & Vol 2 Timbuktu, Sokoto, the Niger, West and Central Soudan*, vol. 1, p. 412.
4. Ibid., p. 425.
5. Ibid., p. 426.
6. Ibid., p. 424.
7. Ibid., p. 477.
8. Ibid., p. 413.
9. Ibid.
10. Ibid., p. 399.
11. Ibid., p. 421.
12. Ibid., p. 423.
13. Ibid., pp. 411, 414.
14. Ibid.
15. Ibid., p. 411.
16. Ibid., p. 416.
17. Ibid., p. 420.
18. Ibid., p. 442.
19. Ibid.
20. Kirk-Greene (ed.), *Barth's Travels in Nigeria*, p. 17.
21. Ibid., p. 2.
22. Ibid., p. 3.
23. Ibid.
24. Something Barth frequently remarks on, for example his entry for 22 December 1851, vol. 1, p. 571.
25. Kopytoff, Igor, *The Reproduction of Traditional African Societies*, Indianapolis: Indiana Univeristy Press, 1987, p. 4.
26. Heinrich, *Barth's Travels in North and Central Africa; Vols 1 & 2*, vol. 2, p. 165.
27. Kirk-Greene (ed.), Anthony, *Barth's Travels in Nigeria*, p. 19.
28. Ibid., p. 6.
29. Johnston, *The Fulani Empire of Sokoto*, p. 150.
30. Barth, *Barth's Travels in North and Central Africa, Vols 1 & 2*, Vol. 1, p. 206.
31. Johnston, *The Fulani Empire of Sokoto*, p. 150.
32. Last, *The Sokoto Caliphate*.
33. Hogben and Kirk Greene (eds), *Emirates of Northern Nigeria*.
34. Barth, Heinrich, *Barth's Travels in North and Central Africa, Vols 1 & 2;* Vol. 1, p. 22.
35. Ibid., p. 82.
36. Ibid., p. 145.
37. Patton, Adell, 'An Islamic Frontier Polity: The Ningi Mountains of Northern Nigeria, 1846—1902' in Kopytoff, Igor (ed.), *The Reproduction of Traditional African Societies*, Indianapolis: Indiana Univeristy Press, 1987, p. 196.

38. Ibid., p. 201.
39. Ibid., p. 6.
40. Ibid., p. 196.
41. Ibid., p. 25.
42. Cruise O'Brien and Coulon, *Charisma and Brotherhood in African Islam.*
43. Last, *The Sokoto Caliphate.*
44. Johnston, *The Fulani Empire of Sokoto*, p. 127.
45. Barth, Heinrich, *Barth's Travels in North and Central Africa; Vols 1 & 2;* p. 267.
46. Johnston, *The Fulani Empire of Sokoto*, p. 126.
47. Ibid.
48. Barth, *Barth's Travels in North and Central Africa*, vol. 1, p. 260.
49. Last, *The Sokoto Caliphate.*
50. Barth, *Barth's Travels in North and Central Africa*, vol. 1, p. 416.
51. Interview with Habila Pudza, September 2014.

3. MODES OF DEALING

1. Pakenham, Thomas, *The Scramble for Africa*, London: Abacus, 1996, pp. 456–7.
2. Ibid., p. 651.
3. Lugard, Frederick, *Colonial Reports Nigeria 1901—1911*, London: British Colonial Office, 1913, p. 365.
4. Lugard, Frederick John Dealtry, Margery Perham and Mary Bull (eds), *The Diaries of Lord Lugard*, Evanston, Illinois: Northwestern University Press, 1959, vol. 3, p. 311.
5. Pakenham, *The Scramble for Africa*, p. 414.
6. Perham and Bull (eds), *The Diaries of Lord Lugard*, p. 388.
7. Pakenham, *The Scramble for Africa*, p. 432.
8. Ibid.
9. Perham and Bull (eds), *The Diaries of Lord Lugard*, vol. 1, p. 57.
10. Ibid, p. 18.
11. Pakenham, *The Scramble for Africa*, p. 419.
12. Ibid., p. 430.
13. Ibid.
14. Perham and Bull (eds), *The Diaries of Lord Lugard*, p. 313.
15. Ibid.
16. Muffet, David, *Concerning Brave Captains*, London: Andre Deutsch, 1964, p. 28.
17. Ibid, p. 36.
18. Ibid., p. 46.
19. Ibid., p. 61.
20. Hogendorn, Jan and Paul Lovejoy, 'Revolutionary Mahdism and resistance to early colonial rule in Northern Nigeria and Niger', Johannesburg: University of Witwatersrand, 1979 p. 7.

21. Glassé, Cyril, *The Concise Encyclopaedia of Islam*, London: Stacey, 2008, p. 411.
22. Hogendorn and Lovejoy, 'Revolutionary Mahdism and resistance to early colonial rule in Northern Nigeria and Niger', p. 11.
23. Hiskett, Mervyn, *The Development of Islam in West Africa*. London: Longman, 1984, p. 272.
24. Hogendorn and Lovejoy, 'Revolutionary Mahdism and resistance to early colonial rule in Northern Nigeria and Niger', p. 8.
25. Ibid., p. 7.
26. Hogben and Kirk Greene, *Emirates of Northern Nigeria*, p. 470.
27. Hogendorn and Lovejoy, 'Revolutionary Mahdism and resistance to early colonial rule in Northern Nigeria and Niger', p. 11.
28. Ibid., p. 12.
29. Hill, Polly, *Rural Hausa: A Village and a Setting*, London: Cambridge University Press, 1972, p. 40.
30. Hogendorn and Lovejoy, 'Revolutionary Mahdism and resistance to early colonial rule in Northern Nigeria and Niger', p. 4.
31. Ibid., p. 16.
32. Muffet, *Concerning Brave Captains*.
33. Hogendorn and Lovejoy, 'Revolutionary Mahdism and resistance to early colonial rule in Northern Nigeria and Niger', p. 4.
34. Ibid., p. 31.
35. Ibid., p. 5.
36. Ozigi, Albert and Lawrence Ocho, *Education in Northern Nigeria*, London: Allen and Unwin, 1981, p. 39.
37. Kane, Ousman, *Muslim Modernity in Postcolonial Nigeria*, Leiden: Brill, 2003, p. 61.
38. Hoechner, Hannah, 'Ambiguous adventures: "Traditional" Qur'anic Students in Kano, Nigeria, Unpublished doctoral thesis, Oxford University, 2014, p. 203.
39. Ozigi, Albert and Lawrence Ocho, *Education in Northern Nigeria*, London: Allen and Unwin, 1981, p. 44.
40. Ibid.
41. Gumi, Abubakar and Ismailia Tsiga, *Where I Stand*, Ibadan: Spectrum Books, 1992.
42. Bello, *My Life*, p. 49.
43. Kane, Ousman, *Muslim Modernity in Postcolonial Nigeria*, Leiden: Brill, 2003.
44. Kukah, Matthew H., *Religion Politics and Power in Northern Nigeria*, Ibadan: Spectrum Books, 2003.

4. HEART ROT

1. Interview, Umar, Hadiza, Kaduna, September 2014
2. Humphreys, Sara, and Lee Crawfurd, *Review of the Literature on Basic Education*

in Nigeria; Issues of Access, Quality, Equity, and Impact, London: Edoren, 2014, p. 55.
3. Ibid., p. 56.
4. Ibid., p. 59.
5. Ibid., p 56.
6. Walker, Andrew, 'Special report: The mixed record of Katsina's development', *Sunday Trust* (17 February 2007).
7. Humphreys and Crawfurd, *Review of the Literature on Basic Education in Nigeria*, p. 117.
8. Interview, Korb, Katrina, Jos, September 2014.
9. Johnson, David, 'An assessment of the development needs of teachers in Nigera—a Kwara state case study', Education Sector Support Programme in Nigeria, Kw301 (December 2008), p. 2.

5. BIG POTATO ON TOP

1. Interview, Attahiru, Kaduna, September 2014.
2. Interview, Shinko, Yahaya, Kaduna, September 2014.
3. Osaghae, Eghosa, *Crippled Giant: Nigeria since Independence*, London: Hurst, 1998, p. 192.
4. Ibid., p. 189.
5. Ibid., pp. 156 and 190 and Siollun, Max, *Soldiers of Fortune*, Abuja: Cassava Republic Press, 2013, p. 74
6. Osaghae, *Crippled Giant*, p. 192
7. Siollun, *Soldiers of Fortune*, p. 62.
8. Ibid., p. 63.
9. Ibid., p. 69.
10. Ibid., p. 75.
11. Ibid., p. 78; and Osaghae, *Crippled Giant*, p. 194.
12. Ibid.
13. Siollun, *Soldiers of Fortune*, p. 93.
14. Osaghae, *Crippled Giant*, p. 192.
15. Ellis, Stephen, *The Mask of Anarchy: The Destruction of Liberia and the Religious Roots of an African Civil War*, London: Hurst, 2001.
16. Eghosa, *Crippled Giant*, p. 195.
17. Siollun, *Soldiers of Fortune*, p. 171.
18. Ibid.
19. Ellis, *The Mask of Anarchy*, p. 176.
20. Ibid., p. 2.
21. Ibid., p 160.
22. Hutchful, Eboe, 'The Ecomog Experience with Peacekeeping in West Afrca', Institute for Security Studies, 36, (1999) p. 6.

23. Interview, Shinko, Yahaya, Kaduna, September 2014.
24. Ellis, *The Mask of Anarchy*, p. 173.
25. Ibid.
26. Ibid., p. 175.
27. Osaghae, *Crippled Giant*, pp. 208, 220.
28. Oliver Owen, 'The Nigerian Police Force; An Institutional Ethnography', unpublished doctoral thesis, Oxford University, 2012, p. 196.
29. Siollun, *Soldiers of Fortune*, p. 118.
30. Ibid.,
31. Interview, Yakubu, Kaduna, September 2014.
32. Yakubu himself is a Christian, but gave the impression he favoured more traditional forms of faith.

6. STOMACH INFRASTRUCTURE

1. Interview, Ladan, Abdullahi Kaduna September 2014.
2. Interview, Sa'ad, Abdulmajid, Kano September 2014.
3. Interview, Sa'ad Abdulmajid, London, February 2015.
4. I am grateful to the academic Grimot Nane for introducing me to this phrase which neatly describes a polical economy based on "chopping".
5. 'Kwankwaso faces major hurdles in denatorial contest', *Daily Trust*, 19 January 2015 http://dailytrust.com.ng/daily/politics/44637-kwankwaso-faces-major-hurdles-in-senatorial-contest accessed 20.01.2015

7. EATING THE CORDS OF SOCIETY

1. Joseph, Richard A., *Democracy and Prebendal Politics in Nigeria: The Rise and Fall of the Second Republic*, Cambridge: Cambridge University Press, 1987, p. 194.
2. Clapham, Christopher S. (ed.), *Private Patronage and Public Power: Political Clientelism in the Modern State*, London: Pinter, 1982.
3. Harnischfeger, Johannes, *Democratization and Islamic Law*, Chicago: University of Chicago Press, 2008.
4. Interview, Rabo, Abubakar, Kano, September 2007.
5. Ibrahim's case was among a number of such adultery accusations that came to light in the early 2000s. The sentences against the women were not carried out after the intervention of the state governors.
6. Thurston, Alex, 'Muslim Politics and Sharia in Kano State Northern Nigeria', *African Affairs*, 114, 454, (2015), pp. 28–51.
7. Küng, Hans, *Islam Past Present and Future*, Oxford: Oneworld, 2007, p. 181.
8. Ibid.
9. Ibid., p. 266.
10. Gumi, Abubakar, Ismailia Tsiga, *Where I Stand*, Ibadan: Spectrum Books, 1992, p. 80.

11. Harnischfeger, *Democratization and Islamic Law.*
12. Larémont, Ricardo R., *Islamic Law and Politics in Northern Nigeria*, New Jersey: Africa World Press, 2011, p. 2.
13. Harnischfeger, *Democratization and Islamic Law.*
14. Ibid.
15. Ibid.
16. Gumi and Tsiga, *Where I Stand*, p. 73.
17. Harnischfeger, *Democratization and Islamic Law.*
18. Kukah, *Religion Politics and Power in Northern Nigeria*, p. 115.
19. Ibid.
20. Ibid.
21. Harnischfeger, *Democratization and Islamic Law*, p. 68.
22. Ibid.
23. Lamb, Venice and Judy Holmes, *Nigerian Weaving*, Roxford: Heartingfordbury, 1980, p. 136.
24. Harnischfeger, *Democratization and Islamic Law.*
25. Kukah, *Religion Politics and Power in Northern Nigeria*, p. 122.
26. Ibid., p. 123.
27. Harnischfeger, *Democratization and Islamic Law*, p. 76.
28. Kukah, *Religion Politics and Power in Northern Nigeria*, p. 123.
29. Ibid.
30. Harnischfeger, *Democratization and Islamic Law*, p. 76.
31. Kukah, *Religion Politics and Power in Northern Nigeria*, p. 118.
32. Kane, Ousman, *Muslim Modernity in Postcolonial Nigeria*, Leiden: Brill, 2003 p. 76.
33. Ibid., pp. 78 and 74.
34. Ibid., p. 75.
35. Isichei, Elizabeth, 'The Maitatsine Risings in Nigeria 1980–85: A Revolt of the Disinherited', *Journal of Religion in Africa*, 17, Fasc. 3 (Oct., 1987), p. 2.
36. Bako, Sabo, *The Maitatsine Revolts: A Socio-political Explanation of the Islamic Insurrections in Northern Nigeria, 1980–85*, Zaria: Ahmadu Bello Uniersity, 1992, p. 160.
37. Isichei, 'The Maitatsine Risings in Nigeria 1980–85', p. 2.
38. Ibid.
39. 'Maitatsine' *BBC Witness* http://www.bbc.co.uk/programmes/p0127jsh
40. Bako, *The Maitatsine Revolts*, p. 305
41. Harnischfeger, *Democratization and Islamic Law.*
42. 'Maitatsine' *BBC Witness* http://www.bbc.co.uk/programmes/p0127jsh
43. Harnischfeger, *Democratization and Islamic Law*, p. 74.
44. Isichei, 'The Maitatsine Risings in Nigeria 1980–85', pp. 194–208.
45. Bako, *The Maitatsine Revolts.*

46. Kane, *Muslim Modernity in Postcolonial Nigeria*, p. 62.
47. Gumi and Tsiga, *Where I Stand.*
48. Ibid., p. 29.
49. Ibid., p. 51.
50. Ibid.
51. Ibid., p. 59.
52. Ibid., p. 60.
53. Ibid., p. 68.
54. Ibid., p. 79.
55. Ibid.
56. Ibid., p. 74.
57. Kukah, *Religion Politics and Power in Northern Nigeria*, p. 11.
58. Kane, *Muslim Modernity in Postcolonial Nigeria*, p. 83.
59. Ibid., p. 88.
60. Gumi and Tsiga, *Where I Stand*, p. 127.
61. Ibid., p. 118.
62. Kane, *Muslim Modernity in Postcolonial Nigeria*, p. 83.
63. Harnischfeger, *Democratization and Islamic Law*, p. 75.
64. Gumi and Tsiga, *Where I Stand*, p. 151.
65. Ibid., p. 86.
66. Kane, *Muslim Modernity in Postcolonial Nigeria*, p. 85.
67. Ibid., p. 210.
68. Ibid., p. 86.
69. Ibid.,p. 216.
70. Ibid., p. 125.
71. Interview Gumi, Ahmed, Kanduna September 2014.
72. Thurston, Alex, 'Muslim Politics and Sharia in Kano State Northern Nigeria', *African Affairs*, 114, 454, (2015), pp. 28–51.
73. Interview, Hamisu Lamido Iyan Tama, Kano, 2007.
74. 'No Justice: Iyan-Tama jailed by corrupt officials', *Free Iyan Tama* http://freeiyantama.blogspot.co.uk/

8. THE REST OF US ARE JUST HAWKING PEANUTS

1. *Achaba* means "double benefit" in Hausa, said to be a bawdy reference to the supposed double benefit the male drivers recieve carrying female passengers; they get paid and sit between the woman's legs. Women riding on *achaba* is not unusual in the north, but is frowned on by some, leading to the purchase of three-wheel tuk-tuk type replacements being promoted in some northern cities.
2. Interview, Zakariyya, Mohammed, Maiduguri, February 2011, with translation by Abdullahi Kaura Abubakar, further translations by Isa Sanusi.

3. Interview, Dujana, Abu, Maiduguri, February 2011, with translation by Abdullahi Kaura Abubakar.
4. From a collection of four speeches by Yusuf anthologised in Arabic as 'A Collction of Speeches by Imam Abu Yusuf RIP', disseminated by the Boko Haram-affiliated Twitter handle @Urwatu_Wutqa—'The Firmest Grip'. These were translated into English by the iihadi monitoring group Jihadology, run by Aaron Zelin.
5. Ibid.
6. Interview, Anon., 2015.
7. Apter, Andrew H., *The Pan-African Nation: Oil and the Spectacle of Culture in Nigeria*, Chicago: University of Chicago Press, 2005.
8. Mohammed, Kyari, 'The Message and Methods of Boko Haram' in Pérouse de Montclos, Marc-Antoine (ed.), *Boko Haram, Islamism, Politics, Security and the State in Nigeria*, Leiden: Institute Francais de Recherche en Afrique, 2014, p. 12.
9. Mustapha (ed.), *Sects and Social Disorder Muslim Identities and Conflict in Northern Nigeria*, p. 168.
10. Interview with Habila Pudza Abuja, September 2014.
11. Higazi, 'Mobilisation Into and Against Boko Haram in North-East Nigeria', p. 14.
12. Ibid., p. 16.
13. 'A collection of speeches of Imam Abu Yusuf, RIP', Yusuf, Mohammed, *al-'Ūrwah al-Wūthqā Foundation*.
14. Harnischfeger, Johannes, 'Boko Haram and its Muslim Critics: Observations from Yobe State' in Pérouse de Montclos (ed.), *Boko Haram, Islamism, Politics, Security and the State in Nigeria*.
15. Interview, Müller-Kosack, Gerhard, Ramsgate, August 2015.
16. Interview, Anon., London, March 2015.
17. Roitman, Janet, 'A Successful life in the Illegal Realm: Smugglers and Bandits in the Chad Basin' in, Geschiere, Peter, Bridgit Meyer and Peter Pels (eds), *Readings on Modernity in Africa*, Bloomington: Indiana University Press, 2008, pp. 214–20.
18. Interview, Anon., Abuja, September 2014.
19. Mohammed, Kyari, 'The Message and Methods of Boko Haram' in Pérouse de Montclos (ed.), *Boko Haram, Islamism, Politics, Security and the State in Nigeria*.
20. 'A collection of speeches of Imam Abu Yusuf, RIP' Yusuf, Mohammed, *al-'Ūrwah al-Wūthqā Foundation*, 2015.
21. Salkida, Ahmad, 'The story of Nigeria's first suicide bomber', *Blueprint Magazine*, http://saharareporters. com/2011/06/26/story–nigerias–first–suicide–bomber–blueprint–magazine
22. 'Islamic group says it was behind fatal Nigeria attack', *New York Times*, http://www.nytimes.com/2011/08/29/world/africa/29nigeria.html?_r=1
23. 'A collection of speeches of Imam Abu Yusuf, RIP' Yusuf, Mohammed, *al-'Ūrwah al-Wūthqā Foundation*, 2015.
24. Ibid.

25. Interview, Dujana, Abu, Maiduguri, February 2011, with translation by Abdullahi Kaura Abubakar.
26. Mohammed, Kyari, 'The Message and Methods of Boko Haram' in Pérouse de Montclos (ed.), *Boko Haram, Islamism, Politics, Security and the State in Nigeria*.
27. 'Nigerian Taliban most likely not tied to Taliban nor Al Qaeda' *Wikileaks* https://wikileaks.org/plusd/cables/04ABUJA183_a.html
28. Interview Isa, Mohammed K, Zaria, September 2014.
29. Interview Salkida, Ahmad, Maiduguri, February 2011.
30. Mohammed, Kyari, 'The Message and Methods of Boko Haram' in Pérouse de Montclos (ed.), *Boko Haram, Islamism, Politics, Security and the State in Nigeria*.
31. Ibid.
32. Interview with Haruna, Mohammed, London 2009.
33. 'Execution of Buji Foi', *YouTube*, https://www.youtube.com/watch?v=oKAtu-vD1Aw
34. 'Life inside the Boko Haram stronghold of Maiduguri', BBC News, http://www.bbc.co.uk/news/world-21775619
35. Mohammed, Kyari, 'The Message and Methods of Boko Haram' in Pérouse de Montclos (ed.), *Boko Haram, Islamism, Politics, Security and the State in Nigeria*.
36. 'Dispatches: Nigeria's Hidden War', *Channel 4*, http://www.channel4.com/programmes/dispatches/on-demand/58946–001
37. Interview, Anon., Abuja, September 2014.
38. Interview with Higazi, Adam, London, July 2015.
39. 'Birom Christian tribe eating the burnt flesh of the Muslims they killed on the 28 08 2011 in Plateau Jos Nigeria', *YouTube*, https://www.youtube.com/watch?v=-3GKm8ik4_o; 'Jos Eid—Cannibal.flv', *YouTube*, https://www.youtube.com/watch?v=ia5HH48iKCM&bpctr=1447124325
40. 'Full transcript of Shekau's latest video on ceasefire deal, Chibok girls', *Premium Times*, http://premiumtimes.com/news/170441-full-transcript-of-shekaus-latest-video-on-ceasefire-deal-chibok-girls.html
41. Higazi, 'Mobilisation into and against Boko Haram in North-East Nigeria', p. 24.
42. Ibid.
43. Interview, Higazi, Adam, London, July 2015.
44. Higazi, Adam, 'Mobilisation into and against Boko Haram in North-East Nigeria'.
45. 'BBC meets gang "paid to join Boko Haram" in Niger', BBC News, http://www.bbc.co.uk/news/world-africa-27107375
46. 'Boko Haram commander's body found with thousands of Euros in Nigeria after foiled attack', *International Business Times*, http://www.ibtimes.com/boko-haram-commanders-body-found-thousands-euros-nigeria-after-foiled-attack-1937716
47. Interview, Barkindo, Atta, London, May 2015.
48. 'Christians caught attempting to bomb COCIN church in Bauchi', *PremiumTimes*, http://www.premiumtimesng.com/news/3955-christians-caught-attempting-to-bomb-cocin-church-in-bauchi.html

49. 'Profile: Who are Nigeria's Ansaru Islamists', BBC News, http://www.bbc.co.uk/news/world-africa-21510767
50. 'Chris McManus killed by kidnappers minutes after rescue mission began', *The Guardian*, http://www.theguardian.com/uk/2013/may/17/chris-mcmanus-killed-by-kidnappers-nigeria
51. 'Nigeria's Boko Haram "got $3m ransom" to free hostages', BBC News, http://www.bbc.co.uk/news/world-africa-22320077
52. 'Boko Haram abducts Cameroon Politician's wife', BBC News, http://www.bbc.co.uk/news/world-africa-28509530
53. Salkida, Ahmad, 'The story of Nigeria's first suicide bomber', *Blueprint Magazine*.
54. Interview, Campbell, John, London, June 2015.
55. 'Full transcript of Shekau's latest video on ceasefire deal, Chibok girls', *Premium Times*.
56. 'Nigerian Islamists kill 59 pupils in boarding school attack', Reuters, http://www.reuters.com/article/2014/02/26/us-nigeria-violence-idUSBREA1P10M20140226#drxY6PxrSZOG1yPL.97
57. 'Northern Nigeria: Boko Haram summarily executes young men who refused to join its ranks', LiveLeak, http://www.liveleak.com/view?i=ebe_1418914796
58. 'Boko Haram massacres young men from Bama, Borno who refused to join the sect', LiveLeak, http://www.liveleak.com/view?i=115_1418995992
59. Sura 3:145 quoted from Haeri, Fadhlalla, *Decree and Destiny*, Shaftesbury,: Element Books, in association with Zahra Publications, 1991.
60. 'Attack on Giwa Barracks, Borno State by Boko Haram Insurgents', LiveLeak, http://www.liveleak.com/view?i=f76_1395917176
61. 'Boko Haram Giwa Barracks attack: Nigerian Army "Killed hundreds"', BBC News, http://www.bbc.co.uk/news/world-africa-26819965
62. Interview, Maiduguri, February 2011 with translation by Abdullahi Kaura Abubakar.
63. 'Boko Haram has kidnapped before—sucessfully', CNN, http://edition.cnn.com/2014/05/12/world/boko-haram-previous-abductions/
64. 'Those terrible weeks in their camp', Human Rights Watch, https://www.hrw.org/report/2014/10/27/those-terrible-weeks-their-camp/boko-haram-violence-against-women-and-girls Accessed 10.11.2015
65. Ibid., p. 22.
66. 'Full English transcript of Boko Haram leader Shekau's latest video', *CKN Nigeria*, http://www.cknnigeria.com/2014/05/full-english-transcript-of-boko-haram.html
67. 'Nigeria kidnapped girls "shown" in new Boko Haram video', *BBC News*, http://www.bbc.co.uk/news/world-africa-27370041
68. Pearson, Elizabeth, 'Boko Haram and Nigeria's female bombers', *RUSI Newsbrief*, 35, 5 (November 2015), pp. 19–21.
69. 'Girls says father gave her to Boko Haram', *Al Jazeera*, http://www.aljazeera.com/

news/africa/2014/12/girl-says-father-gave-her-boko-haram-20141225162449466569.html

70. Interview, Anon., Abuja, 2014.
71. 'Nigerian troops arrest three female undercover operatives of Boko Haram', Sahara Reporters, http://saharareporters.com/2014/07/04/nigerian-troops-arrest-three-female-undercover-operatives-boko-haram
72. 'Nigeria army "relocates" 260 Boko Haram survivors', BBC News, http://www.bbc.co.uk/news/world-africa-32833959
73. Ellis, *The Mask of Anarchy*, 2001, p. 130.

9. KILL ZONES

1. 'White man'.
2. 'Buhari: I cannot change the past, but I can change the present and the future', *The Cable*, https://www.thecable.ng/buhari-cannot-change-past-can-shape-present-future
3. Odeh, Rosaline, *Muhammadu Buhari: Nigeria's Seventh Head of State*, Lagos: Federal Dept. of Information, Domestic Publicity Division, 1984, p. 15.
4. Yar'Adua Foundation, Shehu Musa Yar'Adua: A Life of Service, Abuja: Yar'Adua Foundation, 2004, p. 18.
5. Ibid., p. 18.
6. 'Undated execution of four robbers at Lagos Bar Beach', VidMe, https://vid.me/tBel
7. 'The Crate Escape', *BBC Witness*, http://www.bbc.co.uk/programmes/p0104hmg
8. Interview, Campbell, John, London, June 2015.
9. Harnischfeger, *Democratization and Islamic Law*.
10. 'Insurgency and Buhari's call for full sharia', *Vanguard News*, http://www.vanguardngr.com/2014/12/insurgency-buharis-call-full-sharia/
10. 'Nigerians upset over first lady's flashy watch', BBC News, http://www.bbc.co.uk/news/blogs-trending-32991164
12. 'Switzerland to return Sani Abacha "loot" to Nigeria', BBC News, http://www.bbc.co.uk/news/world-africa-31933083
13. 'Maiduguri: Nigeria's city of fear', BBC News, http://www.bbc.co.uk/news/world-africa-12713739
14. 'Boko Haram's Abu Qaqa gives press conference', The Rat's Head Blog, http://theratshead.blogspot.co.uk/2012/03/boko-harams-abu-qaqa-gives-press.html.
15. 'Boko Haram: How SSS established case against Senator Ndume', *Vanguard*, http://www.vanguardngr.com/2011/11/boko-haram-how-sss-established-case-against-senator-ndume/
16. 'Nigeria Christmas Day bombing suspect arrested', BBC News, http://www.bbc.co.uk/news/world-africa-18551029

17. 'Nigeria army arrests 'Boko Haram commander', BBC News, http://www.bbc.co.uk/news/world-africa-20018670
18. 'Silencing Boko Haram: Mobile Phone Blackout and Counterinsurgency in Nigeria's Northeast region', *Stability Journal*, http://www.stabilityjournal.org/article/10.5334/sta.ey/
19. 'Borno residents want phone network restored as Boko Haram gets deadlier', *PremiumTimes*, http://www.premiumtimesng.com/news/145640-borno-residents-want-phone-network-restored-boko-haram-gets-deadlier.html
20. 'Untold story of how Boko Haram overrun Nigerian soldiers, massacre hundreds in Borno', *PremiumTimes*, http://www.premiumtimesng.com/news/145118-untold-story-of-how-boko-haram-overrun-nigerian-soldiers-massacre-hundreds-in-borno.html
21. Interview, Mohammed, Kyari, London 2014.
22. Preston, Alex, 'Sons of anarchy', *GQ* (February, 2014), p. 166.
23. 'Dispatches: Nigeria's Hidden War', Channel 4, http://www.channel4.com/programmes/dispatches/on-demand/58946–001
24. 'Welcome to hell fire: Torture and other ill-treatment in Nigeria', Amnesty International, https://www.amnesty.org/en/documents/AFR44/011/2014/en/ p. 15.
25. 'Nigeria: Massive destruction, deaths from military raid,' Human Rights Watch, https://www.hrw.org/news/2013/05/01/nigeria-massive-destruction-deaths-military-raid
26. 'Poor conditions at Borno camp of Nigerian soldiers fighting Boko Haram', Sahara Reporters, http://saharareporters.tv/poor-conditions-at-a-borno-camp-of-nigerian-soldiers-fighting-boko-haram/
27. 'VIDEO: Boko Haram declares new caliphate in NorthEastern Nigeria', Sahara Reporters, https://www.youtube.com/watch?v=Rl4IgD—nKg
28. 'Boko Haram did not declare a caliphate', *Foundation for Defence of Democracies*, http://www.defenddemocracy.org/media-hit/gartenstein-ross-daveed-boko-haram-did-not-declare-a-caliphate/
29. Interview, Hall, James, London, May 2014.
30. 'The war against Boko Haram', *Vice News*, https://news.vice.com/video/the-war-against-boko-haram-full-length
31. 'The rise of Islamic State,' BBC Radio 4, http://www.bbc.co.uk/programmes/b050zkrq
32. 'Boko Haram expoits Nigeria's slow military decline', *Reuters*, http://www.reuters.com/article/2014/05/09/us-nigeria-military-insight-idUSBREA4809220140509
33. Interview, Anon., London, January 2014.
34. Adeniyi, Olusegun. *Power, Politics and Death: A Front Row Account of Nigeria Under the Late President Yar'Adua*, Lagos: Prestige, 2011.

35. 'Statement of General Muhammadu Buhari regarding the verdict of the supreme court on Jonathans election', Sahara Reporters, http://saharareporters.com/2011/12/28/statement-general-muhammadu-buhari-regarding-verdict-supreme-court-jonathans-election
36. 'Nigeria: Why FG Opposes Labelling Boko Haram a Terrorist Organisation—Adefuye', *AllAfrica*, http://allafrica.com/stories/201209040065.html
37. 'Nigeria schoolgirl abductions: Protest leader detained', BBC News, http://www.bbc.co.uk/news/world-africa-27283278
38. 'Jonathan gets approval to borrow $1bn to fight Boko Haram', *PremiumTimes*, http://www.premiumtimesng.com/news/168645-jonathan-gets-approval-to-borrow-1billion-to-fight-boko-haram.html
39. 'Announcement: A stable and secure Nigeria, an asset to America', *Embassy of the Federal Republic of Nigeria Washington DC*, http://www.nigeriaembassyusa.org/index.php?mact=News,cntnt01,detail,0&cntnt01articleid=357&cntnt01origid=15&cntnt01detailtemplate=nigeriadet&cntnt01returnid=108
40. Interview, Hall, James, London, May 2014.
41. Interview, anon., March 2014.
42. 'Nigerian soldiers given death penalty for mutiny', BBC News, http://www.bbc.co.uk/news/world-africa-30526725
43. 'We killed Shekau in Nigeria—Cameroon", *Vanguard News*, http://www.vanguardngr.com/2014/09/killed-shekau-nigeria-cameroon/
44. 'Abubakar Shekau killed was one Bashir Mohammed', Sahara Reporters, http://saharareporters.com/2014/09/22/%E2%80%9Cabubakar-shekau%E2%80%9D-killed-was-one-bashir-mohammed
45. Interview, Penney, Joe, London, July 2015.
46. 'Eeben Barlow speaks out; PMC and Nigerian strike force devastates Boko Haram', *Sofrep.com*, http://sofrep.com/40608/eeben-barlow-south-african-pmc-devestates-boko-haram-pt1/
47. 'Boko Haram releases video showing beheading of Nigerian Air Force pilot as terror leader who was thought dead reappears', *Daily Mail*, http://www.dailymail.co.uk/news/article-2780169/Boko-Haram-releases-video-showing-beheading-Nigerian-Air-Force-pilot-terror-leader-declares-Even-kill-not-stop-imposing-Islamic-rule.html
48. 'Three killed in Nigeria military helicopter crash', Reuters, http://af.reuters.com/article/topNews/idAFKCN0IY1CX20141114?pageNumber=1&virtualBrandChannel=0
49. 'Chief of Army staff doing push ups with soldiers (Photo)', *Nairaland*, http://www.nairaland.com/2464757/chief-army-staff-doing-push
50. 'UK to ramp up support to Nigeria in Battle against Boko Haram', *Financial Times*, http://www.ft.com/cms/s/0/22e0d6a0-1130-11e5-abda-00144feabdc0.html#axzz3hm4klT Accessed 03.08.2015.

51. Bako, Sabo, *The Maitatsine Revolts: A Socio-political Explanation of the Islamic Insurrections in Northern Nigeria, 1980–85*, Zaria: Ahmadu Bello University, 1992.
52. Ibid., p. 416.
53. Isichei, Elizabeth, 'The Maitatsine Risings in Nigeria 1980–85: A Revolt of the Disinherited', *Journal of Religion in Africa*, 17, Fasc. 3 (Oct., 1987), pp. 194–208, p. 6.
54. Ibid.
55. Bako, *The Maitatsine Revolts: A Socio-political Explanation of the Islamic Insurrections in Northern Nigeria.*
56. 'General Muhammadu Buhari at the Chatham House (entire speech plus question and answer session)', YouTube, https://www.youtube.com/watch?v=5m4asXkZwRM

10. STRANGE CARTOGRAPHY

1. 'When I met Asari and agreed a peace deal', *Vanguard News*, http://www.vanguardngr.com/2014/09/when-i-met-asari-and-agreed-a-peace-deal-stephen-davis/
2. 'Blood oil dripping from Nigeria', BBC News, http://news.bbc.co.uk/1/hi/world/africa/7519302.stm Accessed 10.11.2015.
3. 'Stephen Davis seven year secret deals with Boko Haram', *Daily Trust*, http://www.dailytrust.com.ng/sunday/index.php/top-stories/18062-stephen-davis-7-year-secret-deals-with-boko-haram
4. 'Exclusive: Boko Haram funded through CBN', *The Cable*, https://www.thecable.ng/exclusive-boko-haram-funded-through-cbn
5. I was given a lesson in radio's massive reach when I went to an annual fishing festival in Argungu, a remote village in Nigeria's far north west. I have the same name as another senior BBC journalist, and when I introduced myself to an elderly fisherman from this very remote town—who many might assume was "illiterate"—he greeted me in Hausa: "Ah! Yes, BBC economic correspondent, well done at your coming."
6. Mustapha, *Sects and Social Disorder Muslim Identities and Conflict in Northern Nigeria*, pp. 147–91.
7. Mustapha, *Sects and Social Disorder*, p. 147.
8. Interview, anon, London, May 2015.
9. Interview Mohammed AS, Zaria, September 2014.
10. 'Helicopters drop arms for insurgents—Borno, Yobe elders', *Punch*, http://punchng.com/news/helicopters-drop-arms-for-insurgents-borno-yobe-elders/
11. 'Former Nigerian Chief Of Defense Staff Badeh Laments Activities Of Fifth Columnists In The Military', Sahara Reporters, http://saharareporters.com/2015/07/30/former-nigerian-chief-defense-staff-badeh-laments-activities-fifth-columnists-military

12. Ellis, *The Mask of Anarchy*.
13. 'Australian Stephen Davis risked life in attempt to rescue kidnapped Nigerian girls', Australian Broadcasting Corporation, http://www.abc.net.au/news/2014–08–27/australian-risks-life-to-rescue-kidnapped-nigerian-girls/5699676
14. 'Arise news Boko Haram exclusive', *YouTube*, https://www.youtube.com/watch?v=K3hOPaB63dk
15. Ibid.
16. '@Contactsalkida on twitter', Twitter, https://twitter.com/ContactSalkida/status/504962747121938434?lang=en
17. 'Alkasim Abdulkadir: Boko Haram, Stephen Davis and the strange tales from Perth', *Ynaija*, http://ynaija.com/alkasim-abdulkadir-boko-haram-stephen-davis-strange-tales-perth-y-frontpage/
18. 'DSS parades seven 'associates' of Stephen Davis as fake Boko Haram members', *The Cable*, https://www.thecable.ng/dss-parades-davis-associates-boko-haram-impostors
19. 'About the blog', Fulan's Sitrep, http://fulansitrep.com/about/ Accessed 17.11.2015.

11. OFF WITH THE RAT'S HEAD

1. 'Moved by Lord Ashdown of Norton-sub-Hamdon 02.07.2015', *Hansard*, http://www.publications.parliament.uk/pa/ld201516/ldhansrd/text/150702–0002.htm#15070243000858 Accessed 18.11.2015
2. 'Interview with Lord Ashdown', *BBC Radio 4 The Week in Parliament*, 11.07.2015
3. 'Boko Haram HQ Gwoza in Nigeria Retaken' *BBC News*, http://www.bbc.co.uk/news/world-africa-32087211
4. 'Buhari to service chiefs: Hunt down Boko Haram in 3 months', *Vanguard*, http://www.vanguardngr.com/2015/08/buhari-to-service-chiefs-hunt-down-boko-haram-in-3-months/
5. 'Seeking to Meet Deadline, Military Pushes into Sambisa', *This Day*, http://www.thisdaylive.com/articles/seeking-to-meet-deadline-military-pushes-into-sambisa/225671/
6. 'Will Boko Haram benefit from an allegiance with Isil?', *Daily Telegraph*, http://www.telegraph.co.uk/news/worldnews/africaandindianocean/nigeria/11459692/The-Big-Question-Will-Boko-Haram-benefit-from-an-allegiance-with-Isil.html
7. 'Islamic State accepts Boko Haram pledge of allegiance', *Daily Telegraph*, http://www.telegraph.co.uk/news/worldnews/islamic-state/11469473/Islamic-State-accepts-Boko-Haram-pledge-of-allegiance.html Accessed 18.11.2015
8. 'Boko Haram's Bin Laden Connection', *The Daily Beast*, http://www.thedailybeast.com/articles/2014/05/11/boko-haram-s-bin-laden-connection.html
9. 'Market attack in Yola challenges claim insurgents close to defeat', *Financial Times*, http://on.ft.com/1HY0RF3
10. 'Global Terrorism Index', *Institute for Economics and Peace*, http://economicsand-

peace.org/wp-content/uploads/2015/11/2015-Global-Terrorism-Index-Report.pdf

11. Robinson, Charles H, *Dictionary of the Hausa Language*, Cambridge: Cambridge University Press, 1925, vol. 1, p. 236.

SELECT BIBLIOGRAPHY

Adeniyi, Olusegun, *Power, Politics and Death: A Front Row Account of Nigeria Under the Late President Yar'Adua*, Lagos: Prestige, 2011.

Apter, Andrew H., *The Pan-African Nation: Oil and the Spectacle of Culture in Nigeria*, Chicago: University of Chicago Press, 2005.

Bako, Sabo, *The Maitatsine Revolts: A Socio-political Explanation of the Islamic Insurrections in Northern Nigeria, 1980–85*, Zaria: Ahmadu Bello Uniersity, 1992.

Barth, Heinrich, *Barth's Travels in North and Central Africa; Vol 1 Tripoli, The Sahara and Bornu & Vol 2 Timbuktu, Sokoto, the Niger, West and Central Soudan*, London: Ward, Lock and Co, 1890.

Bello, Ahmadu, *My Life*, Cambridge: Cambridge University Press, 1962.

Bello, Muḥammad, and E. J. Arnett, *The Rise of the Sokoto Fulani*, Kano: Kano Emirate Printing, 1922.

Clapham, Christopher (ed.), *Private Patronage and Public Power: Political Clientelism in the Modern State*, London: Pinter, 1982.

Clarke, Christa, *Power Dressing*, Newark: The Newark Museum, 2005.

Cruise O'Brien, Donal and Christian Coulon, *Charisma and Brotherhood in African Islam*, Oxford: Clarendon Press, 1988.

de Saint Croix, F.W., and Garba Kawu Daudu, *Life On the Move With Pastoral Fulani*, Kano: Bayero University, Centre for the Study of Nigerian Languages, 1999.

Ellis, Stephen, *The Mask of Anarchy: The Destruction of Liberia and the Religious Roots of an African Civil War*, London: Hurst, 2001.

Glassé, Cyril, *The Concise Encyclopaedia of Islam*, London: Stacey, 2008.

Gumi, Abubakar, Ismailia Tsiga, *Where I Stand*, Ibadan: Spectrum Books, 1992.

Haeri, Fadhlalla, *Decree and Destiny*, Shaftesbury, Dorset: Element Books, 1991.

Hailey, Malcolm, *Native Administration in the British African Territories pt3*, London: British Colonial Office, 1951.

Harnischfeger, Johannes, *Democratization and Islamic Law*, Chicago: University of Chicago Press, 2008.

Hill, Polly, *Rural Hausa: A Village and a Setting*, Cambridge: Cambridge University Press, 1972.

Hiskett, Mervyn, *The Sword of Truth, the life and times of the Shehu Usuman dan Fodio*, London: Oxford University Press, 1973.

——— *The Development of Islam in West Africa*, London: Longman, 1984.

Hodgkin, Thomas, *Nigerian Perspectives: An Historical Anthology*, London: Oxford University Press, 1975.

Hoechner, Hannah, 'Ambiguous adventures: "Traditional" Qur'anic students in Kano, Nigeria', Unpublished doctoral thesis, Oxford University, 2014.

Hogben, S.J., Anthony Kirk-Greene, *Emirates of Northern Nigeria*, London: Oxford University Press 1966.

Hogendorn, Jan, Paul Lovejoy, '*Revolutionary Mahdism and resistance to early colonial rule in Northern Nigeria and Niger*', Johannesburg: University of Witwatersrand, 1979.

——— *Slow Death for Slavery: The Course of Abolition in Northern Nigeria 1897–1936*, Cambridge: Cambridge University Press, 1993.

Humphreys, Sara, Lee Crawfurd, *Review of the Literature on Basic Education in Nigeria: Issues of access, quality, equity, and impact*, London: Edoren, 2014.

Johnston, Hugh, *The Fulani Empire of Sokoto*, London: Oxford University Press, 1967.

Joseph, Richard A., *Democracy and Prebendal Politics in Nigeria: The Rise and Fall of the Second Republic*, Cambridge: Cambridge University Press, 1987.

Kane, Ousman, *Muslim Modernity in Postcolonial Nigeria*, Leiden: Brill, 2003.

Kirk-Greene, Anthony (ed.), *Barth's Travels in Nigeria*, London: Oxford University Press, 1962.

Kirk Greene, Anthony, and Paul Newman (eds), *West African Travels and Adventures*, New Haven: Yale University Press, 1971.

Kopytoff, Igor (ed.), *The Reproduction of Traditional African Societies*, Bloomington: Indiana University Press, 1987.

Kukah, Matthew H., *Religion Politics and Power in Northern Nigeria*, Ibadan: Spectrum Books, 2003.

Küng, Hans, *Islam Past Present and Future*, Oxford: Oneworld, 2007.

Lamb, Venice and Judy Holmes, *Nigerian Weaving*, Roxford: Heartingfordbury, 1980.

Larémont, Ricardo R., *Islamic Law and Politics in Northern Nigeria*, Trenton: Africa World Press, 2011.

Last, Murray, *The Sokoto Caliphate*, London: Longmans, 1967.

Lugard, Frederick, *Colonial Reports Nigeria 1901—1911*, London: British Colonial Office, 1913.

Perham, Margery, Mary Bull (eds), *The Diaries of Lord Lugard*, Evanston: Northwestern University Press, 1959.

Meijer, Roel (ed.), *Global Salafism: Islam's New Religious Movement*, London: Hurst, 2009.

Muffet, David, *Concerning Brave Captains*, London: Andre Deutsch 1964.

Mustapha, Abdul R. (ed.), *Sects and Social Disorder: Muslim Identities and Conflict in Northern Nigeria*, Woodbridge: James Currey, 2014.

Odeh, Rosaline, *Muhammadu Buhari: Nigeria's Seventh Head of State*, Lagos: Federal Dept. of Information, Domestic Publicity Division, 1984.

Osaghae, Eghosa, *Crippled Giant: Nigeria since Independence*, London: Hurst, 1998.

Owen, Oliver, 'The Nigerian Police Force: An Institutional Ethnography', unpublished doctoral thesis, University of Oxford, 2012.

Ozigi, Albert and Lawrence Ocho, *Education in Northern Nigeria*, London: Allen and Unwin, 1981.

Pakenham, Thomas, *The Scramble for Africa*, London: Abacus, 1996.

Pérouse de Montclos, Marc-Antoine (ed.), *Boko Haram, Islamism, Politics, Security and the State in Nigeria*, Leiden: Institute Francais de Recherche en Afrique, 2014.

Riesman, Paul, *Freedom in Fulani Social Life*, Chicago: University of Chicago Press, 1998.

Robinson, Charles H., *Dictionary of the Hausa Language*, Cambridge: Cambridge University Press, 1925, vol. 1, p. 236.

Sattin, Anthony, *The Gates of Africa; Death, Discovery and the Search for Timbuktu*, London: HarperCollins 2004.

Siollun, Max, *Soldiers of Fortune*, Abuja: Cassava Republic Press, 2013.

Smith, Michael, *Government in Zazzau, 1800–1950*, London: Oxford University Press, 1960.

Tremearne, Arthur, *The Ban on the Bori*, London: Heath, Cranton and Ouseley, 1914.

Trimmingham, John S., *Islam in West Africa*, Oxford: Clarendon Press, 1959.

Whitehead, Clive, *Colonial Educators: The British Indian and Colonial Education Service 1858–1983*, London: IB Tauris, 2003.

Yar'Adua Foundation, *Shehu Musa Yar'Adua: A Life of Service*, Abuja: Yar'Adua Foundation, 2004.

Articles

Higazi, Adam, 'Mobilisation into and against Boko Haram in North-East Nigeria', in Michel Cahen, Marie Emmanuelle Pommerolle, Kadya Tall (eds), *Collective Mobilisations in Africa: Contestation, Resistance, Revolt*, Leiden: Brill.

Hutchful, Eboe, 'The Ecomog Experience with Peacekeeping in West Africa', *Institute for Security Studies*, 36, (1999).

Isichei, Elizabeth, 'The Maitatsine Risings in Nigeria 1980–85: A Revolt of the Disinherited', *Journal of Religion in Africa*, 17, Fasc. 3 (Oct., 1987), pp. 194–208.

Johnson, David, 'An assessment of the development needs of teachers in Nigera—a Kwara state case study', *Education Sector Support Programme in Nigeria*, Kw301 (December 2008).

Last, Murray, 'From Dissent to Dissidence: The genesis & development of reformist Islamic groups in northern Nigeria' in Mustapha, Abdul R. (ed.), *Sects and Social Disorder Muslim Identities and Conflict in Northern Nigeria*, Woodbridge: James Currey, 2014.

Pearson, Elizabeth, 'Boko Haram and Nigeria's female bombers', *RUSI Newsbrief*, 35, 5 (November 2015), pp. 19–21.

Preston, Alex, 'Sons of Anarchy', *GQ* (February, 2014), p. 166.

Roitman, Janet, 'A Successful life in the Illegal Realm: Smugglers and Bandits in the Chad Basin' in Geschiere, Peter, Bridgit Meyer, Peter Pels (eds), *Readings on Modernity in Africa*, Bloomington: Indiana University Press, 2008, pp. 214–20.

Thurston, Alex, 'Muslim Politics and Shari'a in Kano State Northern Nigeria', *African Affairs*, 114, 454, (2015), pp. 28–51.

Walker, Andrew 'Special report: The mixed record of Katsina's development', *Sunday Trust* (17 February 2007).

Website Resources

'@Contactsalkida on twitter', *Twitter*, https://twitter.com/ContactSalkida/status/504962747121938434?lang=en Accessed 10.11.2015.

'A collection of speeches of Imam Abu Yusuf, RIP', Yusuf, Mohammed, *al-'Ūrwah al-Wūthqā Foundation* http://jihadology.net/2015/03/03/al-urwah-al-wuthqa-foundation-presents-a-new-release-from-jamaat-ahl-al-sunnah-li-l-dawah-wa-l-jihad-boko-%E1%B8%A5aram-grouping-of-sermons-of-the-imam-abu-yusuf-mu/ Accessed 10.11.2015.

'Abubakar Shekau killed was one Bashir Mohammed', Sahara Reporters, http://saharareporters.com/2014/09/22/%E2%80%9Cabubakar-shekau%E2%80%9D-killed-was-one-bashir-mohammed Accessed 10.11.2015.

'Alkasim Abdulkadir: Boko Haram, Stephen Davis and the strange tales from Perth', *Ynaija*, http://ynaija.com/alkasim-abdulkadir-boko-haram-stephen-davis-strange-tales-perth-y-frontpage/ Accessed 10.11.2015.

'Announcement: A stable and secure Nigeria, an asset to America', *Embassy of the Federal Republic of Nigeria Washington DC*, http://www.nigeriaembassyusa.org/index.php?mact=News,cntnt01,detail,0&cntnt01articleid=357&cntnt01origid=15&cntnt01detailtemplate=nigeriadet&cntnt01returnid=108 Accessed 10.11.2015

'Arise news Boko Haram exclusive', *YouTube*, https://www.youtube.com/watch?v=K3hOPaB63dk Accessed 10.11.2015.

'Attack on Giwa Barracks, Borno state by Boko Haram Insurgents', LiveLeak, http://www.liveleak.com/view?i=f76_1395917176 Accessed 10.11.2015.

'Australian Stephen Davis risked life in attempt to rescue kidnapped Nigerian girls', Australian Broadcasting Corporation, http://www.abc.net.au/news/2014–08–27/australian-risks-life-to-rescue-kidnapped-nigerian-girls/5699676 Accessed 10.11.2015

'BBC meets gang "paid to join Boko Haram" in Niger', BBC News, http://www.bbc.co.uk/news/world-africa-27107375 Accessed 10.11.2015.

'Birom Christian tribe eating the burnt flesh of the Muslims they killed on the 28 08 2011 in plateau Jos Nigeria', YouTube, https://www.youtube.com/watch?v=-3GKm8ik4_o Accessed 10.11.2015.

'Blood oil dripping from Nigeria', BBC News, http://news.bbc.co.uk/1/hi/world/africa/7519302.stm Accessed 10.11.2015.

'Boko Haram abducts Cameroon Politician's wife', BBC News, http://www.bbc.co.uk/news/world-africa-28509530 Accessed 10.11.2015.

'Boko Haram commander's body found with thousands of Euros in Nigeria after foiled attack', *International Business Times*, http://www.ibtimes.com/boko-haram-commanders-body-found-thousands-euros-nigeria-after-foiled-attack-1937716 Accessed 10.11.2015.

'Boko Haram did not declare a caliphate', Foundation for Defence of Democracies, http://www.defenddemocracy.org/media-hit/gartenstein-ross-daveed-boko-haram-did-not-declare-a-caliphate/ Accessed 10.11.2015.

'Boko Haram expoits Nigeria's slow military decline', Reuters, http://www.reuters.com/article/2014/05/09/us-nigeria-military-insight-idUSBREA4809220140509 Accessed 10.11.2015.

'Boko Haram Giwa Barracks attack: Nigerian Army "Killed hundreds"', BBC News, http://www.bbc.co.uk/news/world-africa-26819965 Accessed 10.11.2015.

'Boko Haram has kidnapped before—sucessfully', CNN, http://edition.cnn.com/2014/05/12/world/boko-haram-previous-abductions/ Accessed 10.11.2015

'Boko Haram massacres young men from Bama, Borno who refused to join the sect', LiveLeak, http://www.liveleak.com/view?i=115_1418995992 Accessed 10.11.2015

'Boko Haram releases video showing beheading of Nigerian Air Force pilot as terror leader who was thought dead reappears', *Daily Mail*, http://www.dailymail.co.uk/news/article-2780169/Boko-Haram-releases-video-showing-beheading-Nigerian-Air-Force-pilot-terror-leader-declares-Even-kill-not-stop-imposing-Islamic-rule.html Accessed 10.11.2015.

'Boko Haram: How SSS established case against Senator Ndume', *Vanguard*, http://www.vanguardngr.com/2011/11/boko-haram-how-sss-established-case-against-senator-ndume/ Accessed 10.11.2015.

'Boko Haram; What's in a name?', Thurston, Alex, SahelBlog https://sahelblog.wordpress.com/2013/01/07/boko–haram–whats–in–a–name/ accessed 07.10.2015

'Boko Haram's Abu Qaqa gives press conference', The Rat's Head Blog, http://theratshead.blogspot.co.uk/2012/03/boko-harams-abu-qaqa-gives-press.html Accessed 10.11.2015.

'Borno residents want phone network restored as Boko Haram gets deadlier', *PremiumTimes*, http://www.premiumtimesng.com/news/145640-borno-residents-want-phone-network-restored-boko haram gets deadlier.html Accessed 10.11.2015.

'Buhari: I cannot change the past, but I can change the present and the future', The Cable, https://www.thecable.ng/buhari-cannot-change-past-can-shape-present-future Accessed 10.11.2015.

'Chief of Army staff doing push ups with soldiers (Photo)', *Nairaland*, http://www.nairaland.com/2464757/chief-army-staff-doing-push Accessed 10.11.2015.

'Chris McManus killed by kidnappers minutes after rescue mission began', *The Guardian*, http://www.theguardian.com/uk/2013/may/17/chris-mcmanus-killed-by-kidnappers-nigeria Accessed 10.11.2015.

'Christians caught attempting to bomb COCIN church in Bauchi', *PremiumTimes*, http://www.premiumtimesng.com/news/3955-christians-caught-attempting-to-bomb-cocin-church-in-bauchi.html Accessed 10.11.2015.

'Dispatches: Nigeria's Hidden War', Channel 4, http://www.channel4.com/programmes/dispatches/on-demand/58946–001 Accessed 10.11.2015.

'DSS parades seven 'associates' of Stephen Davis as fake Boko Haram members', The Cable, https://www.thecable.ng/dss-parades-davis-associates-boko-haram-impostors Accessed 10.11.2015.

'Eeben Barlow speaks out; PMC and Nigerian strike force devastates Boko Haram', *Sofrep.com*, http://sofrep.com/40608/eeben-barlow-south-african-pmc-devestates-boko-haram-pt1/ Accessed 10.11.2015.

'Exclusive: Boko Haram funded through CBN', The Cable, https://www.thecable.ng/exclusive-boko-haram-funded-through-cbn Accessed 10.11.2015.

'Execution of Buji Foi" YouTube, https://www.youtube.com/watch?v=oKAtu-vD1Aw Accessed 10.11.2015.

'Former Nigerian Chief Of Defense Staff Badeh Laments Activities Of Fifth Columnists In The Military', Sahara Reporters, http://saharareporters.com/2015/07/30/former-nigerian-chief-defense-staff-badeh-laments-activities-fifth-columnists-military Accessed 10.11.2015.

'Full English transcript of Boko Haram leader Shekau's latest video', *CKN Nigeria*, http://www.cknnigeria.com/2014/05/full-english-transcript-of-boko-haram.html Accessed 10.11.2015.

'Full transcript of Shekau's latest video on ceasefire deal, Chibok girls', *Premium Times*, http://premiumtimes.com/news/170441-full-transcript-of-shekaus-latest-video-on-ceasefire-deal-chibok-girls.html Accessed 03.10.2015.

'General Muhammadu Buhari at the Chatham House (entire speech plus question and answer session)', YouTube, https://www.youtube.com/watch?v=5m4asXkZwRM Accessed 10.11.2015.

'Girls says father gave her to Boko Haram', Al Jazeera, http://www.aljazeera.com/news/africa/2014/12/girl-says-father-gave-her-boko-haram-20141225162449466569.html Accessed 10.11.2015.

'Helicopters drop arms for insurgents—Borno, Yobe elders', *Punch*, http://punchng.com/news/helicopters-drop-arms-for-insurgents-borno-yobe-elders/ Accessed 10.11.2015.

'How it went, Buhari speaks at Chatham House', The Cable, https://www.thecable.ng/live-buhari-speaks-chatham-house Accessed 10.11.2015.

'Insurgency and Buhari's call for full shari'a', *Vanguard News*, http://www.vanguardngr.com/2014/12/insurgency-buharis-call-full-sharia/ Accessed 10.11.2015.

'Islamic group says it was behind fatal Nigeria attack', *New York Times*, http://www.nytimes.com/2011/08/29/world/africa/29nigeria.html?_r=1 Accessed 10.11.2015.

'Jonathan gets approval to borrow $1bn to fight Boko Haram', *PremiumTimes*, http://www.premiumtimesng.com/news/168645-jonathan-gets-approval-to-borrow-1billion-to-fight-boko-haram.html Accessed 10.11.2015.

'Jos Eid—Cannibal.flv', *YouTube*, https://www.youtube.com/watch?v=ia5HH48iKCM&bpctr=1447124325 Accessed 10.11.2015.

'Kwankwaso faces major hurdles in senatorial contest', *Daily Trust* http://dailytrust.com.ng/daily/politics/44637-kwankwaso-faces-major-hurdles-in-senatorial-contest Accessed 20.01.2015.

'Life inside the Boko Haram stronghold of Maiduguri', BBC News, http://www.bbc.co.uk/news/world-21775619 Accessed 10.11.2015.

'Maiduguri: Nigeria's city of fear', BBC News, http://www.bbc.co.uk/news/world-africa-12713739 accessed 10.11.2015.

'Maitatsine', *BBC Witness* http://www.bbc.co.uk/programmes/p0127jsh Accessed 09.11. 2015.

'Nigeria army "relocates" 260 Boko Haram survivors', BBC News, http://www.bbc.co.uk/news/world-africa-32833959 Accessed 10.11.2015.

'Nigeria army arrests 'Boko Haram commander', BBC News, http://www.bbc.co.uk/news/world-africa-20018670 Accessed 10.11.2015.

'Nigeria Christmas Day bombing suspect arrested', BBC News, http://www.bbc.co.uk/news/world-africa-18551029 Accessed 10.11.2015.

'Nigeria kidnapped girls "shown" in new Boko Haram video', BBC News, http://www.bbc.co.uk/news/world-africa-27370041 Accessed 10.11.2015.

'Nigeria schoolgirl abductions: Protest leader detained', BBC News, http://www.bbc.co.uk/news/world-africa-27283278 Accessed 10.11.2015.

'Nigeria: Massive destruction, deaths from military raid,' Human Rights Watch, https://www.hrw.org/news/2013/05/01/nigeria-massive-destruction-deaths-military-raid Accessed 10.11.2015.

'Nigeria: Why FG Opposes Labelling Boko Haram a Terrorist Organisation—Adefuye', *AllAfrica*, http://allafrica.com/stories/201209040065.html Accessed 11.11.2013.

'Nigeria's Boko Haram "got $3m ransom" to free hostages', BBC News, http://www.bbc.co.uk/news/world-africa-22320077 Accessed 10.11.2015.

'Nigerian Islamists kill 59 pupils in boarding school attack', Reuters, http://www.reuters.com/article/2014/02/26/us-nigeria-violence-idUSBREA1P10M20140226#drxY6PxrSZOG1yPL.97 Accessed 10.11.2015.

'Nigerian soldiers given death penalty for mutiny', BBC News, http://www.bbc.co.uk/news/world-africa-30526725 Accessed 10.11.2015.

'Nigerian Taliban most likely not tied to Taliban nor Al Qaeda', Wikileaks https://wikileaks.org/plusd/cables/04ABUJA183_a.html Accessed 10.11.2015.

'Nigerian troops arrest three female undercover operatives of Boko Haram', Sahara Reporters, http://saharareporters.com/2014/07/04/nigerian-troops-arrest-three-female-undercover-operatives-boko-haram Accessed 10.11.2015.

'Nigerians upset over first lady's flashy watch', BBC News, http://www.bbc.co.uk/news/blogs-trending-32991164 Accessed 10.11.2015.

'No Justice: Iyan Tama jailed by corrupt officials', Free Iyan Tama http://freeiyantama.blogspot.co.uk/ Accessed 09.11.2015.

'Northern Nigeria: Boko Haram summarily executes young men who refused to join its ranks', LiveLeak, http://www.liveleak.com/view?i=ebe_1418914796 Accessed 10.11.2015.

'Poor conditions at Borno camp of Nigerian soldiers fighting Boko Haram', Sahar Reporters, http://saharareporters.tv/poor-conditions-at-a-borno-camp-of-nigerian-soldiers-fighting-boko-haram/ Accessed 10.11.2015.

'Profile: Who are Nigeria's Ansaru Islamists', BBC News, http://www.bbc.co.uk/news/world-africa-21510767 Accessed 10.11.2015.

'Shekau proclaims Islamic Caliphate', *Daily Trust* http://www.dailytrust.com.ng/daily/top–stories/32604–shekau–proclaims–islamic–caliphate accessed 08.10.2015.

'Silencing Boko Haram: Mobile Phone Blackout and Counterinsurgency in Nigeria's Northeast region', *Stability Journal*, http://www.stabilityjournal.org/article/10.5334/sta.ey/ Accessed 10.11.2015.

'Statement of General Muhammadu Buhari regarding the verdict of the supreme court on Jonathans election', Sahara Reporters, http://saharareporters.com/2011/12/28/statement-general-muhammadu-buhari-regarding-verdict-supreme-court-jonathans-election Accessed 10.11.2015.

'Stephen Davis seven year secret deals with Boko Haram', *Daily Trust*, http://www.dailytrust.com.ng/sunday/index.php/top-stories/18062-stephen-davis-7-year-secret-deals-with-boko-haram Accessed 10.11.2015.

'Switzerland to return Sani Abacha "loot" to Nigeria', BBC News, http://www.bbc.co.uk/news/world-africa-31933083 Accessed 10.11.2015.

'The Crate Escape', BBC Witness, http://www.bbc.co.uk/programmes/p0104hmg accessed 10.11.2015.

'The rise of Islamic State,' BBC Radio 4, http://www.bbc.co.uk/programmes/b050zkrq Accessed 10.11.2015.

'The story of Nigeria's first suicide bomber', Salkida, Ahmad, *Blueprint Magazine*, http://saharareporters.com/2011/06/26/story–nigerias–first–suicide–bomber–blueprint–magazine Accessed 01.10.2015.

'The war against Boko Haram', *Vice News*, https://news.vice.com/video/the-war-against-boko-haram-full-length Accessed 10.11.2015.

'Those terrible weeks in their camp', Human Rights Watch, https://www.hrw.org/report/2014/10/27/those-terrible-weeks-their-camp/boko-haram-violence-against-women-and-girls Accessed 10.11.2015.

'Three killed in Nigeria military helicopter crash', Reuters, http://af.reuters.com/article/topNews/idAFKCN0IY1CX20141114?pageNumber=1&virtualBrandChannel=0 Accessed 10.11.2015.

'UK to ramp up support to Nigeria in Battle against Boko Haram', *Financial Times*, http://www.ft.com/cms/s/0/22e0d6a0-1430-11e5-abda-00144feabdc0.html#axzz3hm4klT Accessed 03.08.2015.

'Undated execution of four robbers at Lagos Bar Beach', VidMe, https://vid.me/tBel Accessed 10.11.2015.

'Untold story of how Boko Haram overrun Nigerian soldiers, massacre hundreds in Borno', *PremiumTimes*, http://www.premiumtimesng.com/news/145118-untold-story-of-how-boko-haram-overrun-nigerian-soldiers-massacre-hundreds-in-borno.html Accessed 10.11.2015.

'VIDEO: Boko Haram declares new caliphate in NorthEastern Nigeria', Sahara Reporters, https://www.youtube.com/watch?v=Rl4IgD—nKg Accessed 10.11.2015.

'We killed Shekau in Nigeria—Cameroon", *Vanguard News*, http://www.vanguardngr.com/2014/09/killed-shekau-nigeria-cameroon/ Accessed 10.11.2015.

'Welcome to hell fire: Torture and other ill-treatment in Nigeria', Amnesty International, https://www.amnesty.org/en/documents/AFR44/011/2014/en/ Accessed 10.11.2015.

'When I met Asari and agreed a peace deal', *Vanguard News*, http://www.vanguardngr.com/2014/09/when-i-met-asari-and-agreed-a-peace-deal-stephen-davis/ Accessed 10.11.2015.

INDEX